Platinum, gold and diamonds –
The adventure of Hans Merensky's discoveries

# Platinum, gold and diamonds –
## The adventure of Hans Merensky's discoveries

Eberhard W. Machens

Protea Book House
Pretoria

First edition, first impression in 2009 by Protea Book House
First edition, second impression in 2013 by Protea Book House
PO Box 35110, Menlo Park, 0102
1067 Burnett Street, Hatfield, Pretoria
8 Minni Street, Clydesdale, Pretoria
protea@intekom.co.za
www.proteaboekhuis.co.za

Translated from the original German by Idette Noomé
Editor: Amelia de Vaal
Cover design: Hanli Deysel
Set in 12 on 14 pt Times New Roman by Ada Radford
Printed and bound by Interpak Books

© 2009 Eberhard W. Machens
ISBN 978-1-86919-200-6

No part of this book may be reproduced or transmitted in any form or by any electronic or mechanical means, including photocopying and recording, or by any other information storage or retrieval system, without written permission from the publisher.

**Graphic material courtesy of the following individuals and institutions:**
Hans Merensky Foundation: Figures 1, 2, 3, 5, 11, 12, 13, 15, 16, 18, 19, 21, 22, 24, 25
Geological Society of South Africa: Figure 6
Prof. David L. Reid, University of Cape Town: Figure 20
University of Pretoria: Figure 27
Mr. Jos Deen, The Netherlands: Figure 9
Dr Gabriele Machens: Figures 7, 23, 26
E.W. Machens: Figures 4, 8, 10, 14, 17 and 2 maps inside the cover

# Contents

Preface and acknowledgements  7

Chapter 1: The life of a discoverer  13
    Textbox 1: What is a mineral deposit?  15

Chapter 2. The missionary's son  17
    Textbox 2: The land of gold – Ophir  25
    Textbox 3: Carl Mauch discovers the Zimbabwe Ruins  28

Chapter 3: Lieutenant of the Guard and mining assessor  33

Chapter 4: Consulting geologist in South Africa  41
    Textbox 4: What is the difference between prospecting and exploration?  46

Chapter 5: The Madagascar gold  53
    Textbox 5: "Primary" and "secondary" deposits  61

Chapter 6: Bankruptcy  65

Chapter 7: Interned  73

Chapter 8: The art of getting into debt  79

Chapter 9: Light at the end of the tunnel  85
    Textbox 6: The history of platinum  90

Chapter 10: Platinum in the Bushveld  97

Chapter 11: Platinum, platinum without end  113

Chapter 12: To the Adlon in Berlin and back to the Transvaal  127
    Textbox 7: The history of diamonds  139

Chapter 13: Diamonds in Namaqualand  143
    Textbox 8: "Like Argus of the Ancient Times"  161

Chapter 14: The struggle for mining rights  163
    Textbox 9: The diamond cartel  179

Chapter 15: The turning point in Merensky's life  183

Chapter 16: A summer in Mecklenburg  189

Chapter 17: The creative farmer  201
    Textbox 10: Eucalyptus as timber  217

Chapter 18: Gold in the Orange Free State  219
    Textbox 11: Chrome ore deposits  226
Chapter 19: New successes: chrome ores and vermiculite  229
    Textbox 12: Vermiculite  237
Chapter 20: The last coup  239
Chapter 21: The last years  253
Chapter 22: A lasting legacy  265
Bibliography  281
Index of people  289
Index of places, companies and institutions  293
Index of concepts and events  301

# Preface and acknowledgements

Olga Lehmann's biography of Hans Merensky, *Look beyond the Wind. The Life of Dr. Hans Merensky, 1871–1952* (thus far the first and only extensive work on his life), appeared 53 years ago. The book was reprinted unchanged in 1956, 1959 and 1989; and a German translation was published in 1965.

Merensky's scientific achievements were justly celebrated in 1999 in a special edition of the much-respected *South African Journal of Geology*, which is read worldwide, and which was edited by R.G. Cawthorn.

However, hitherto there has been little recognition of the value and importance of Hans Merensky's politico-economic contributions. There has also been no comprehensive overview of the life's work of this great explorer and discoverer. Several occasional articles have appeared, but neither on the occasion of what would have been his 100th birthday (in 1971) nor on the occasion of the 50th anniversary of his death (in 2002) were there any particular commemorative events on a scale worthy of his achievements. This seems strange, especially since, in the past fifty years or so, the economic value of many raw materials has changed dramatically and the main centres of production have shifted.

With regard to Hans Merensky, these changes imply that – from an economic point of view – the discoveries he made between 1924 and 1950 are much more significant today than they were 60 or 80 years ago. Back then, the ever-inventive press dubbed Hans Merensky "the Wizard Geologist". Today, it is obvious that he was much more – he was also an extremely far-sighted economic strategist to whom South Africa is vastly indebted. Without his visionary thinking and planning, South Africa would undoubtedly be a considerably poorer country.

In the first few years after Merensky discovered platinum in South Africa, it was difficult for South African platinum to break into the world market. Today, South Africa is the world's most prominent platinum producer. Merensky always believed that this would be the case. When the chrome ores of the Bushveld were first found, there was no market for them at all, but Merensky was utterly and unshakably convinced that one day, these ores would dominate the global market. Once again, he has been proven right. In the decades since his discoveries, the Phalaborwa region, where Merensky discovered a vast phosphate deposit, has also developed very much along the lines which the discoverer envisioned and sketched out for his associates when they had concluded the prospecting work. Perhaps the most far-sighted of Merensky's visions is embodied in the way he drew up his will to ensure that his great fortune would be well employed to serve progress in general and to benefit South Africa in particular. He planned 100 years ahead. If one looks at what his legacy has wrought and at the way in which the Merensky Foundation functions today, benefiting both South Africa and the international community, one has to accord Merensky the highest possible praise for his visionary planning.

So, there is much that needs to be told.

How does one come to write a book such as this? Who provided the impetus and how did the task proceed? The answer to the first part of the latter question is simple, but the answer to the last part could fill volumes.

The impetus came from my wife. When I prepared my first lecture on Africa, 45 years ago, she read the manuscript. Of course, I mentioned South Africa's diamonds. To add a little personal interest to the text at that point, I added the anecdote that I retell in Chapter 17 of this book, about Merensky's gallant treatment of society ladies and his generous gestures in giving away diamonds. My wife loved this story, and instantly became a "Merensky fan". My female students were just as charmed by this anecdote. Their enthusiasm prompted me to trace more elements of Merensky's private life. It did not take me long to discover that the "later" Merensky (after he had purchased Westfalia) was a highly fascinating personality, in human terms. One day, a few years after I had retired, my wife said: "You have entertained our guests and the children with your stories about Merensky all our lives – why don't you sit and write them all down?"

If one already has all the material in one's mind that is easy to do. But then, in the course of this labour of love, one weaves together such a complex tapestry of information, advice, assistance in many forms, and of well-meant encouragement, that after 2 or 3 years it is almost impossible to thank all those whose help contributed to this work. It is undeniable that a book of this nature is not written just by the author. I would therefore like to mention a few of the most important of the many people who assisted me.

My erstwhile assistant, Professor Rainer Herd, looked at the manuscript from a geological perspective and suggested some corrections. Our erstwhile technical draughtswoman, Mrs Sabine Printschitsch, drew the maps. My friend Gerd Kähler edited the language of the German version a number of times. Relatively late in the process – the first draft of the book was already complete – when I was looking for photographs, I came into contact with the Merensky Foundation and its erstwhile president, Dr Viktor Hesse; the executive manager of Agribusiness, Claus Lippert; the director of the farm Westfalia, Dr. Stefan Koehne and his wife Sylvie, who runs the research station on Westfalia. The Foundation offered to pay for the translation of the book into English, and that is why the book is published in South Africa first. The Foundation also enabled me to visit Merensky's farm Westfalia and to make use of the Merensky Archive there. It was an unforgettable and moving experience to hold Merensky's original reports on the platinum exploration and many other artefacts in my hands.

Then came the task of translating and editing the manuscript. Mrs Idette Noomé, a lecturer at the University of Pretoria, produced an empathetic translation and even managed to make the translated text some 20 pages shorter than the original without changing the text. Dr Hans Ulrich Bantz, like Merensky a geologist who was trained in Germany and then emigrated to South Africa, gave me his generous assistance and checked the correctness of the translation of all the geological and mining terminology. Finally, Ms Amelia de Vaal, an editor at Protea Boekhuis, took in hand the final preparation for the publication of the book. I would like to thank them and the many others that I could not all mention by name for their help and their engagement with this project.

Finally, I would like to pay one last tribute, one that may seem a little unusual. However, it is a tribute very close to my heart. It is a tribute to the work done by Olga Lehmann, Hans Merensky's first biographer. She did the research for her book very soon after Merensky's death and spoke to incredibly many of Merensky's friends, to mine managers and politicians who had come into contact with him. Consequently, the acknowledgement of the sources of her information that prefaces her biography reads like a *Who's Who* of the South African mining community around the middle of the 20$^{th}$ century. Olga Lehmann also did very thorough legal archival and newspaper research and finally also collected a large number of anecdotes about Hans Merensky. Nobody writing about Merensky after her can ignore her pioneering work – at best one can shift the emphasis on and evaluation of specific events somewhat.

Olga Lehmann made another and, in my opinion, even more vital contribution. In the course of her research, she recognised the significance of Merensky's father, the missionary Alexander Merensky, to the development of his son. It is generally known that in the years between 1860 and 1890, Alexander Merensky was one of the most energetic pioneers in South Africa. His son, the geologist who became famous as a discoverer, is a completely independent personality. Both in his choice of career, and in the important decisions he made in the years after he purchased Westfalia and in the wording of his will, he followed his own mind. He was not influenced in these choices by the memory of his father's career and life. However, the imprint of his parental home is very visible in the way in which he made his decisions. Olga Lehmann sensed this and at least part of her book was devoted to the history of Merensky's family. In my biography I consciously followed her example in this, because I believe that she is quite correct. One cannot understand and appreciate Hans Merensky without a detailed look at his origins, his parents and their home, his education and the example set by his father.

Eberhard W. Machens
Bonn, July 2008

*Only personalities move the world, never principles.*
                                            Oscar Wilde

CHAPTER 1

# The life of a discoverer

*Hans Merensky*. This name is probably familiar only to a few people, unless they have studied mining or geology. If they have, they would probably have heard that name in their very first lecture on mineral deposits, on where and how they are found. Or they might have heard it while travelling extensively in South Africa and Namibia, because there that name is attached to several public places. Dams, streets, a game reserve connected to a luxury lodge, a high school in Tzaneen, university institutes in Stellenbosch and the library of the University of Pretoria are all named after Merensky. The reason is simple: Hans Merensky was the most successful discoverer of mineral deposits and diamonds that has ever lived, anywhere.

Hans Merensky was born in quite modest circumstances on his parents' farm in what was then the Transvaal, in 1871. His parents were missionaries from Brandenburg. Later he went to Germany, where he was educated in the German education system, did his military service, became a lieutenant in the Guard, studied mining and geology and became a Prussian mining assessor, which placed him among the elite of the German mining fraternity. At the age of 33, he returned to South Africa and soon became one of the leading geologists in the country. In the years that followed, he had a number of large successes, but also several financial disasters; and he was eventually even declared bankrupt. The years during the First World War and the period immediately after the war were extremely difficult for him. In the mid-1920s his discovery of platinum in South Africa was his first really big success, one that made him world famous. But not long after that, he was again in financial difficulties. A mere two years later, he had a second huge success: he discovered the diamond deposits at Alexander Bay, at the mouth of the Orange River. It was the largest deposit of diamonds of gemstone quality ever found. This discovery at last allowed him to join the elite ranks of South African mining magnates.

He spent the last 22 years of his life farming his large farm Westfalia, which he developed into a model farm. In those years he became a universally respected proponent of scientifically and ecologically sound agriculture and a trendsetter in the struggle against soil erosion and the destruction of the landscape. Every now and again he went off on prospecting journeys on which he discovered numerous mineral deposits of world significance. Merensky died in 1952, aged 81, on his farm Westfalia, a very wealthy man indeed; an industrially sought-after adviser on issues regarding natural resources. More than that, he was a patron of the arts engaged in multiple projects and a promoter of the sciences, where his influence remained strong in South Africa even after his death, because of the legacies set out in his will.

His life story is worth telling for various reasons: it is exciting and even dramatic in places. There are few authors who would have an imagination fantastic enough to dream up such a multifaceted life. But his life story is also worth recording because many of his discoveries were of global significance. Again and again, Merensky set in motion changes in the international raw materials markets and his finds made headlines. His work had a critical effect on the world's industrial history. And finally, his life should also be recorded because Hans Merensky was one of the defining personalities in South Africa in the first half of the 20th century. Without Hans Merensky's contributions, both South Africa and Namibia would have looked very different today. Were it not for his discoveries, both these countries would have been considerably poorer than they are now.

**Note:**

Throughout this book several expressions and terms specific to mining, geology and mineralogy are used. To assist the reader, some more detailed explanations are provided. If such explanatory notes were to be woven into the main text, they would interrupt the flow of the narrative. To prevent that from happening, these explanations have been removed from the main text and placed in textboxes. The same applies to any historical or cultural historical notes. Readers can choose to skip the textboxes if they want to focus on Hans Merensky's life story, but if they want to go back to a particular item of specialist background in an earlier textbox, they can find that information very easily.

---

**Textbox 1 – What is a mineral deposit?**

When useful minerals and their mineral concentrations in various places in the earth's crust are mentioned, terms such as "occurrence", "mineral deposit" and "economically viable deposit" are used. These terms can be defined as follows:

An **occurrence** refers to the localised presence of a mineral substance or of a particular type of rock. This expression is the most common way to describe such a presence. The term gives no indication of the amount of the mineral substance or of the type of rock in question present in the deposit, nor of its value or its economic significance.

A **mineral deposit** refers to a spatially limited geological body in the crust of the earth which contains a particular concentration of specific chemical elements or of a particular type of rock. This concentration has come about naturally, and the concentration of the substance is clearly above the average distribution of the substance in question in the crust of the earth, in so far as this mineral concentration can be accessed by means of mining activities.

An **economically viable deposit** is a deposit as defined above, to which a further criterion is added, namely the viability of the economic exploitation of the mineral concerned. This possibility arises when the mineral deposit contains a raw material for which there is an economic demand and which would be profitable to mine and market. The amount and value of the raw material present must be high enough for the value of the sales of the material to exceed the total cost of the infrastructure, the mining operation, the dressing and preparation of the material, and the transport etc. of the raw material.

It is important in terms of this definition that one should recognise that the "economic viability" of a mineral deposit is a variable factor. This implies that mineral deposits that have long been economically uninteresting can join the class of deposit that can be profitably exploited when the demand for the mineral concerned increases, or when other suppliers fall away. Such deposits can then become "economically viable deposits". On the other hand, deposits that are already being mined can also drop out of this category. That would be the case, for example, when new competitors can produce the material concerned more economically, or when the end product made from this raw material is replaced in the market by another end product.

It should be noted that most geologists leave out the description "economically viable" and usually simply refer to "mineral deposits". This applies particularly in cases where the context makes it clear that the deposit in question is sufficiently significant to be mined or is already being mined.

CHAPTER 2

# The missionary's son

When one immerses oneself in the details of the life of a famous person who has achieved something extraordinary, it is always interesting to learn something more about that person's early years. We all want to know whether there were some special circumstances or an impetus in the person's childhood, be it in his parents' home, in the circle of his friends or somewhere else, which played a significant role in his later life. So what happened to the young Hans Merensky?

Early influences can be clearly discerned: his interest in the natural sciences was aroused when he was quite young. At the same time, he was taught the art of making accurate observations and the skill of not overlooking even the tiniest of details. Both these influences came from his father, Alexander Merensky, a missionary. Moreover, he spent some of his childhood on his parents' mission station, where the circumstances of his life were such that the boy grew up with a sense of living in a country in which there was still incredibly much to discover. The long discussions in the evenings between his father and his father's friends, or even with strange visitors, became a catalyst for – or, to be more precise, crystallised – this sense in the young boy of the vast potential of the country he lived in. For us to understand the real significance of these discussions in the evenings, it is perhaps important to know a little more about Hans Merensky's father, the missionary Alexander Merensky.

Alexander Merensky was born in 1837. His father died early and so he grew up in Schindler's orphanage in Berlin, where he received his high school education at the local *Gymnasium*. There, he was still very young when he developed a lively faith and decided to become a missionary. At the age of 18, he began with suitable training in the house of the Berlin Mission Society. As early as 1858 – aged only 21 – he was sent to South Africa.

At that time, travelling in southern Africa was a strenuous undertaking and often turned out to be quite an adventure. Partly on foot, partly in ox wagons, the young missionary, with one companion, journeyed 1400 kilometres to the northeast from Cape Town, to the Emmaus Mission Station in Zululand. From there he went even further north, into the tribal lands of the Swazi in the Drakensberg. Swaziland is today a small kingdom wedged between the eastern Transvaal area (now called Mpumalanga) and Mozambique. Back then, the land of the Swazi lay far beyond the sphere of influence of any of the large European powers. Missionaries had to be self-reliant, as they had no special protection whatsoever. Thus it was no wonder that the mission was unable to get any proper foothold in Swaziland.

Consequently, Alexander Merensky turned to the west, to the area inhabited by the Sotho, in the land bordering what was then the Transvaal. There he was able to establish a number of small congregations. But even here the continued presence and safety of a resident missionary depended largely on the benevolence of the local tribal chieftains. Initially, the missionary was received with great friendliness, because of his many skills and the little gifts that he brought with him. But when the tribal elders gradually became aware of how much their subjects were changed by their baptism, this benevolence disappeared rapidly, and was soon replaced by open animosity. For those who were baptised, becoming Christians meant a release or even salvation from numerous evil powers that had thus far surrounded them. They became freer and, at the same time, more independent, and they were liberated from many of the dark bonds that had constrained their lives hitherto. But, of course, the sangomas (traditional healers within the Zulu, Swazi and Xhosa communities) and tribal elders saw things differently. For them, it was the start of the destruction not only of ancient social structures, but also of the dependencies that created their power base – and that was not something they could permit. King Sekhukhune, who was afraid that he might lose some of his power, reacted vehemently. Soon it was not only a matter of mere friction: a very real persecution of the baptised members of the tribe began. For this reason, the young missionary thrice had to abandon a newly founded mission station.

The third expulsion of the missionary took place under dramatic circumstances. At the time, Alexander Merensky was much less concerned for his own life than for those of the baptised families that had entrusted themselves to him and that he could barely protect. So, he and his congregation fled, in the middle of the night, along remote and hidden paths, skirting all the villages, through the barely passable gorges of the Drakensberg toward the west, to the Transvaal. By then, Alexander Merensky was already married, and his wife had given birth to their first child only two days earlier. In her condition she could obviously neither ride nor walk, so she had to be carried on a chair through the pitch-dark night. A black servant carried the two-day-old little girl, Paula, Hans Merensky's older sister, over the stony paths. The missionary was accompanied by 12 of the African families he had baptised, and who had left the tribal area with him. These refugees, no fewer than 70 souls, found temporary refuge in a mission station in the Lydenburg district. Then Alexander Merensky began to look for a place to build a new mission station. He crisscrossed the eastern Transvaal in his search for a suitable place, and eventually found the ideal site for a new mission in the Middelburg district. He called the new mission *Botshabelo*, which means "place of refuge". That was in 1865. By that time, he had already had seven years of hard missionary work behind him, years that had, as he saw it, brought him but little success.

At his newly founded mission station things were quite different, because Alexander Merensky had a lot of organisational talent which he was now able to put to full use. The development of the new mission station became a lasting success. It therefore came as no surprise that, a few years later, when the congregations of the Berlin Mission in the Transvaal were reorganised, Alexander Merensky was nominated as superintendent. But this was not the only success story in his life; this achievement was followed by others.

The first days on the new premises were difficult. The congregants stayed in simple huts made from grass and branches. They immediately began to build fixed rondavels – round huts with thatched roofs. The work progressed swiftly. Building huts from materials gleaned from nature in the surrounding area was a craftsman's skill that the refugees possessed in abundance. Each of them, men and women, had practised these skills in their home villages often enough, and even the children helped. They were all cheerful, as Alexander Merensky had been able to purchase the premises for a good price, namely £75, and his protégés felt that they now had a home in which they could live without oppressive constraints.

After some time, the first solid house was erected according to the missionary's plans. Next came a church and, by and by, more buildings. When Alexander Merensky eventually returned to Germany 17 years later, he left behind a flourishing enterprise, consisting of a farm house, a mill, a smithy and a viable agricultural enterprise that could feed one missionary's family. During these 17 years the mission had become not only a spiritual centre, but also a cultural and economic centre. A large number of African families lived in its environs in a well-structured community in which each person had his or her own means of subsistence.

It was in this mission station that the young Hans Merensky was born in 1871, in the sixth year after it had been founded, and this was where he grew up until his 11$^{th}$ year. He was the third child in a merry string of four girls and four boys. A governess who had been sent for from Germany taught the children arithmetic, reading, writing, German, English and music. Of course, the children also spoke Afrikaans, the language spoken by the local Boers. Their father himself taught the children Latin and natural science. The children's enthusiasm for their Latin lessons was somewhat limited, but they loved their nature study lessons. These lessons were done without textbooks and were quite unique. Their father took the children out into the bush to show them and explain to them where and why which plants grew where they did, and what the plants needed in order to grow. The children could soon identify 15 different types of grass by name, and were able to deduce the humidity levels and the soil types from the presence of certain types of grass. He explained the relationships and symbiosis between the various kinds of animal groups starting with the dung beetle that they saw on a dead field mouse, the antelopes that gathered at the waterholes and the predators that came there to find their prey, to the vultures that soared in the sky above them, waiting for an opportunity to snatch some carrion. This was not conventional education in the European sense, but almost the perfect training for young Red Indians who had to learn to inhabit nature and to be absorbed in it. But above all, their father exhorted the children to observe nature closely and to learn to recognise the tiniest variations. Hans Merensky, who was later to achieve such huge successes as a prospector thanks to his exceptionally well-developed skills of observation, later said repeatedly that the basis for his phenomenal skills of observation had been laid in his childhood. In one place he wrote almost poetically about his father, saying: " ... *er lehrte uns die Sprache des Windes zu verstehen und ließ den verwitterten Felsen seine Geschichte erzählen*" [" ... he taught us to understand the language of the wind and let the weathered rock tell us its history"].

But Alexander Merensky was an interesting man in yet another sense. Before he left Germany, he had been trained in First Aid. Later he learnt more and practised in the hospital in Pretoria, where he also participated in a number of operations. In the Middelburg district, he was eventually regarded as the only really qualified doctor that one could call when there had been an accident. During the First Anglo-Boer War (1880–1), he distinguished himself while working on the Boer side as a military doctor.

Alexander Merensky was the author of a number of books on Africa. He wrote about the tasks and the history of the missionary movement, but also about themes such as the geographical and cultural aspects of the regions he lived and worked in. When his principal work – *Erinnerungen aus dem Missionsleben in Transvaal 1859–1882* [Memories of missionary life in the Transvaal 1859–1882] – appeared, it was even compared with Livingstone's famous accounts of his travels. In addition he became, with Frederick Jeppe, an old Transvaal pioneer, the compiler and publisher of the first map of the Transvaal in 1868. An improved second edition appeared in 1875. For over 20 years, this map was regarded as the standard map for the country. This was followed in 1884, from Germany, by the publication of a map of the whole of South Africa which reflected the rapidly changing colonial possession of the time.

In combination with this, Alexander Merensky also had a very intriguing personal hobby: he was fascinated by the history of the exploration and discovery of southern Africa. If one looks at the maps of the 15$^{th}$ and 16$^{th}$ centuries, one can see that the coastline of southern Africa, as well as the western and eastern side of the continent, had been represented fairly accurately quite soon after Portuguese explorer Bartholomeu Dias first sailed around the tip of Africa in 1488. Along the western and eastern shores of the continent, numerous landing points and small Portuguese settlements were marked on these maps. By contrast, for the interior of Africa, for quite some time, there were only a number of imaginary and fantastic names.

As time passed knowledge of the interior increased, because wherever there was a Portuguese settlement, there were also missionaries, and they recorded any reports they could collect about the interior. There was no shortage of reports, since traders, ivory hunters and adventurers continuously tried to penetrate into the wilderness. It was probably already at the start of the 17$^{th}$ century that the first expeditions crossed the continent from Mozambique to Angola. But the scientific value of such ventures was minimal. The adventurers who undertook these journeys were not really in a position to make useful notes about the geographical and cultural phenomena they encountered or to compile helpful route descriptions. Some of the stories they told were probably the products of sheer fantasy. Nevertheless, the sum of such reports gave the first insights into the interior of the continent.

Alexander Merensky, who had learnt Portuguese especially for this purpose, collected such documents. He visited other mission stations and copied these early travel descriptions for his archive. In his own travels he also questioned the old people in the villages he came across about what they knew about the as yet unexplored areas to the north of the Limpopo or further to the west, in Bechuanaland (what is today Botswana), or about what they had heard from their fathers. And naturally he also questioned all European travellers, big game hunters and gold prospectors who came back from the areas to the north of the Limpopo, and who spent a night or two at his mission station. Looking at his notes, he realised — and this was confirmed by many a tale — that there had to be a city built of stone somewhere between the Limpopo and the Zambezi, surrounded by walls set with towers. This city was supposed to lie in a land in which gold had been mined in many places.

The notion that there was a city built of stone in the middle of the African bush was in itself quite unusual. The claim that this city was also situated in a land rich in gold made the missionary prick up his ears. As a man of the church well-versed in the Bible, he connected these reports with the land of Ophir, the source of King Solomon's gold, mentioned in 1 Kings in the Old Testament.

The notion of connecting southern Africa with the biblical land of Ophir was not, of course, completely new. In Germany, this idea had already been ventured by the professor of history and philosophy at Göttingen, Arnold H. Heeren (1760–1842), in his then very well-known work on the politics of the peoples of the Ancient World and the trade and communication between them. Around the same time, in France, the famous orientalist Etienne Marc Quatremère published similar conclusions. One has to assume that Alexander Merensky knew at least the work of Arnold H. Heeren. However, Heeren's references to southern Africa were not very precise and did not indicate a particular region. The credit for drawing attention to Matabeleland and the area where the Zimbabwe Ruins were eventually found must almost certainly go to the missionary Alexander Merensky.

He was convinced that this city really had to have existed, and he twice planned to go in search of it. He did not have much luck in his endeavours, though. His first attempt was frustrated by an outbreak of smallpox in some villages north of the Limpopo. His companions were terrified of contracting this disease. Because his black companions refused to go any further, he had to return to Botshabelo. His second attempt to put together a small expedition also came to nothing. While he was still preparing for the journey, he had to abandon his plans, as Botshabelo was attacked.

It was a motley crowd of people who visited Alexander Merensky's mission station over the years, and who were always treated with hospitality. But there were also men among these people who had something to tell him. The missionary gained much from his exchange of ideas with them. One of the people he spoke to a lot – a frequent visitor to the Merenskys, and eventually a good friend of the family – was a German explorer of Africa, Carl Mauch. Today he is almost forgotten in Germany, because he travelled exclusively in regions that were later to become British colonial possessions. Furthermore his work did not lead to the proclamation of a German protectorate. One of the topics that the missionary and Carl Mauch often debated hotly was the existence of a city built of stone mentioned in the old Portuguese writings. Carl Mauch came to accept the missionary's theory that this city must have been the capital of the land of Ophir.

At last, in 1871, Carl Mauch departed on a march into the areas to the north of the Limpopo. Alexander Merensky had made available to him the reports and data that he had gathered on this city surrounded by myth. And indeed, the explorer did discover the ruins that the local people called *Zimbabwe*, a word that was adopted from a local Bantu language. These ruins are one of the most impressive testimonies to a high level of early African civilisation. Today we know that these structures do not go back to biblical times (King Solomon reigned between 965 and 926 BC), but date from the 14$^{th}$ to the 15$^{th}$ century AD. But that does not change the exceptional intellectual and physical achievement of Carl Mauch, who purposefully sought and eventually found the ruins of this city in the bush.

The young Hans Merensky – the hero of this story – had only just been born when Carl Mauch departed on his last expedition. He was therefore too young to remember the explorer. But since the nightly discussions in the Merensky household continued for many years to centre on the topic of the land of Ophir, the Zimbabwe Ruins and the successes of Carl Mauch's expedition, the subject was very real to the boy throughout his childhood. (Carl Mauch has only been discussed in such detail here as an example of one of the missionary's guests and to demonstrate the kind of discussion that tended to dominate around the family dinner table after nightfall.)

Perhaps we should pause here briefly to try to sketch some of the evenings in the house of the missionary. Botshabelo was situated on the 25$^{th}$ latitude south. In the northern hemisphere, that would correspond to the central Sahara or the southern tip of Florida. At that latitude, there are no long, late-lit summer evenings, as one gets in central Europe. Night falls quickly, and the dark nights are long. Of course, there was no electric light then, and even candles tended to be used sparingly. The men sat around the large table, barely lit by light from the fireplace or a small oil lamp. The children would sit outside the circle of light, silent as mice, on the benches along the walls or on the floor and they listened to the men's conversation. They would hear of incredibly beautiful places in nature, of unexploited treasures and many other wonderful things. Often the children might not have understood what the adults were talking about, but they listened to the tales with bated breath. Of course, the men also spoke about diamonds. Since the Berlin Mission owned land in the diamond area on the Vaal River, 25 men had been sent from Botshabelo to prospect for diamonds on the mission's own land. But their success was modest. In five months, the men only found eight small stones and so they returned to Botshabelo. Alexander Merensky went to their encampment to oversee them and to take care of them – at least from time to time. It is unclear from his memoirs whether he himself panned for diamonds, but it is certain that he knew the diamond fields along the Vaal River quite well, and it is very likely that he would have spoken to his guests about this topic on such evenings.

The conversations in the evenings between his father and the adventurers, ivory hunters and gold prospectors that passed through the mission station undoubtedly had an early influence on the young Merensky. Not, of course, that he decided even then to become a geologist. But in the 10-year-old boy a diffuse sense grew that he was living in a land that was infinitely wide, in which, beyond the mountains that surrounded the farm, there were still plenty of wonderful things to discover. He was to take this diffuse sense of the potential of the land with him to Europe, when his father and the family left South Africa in 1882. At that time, Hans Merensky was 11 years old.

---

**Textbox 2 – The land of gold – Ophir**

The land of gold, Ophir, is mentioned in the Old Testament, in 1 Kings 9:
 [26]And King Solomon made a navy of ships in Ezion-geber,
 which is beside Eloth, on the shore of the Red Sea,
 in the land of Edom.

> ²⁷And Hiram sent the navy his servants, shipmen that had knowledge of the sea,
> with the servants of Solomon.
> ²⁸And they came to Ophir, and fetched from thence gold,
> four hundred and twenty talents, and brought it to King Solomon.

Today we know that such reports may well have had a real background, just as we know that King Solomon was a real historical figure.

Solomon was one of the sons of David, the greatest king of Israel, who reigned from about 1000 BC and who was a notable statesman and military commander. Under his long leadership, Israel developed into a complex state structure. David was king of Judea, Israel and Ammon and he ruled over the province of Aram (Damascus), the land of Edom in the south and the vassal kingdom Moab. Toward the end of his reign there was a bloody succession war. King David's oldest son Amnon was murdered by his brother Absalom, who was killed in his turn by some of his father's soldiers when Absalom fled after losing a battle.

At the prompting of Bathsheba, one of David's secondary wives famed for her beauty, the ageing king eventually named as his successor, not his next son Adonijah, but Solomon, his son by Bathsheba. David gave him the regency while David was still alive. Solomon reigned for forty years from 965 BC. Unlike his father, he did not go to war. He was a king of peace. Nevertheless, he managed to maintain David's large kingdom more or less as it was. He became famed as the wisest of all the rulers of whom the Old Testament speaks. His wisdom was spoken of not only in Israel, but became known far beyond the borders of his kingdom in many far-off lands. That eventually led to the famous visit of the Queen of Sheba, who came from the south-west of the Arabian Peninsula to meet him, but who may also have been pursuing her own political objectives, such as establishing trade links.

In this account we also learn that Solomon's court was magnificent, and that he could lay claim to fabulous wealth for his time. That raises the question of where this wealth came from, considering that Solomon did not indulge in predatory wars of conquest. Israel and Judea were essentially agrarian states and they were not naturally so fortunately endowed that one could assume that this wealth could have been generated from the land itself. Even if one argues that in those days the land received more rain and that the pasture was much greener than today because of temporary post-ice age climate changes, the wealth described in the Bible must have come from elsewhere – that is, from trade.

The Israelites in this flowering period under the rule of King Solomon were indeed a very successful trading nation which was engaged in lively trade abroad. The trading products that the king could offer were iron and copper. He mined both of these in local mines. The accompanying smelting sites were excavated by the American archaeologist Nelson Glueck at Tell el-Kheleifeh, very near ancient Eloth, in 1938. Eloth lay 45 kilometres to the north of what is today the northern tip of the Gulf of Akaba and modern Eloth – an indication of how much land has been claimed at the northern end of the Red Sea in the past 3000 years. The smelting sites – they are, in fact, real smelters – were part of a huge complex, perhaps the largest smelting complex in the known world at that time. This suggests that Solomon was not only a wise king, but also a copper magnate, an industrialist, a shipping magnate and royal businessman. There was one thing the Israelites of that time were not – they were not a nation of seafarers. For that reason, they engaged the assistance of the Phoenicians, then the most experienced sailors. King David had already done so, and had maintained friendly relations with Hiram, the King of Tyre, and Solomon continued these relations. With the assistance of the Phoenicians the "servants of Solomon" could reach every coastal strip and every port in the known world, in the Mediterranean, the Red Sea or in the Indian Ocean. For the southern route, Eloth was the port, and nearby, in Ezion-geber, ships were built.

These are the historical facts. To this day, it is unclear where the land of Ophir was situated. Ophir is mentioned in various places in the Old Testament, aside from the verses quoted above, and it seems fairly certain that such journeys were undertaken on several occasions. The expeditions took three years each and they are not described as wars or plundering expeditions. This implies that they were trading expeditions. From these journeys, the travellers brought back gold, precious stones, sandalwood and spices. Since there are no further geographic indications, it is not surprising that historians have connected the land of Ophir with one of the countries that still produce gold and precious stones.

Some possibilities are the Arabian Peninsula, where several small gold deposits have been found; India, where gold is found in the regions around Mysore, Madras and Hyderabad; and, finally, southern Africa, where, in the hinterland of Mozambique, in what is today Zimbabwe, there are many gold deposits. Each of these areas has attracted a number of proponents as the land of Ophir.

There are a large number of scientific publications on the topic and popular semi-scientific works on the topic are legion. It is not the intention of this book to add to their number. However, it must perhaps be mentioned that it is very doubtful that Ophir was on the Arabian Peninsula, because the well-developed system of caravans would have been able to carry the gold overland. Since Solomon's kingdom was also a military power, Solomon's soldiers would have been able to protect the caravans from the attacks of robbers. After all, the Queen of Sheba, with all her valuable gifts, arrived safely in Solomon's court. The strongest argument against

India as the site of the land of Ophir is that India never really exported gold. Whatever was produced there was also consumed there.

If one looks at the length of the expeditions, namely three years, then that would strengthen the argument that the biblical land of Ophir may have been in what is today Zimbabwe. Solomon's people were unlikely to have penetrated deeply into the interior of the continent to purchase gold there, but they probably sent messengers from their anchorage on the coast at Sofala (where Beira is today) into the interior. This meant a route of more than 600 kilometres. By the time the answer had been sent and the gold had been transported to the coast and the trade was completed, several months would have passed. This would provide a plausible explanation for the length of these trading expeditions. Nevertheless, Zimbabwe remains only one option among many for the location of the land of Ophir, and there is no proof that it was the original site.

It should also be mentioned that there is a fourth possibility, namely that the Ophir in the biblical text is not meant to be a geographical place at all, but that the name represents a generic term for a "distant, rich land" or Eldorado of sorts. This opinion was held by several famous explorers, including Alexander von Humboldt, and the researcher who deciphered Assyrian cuneiform script, Jules Oppert.

**Textbox 3 – Carl Mauch discovers the Zimbabwe Ruins**

Carl Mauch is regarded as one of the most significant 19$^{th}$ century explorers in southern Africa. In Germany he has been almost completely forgotten, because he explored regions that later became British colonies and because his work did not lead to the declaration of a German protectorate. But in South Africa, his name is still honoured. So, for example, the highest elevation of the northern Drakensberg, the Mauchberg, with an elevation of 2116 metres above sea level, is named after him.

Carl Mauch was born in Stetten in the Rems Valley in 1837. He had a solid training as a teacher, sound geological knowledge (not unusual among teachers in Swabia) and was able to do geodetical surveying. At the age of 28 he came to South Africa at his own expense and then travelled northward from Durban. From 1865, he explored large parts of what became the Transvaal, Bechuanaland and what was later to become Southern Rhodesia (today Limpopo/Mpumalanga, Botswana and Zimbabwe respectively). Wherever he was, he examined the local types of rock, used his sextant to determine the exact locations and sketched the lay of the land, entering his geological observations.

He became famous in South Africa especially as the discoverer of a number of later very productive gold fields and as one of the first explorers to point out how rich the Transvaal and the neighbouring regions were in gold. In 1867, he discovered the first gold deposit – Inyati near Bulawayo, in the southern part of what is today Zimbabwe. On one of his trips he stumbled upon some diggings, that is, areas in which in pre-European times, minerals had been mined. Such a man-made thing in a landscape otherwise largely untouched by humans did not escape his trained eye, and he made several other similar finds in the years to come in many other places. Often, he also found ancient smelting sites in the vicinity.

Generally, these pre-European diggings did not go far below the surface and were eventually abandoned. In many cases, beneath such ancient diggings there was a deeper mineral deposit. For European gold prospectors and for the businesses that followed on their heels and that wanted to prospect for gold on a large scale, Carl Mauch's discoveries were very interesting indeed. The only problem was that he never saw himself as a prospector and gold-seeker. Once, after he had discovered the gold deposits at Tati, about 500 kilometres to the north of Johannesburg, some people wanted to nominate him as General Director of a newly founded outfitting firm. Since at the time he had some money – the German geographer Dr Petermann, who occasionally supported him, had just sent him a small sum from Gotha – he refused. His urge to explore drove him on.

And so it continued. Carl Mauch never profited from the gold deposits he discovered. He never wanted to stay in any single place for a long time, and he never took the time to work as a gold digger. Although he was often in dire financial straits and often went hungry, he always walked on to discover something new.

On one of his expeditions, he passed the Botshabelo mission station (near today's Middelburg in Mpumalanga), asked whether he could stay overnight and was cordially received by Alexander Merensky. Later, he often returned to Botshabelo, and since the two men had many interests in common, a genuine friendship developed between them. Carl Mauch put his positioning (latitude and longitude) and his sketched maps at the missionary's disposal. The data in these documents were eventually used in the first maps of the Transvaal which Alexander Merensky published in 1868 and 1875. In return, Mauch got some insight into the documents written by the early Portuguese missionaries that Alexander Merensky had collected, and in which there were reports of a city built of stone to the north of the Limpopo. The city was said to be in the middle of a land rich in gold. In the old Portuguese reports, the city was referred to as the capital of the kingdom of Monomotapa. The missionary firmly believed that this was what the Old Testament called the land of Ophir. The Book of Kings said that King Solomon had received his gold from this land. Carl Mauch also adopted this notion, and the two men agreed on a joint expedition to find this fabled city. Unfortunately, the missionary was prevented from joining him, which meant that Carl Mauch had to go alone.

It was his last big journey of discovery, but also his most successful one. It was on this trip, in 1871, that Carl Mauch found the Zimbabwe Ruins to the north of the Limpopo, in Matabeleland. But it was a march full of hardships and great obstacles, because the local tribal chieftains did not want to allow a European to see this city. Although the inhabitants in the surrounding villages at this time no longer knew who had lived in this fortified city and who had built it, they regarded the place as a kind of supernatural or sacred place. Eventually, Mauch met a German-American hunter, Adam Renders, who, four years previously, during a hunting expedition, had come across this ruined city built of stone – probably without realizing the archaeological significance of this discovery. Renders showed Carl Mauch the way to this city. When he finally reached the Zimbabwe Ruins, Mauch was physically almost at the end of his tether. Constant malnutrition had brought him to the verge of a breakdown.

The ruined city impressed him enormously. For more than 200 years no European had seen this city, but the old Portuguese reports were proven to have been correct. The city was indeed surrounded by stone walls, set with towers. It was a large construction with a fortress on a hill; and – there was no doubt about it – the city was indeed situated in an area in which there was gold. On his way to Zimbabwe, Carl Mauch had seen a string of ancient diggings, and in the Matabele villages along his route he had encountered many gold diggers. He believed that he had indeed found the land of Ophir.

Because he was so exhausted, Carl Mauch had to stay in Zimbabwe for some time. At last, he continued his journey. Ill and shaking with fever, accompanied by only one companion, he dragged himself 900 kilometres right across what is today Zimbabwe to the lower reaches of the Zambezi River. He hoped to find in Sena, a small Portuguese settlement, some mail and a little money from Dr Petermann, but he was disappointed. He was now completely without funds. The Portuguese took him in and looked after him. At last, they took him 200 kilometres downriver to the mouth of the Zambezi, from where a French ship took him to Europe. Carl Mauch lived another three years in very modest circumstances in Württemberg. He died in Stuttgart in 1875, only 37 years old, after falling out of a window.

Before he died, he was able to publish his discovery of the Zimbabwe Ruins or the "Goldland of Ophir". As so often in his life, he did not profit from his discoveries at all. But others did. Matabeleland was soon swamped with gold seekers, and soon thereafter the area was declared a British sphere of influence. In 1889, Cecil John Rhodes started the British South Africa Company, which acquired large tracts of land in the next few years. The path to the foundation of the colony of Southern Rhodesia was paved. These political developments meant that in Germany interest in Carl Mauch's discoveries faded, and so his name was forgotten.

By contrast, anglophone archaeologists began intensive research on the ruined stone city. Initially, they were firmly convinced of the truth of the hypothesis that the Zimbabwe Ruins were the vestiges of a Phoenician settlement and that they were indeed the remains of the biblical land of Ophir, as was argued, for example, in the comprehensive works of Richard Nicklin Hall (1902) and W.G. Neal (1907). Then Egyptologist David Randall MacIver (1906) undertook an objective new evaluation of all finds and concluded that the Ruins were considerably younger than had previously been assumed and that they were of purely African origin. None of the objects that he was able to recover was any older than the $14^{th}$ or $15^{th}$ centuries, and he could not discover any elements of European or Oriental style in the Ruins. Moreover, there were no inscriptions in the city. Clearly, its inhabitants had not yet developed the art of writing. Little more than 20 years later, British archaeologist Gertrude Canton-Thompson undertook research on a much wider scale. By that time, it had become much easier to move about in the colony of Southern Rhodesia, and so she counted no fewer than 500 sites with ruins between the Zambezi and the Limpopo. Among them were the Ruins of Inyanga, which covered an even bigger area than the Zimbabwe Ruins. This implies that the Zimbabwe Ruins should not be looked at in isolation, but as forming part of a large settlement area inhabited by an African people, possibly advanced Bantu tribes.

The mystery of Zimbabwe appears to have been largely solved. But that does not mean that King Solomon's gold did not come from this region after all. Among the finds in the excavations at Zimbabwe, there were necklaces of Indian and Malaysian origin. They prove that trade relations existed between Zimbabwe and the coast and that these stretched right across the Indian Ocean in the $14^{th}$ and $15^{th}$ centuries. We can therefore assume that these Indian and Malaysian wares were paid for in gold. And what was possible 500 years ago, namely gold export from the region, could also have been possible 2400 years earlier, in the time of Solomon, whether or not the stone walls of Zimbabwe already stood then.

CHAPTER 3

# Lieutenant of the Guard and mining assessor

The family returned to Berlin, where Alexander Merensky began a second career that was just as successful as the first. From 1883 he first worked as Inspector of the Berlin City Mission and from 1886 to 1909 he worked as Mission Inspector for the entire Berlin Mission Society.

Alexander Merensky became a much sought-after man almost immediately after his arrival, because it was at this time that German colonial development was starting to accelerate. Hanseatic merchants had long argued that Germany should not only trade abroad but should, like the British, also build settlements that would enjoy the protection of the German government. Several attempts were made. In 1883, on the coast of South West Africa, a wholesale merchant from Bremen, Adolf Lüderitz, acquired the small bay called Angra Pequeña, which is now known as Lüderitz (and which, in Merensky's day, was still referred to as "Lüderitzbucht"). The Chancellor of the German Empire, Otto von Bismarck, who had thus far refused to consider the wishes of the merchants, changed his mind. In 1884 the government gave permission for this acquisition. This made Lüderitzbucht (Lüderitz Bay) the germ of German South West

Africa. In the same year Carl Peters acquired German East Africa, which soon after that also became a German Protectorate. Everybody in Germany was suddenly interested in overseas regions, but nobody knew exactly how to establish trade there or what difficulties would be encountered. It was precisely at that moment that a missionary returned from Africa – someone who had worked there successfully for 24 years. He could report on how the British acquired and established colonies, and he knew much about British administrative practice. But he could also tell people about the locals, about their character and about the possibility of using them as labourers. These were highly current topics. In short, the experienced missionary Alexander Merensky was swamped with invitations to address people on conditions in Africa, and such invitations increased when, in 1884, it became known that he had published a map of South Africa. Indeed, he was happy to provide such information, because in principle he supported the colonial movement. He did so without making any concessions with regard to the Gospel. Like many others, he was firmly convinced that it was one of the tasks of German Christians to acquaint Africans who had come under German rule with the Christian faith. Hence, he did not hesitate when in 1891 he was again sent to Africa. At that time, the Berlin Mission opened a new field of activity in the southern part of German East Africa and there was no one who was better equipped for this task than he. At the age of 54 he was admittedly much older than most people who went into the tropics, but he did not refuse and led the process of building up the new mission for several years and with great success.

Alexander Merensky did not only share his vast knowledge about Africa with others in his talks and in discussions, but also in the form of numerous scientific publications. He proved to be an all-round expert. His most comprehensive and probably his most significant contributions were his texts on the geography of South Africa, and his maps of the Transvaal. He also published on the climate, on malaria, leprosy and other tropical diseases, as well as on veterinary matters such as the acclimatisation of European horses to South Africa. There were also numerous publications on the principles of missionary work and the problem, then very acute in Africa, of the clash between Christianity and other religions. His unusually wide engagement with such topics was accorded high honours by the scientific community. The universities of Heidelberg and Berlin awarded Alexander Merensky a doctorate honoris causa and as a very exceptional and rare honour, the Leopoldina, the oldest and most famous German academy of science, made him an honorary member.

Meanwhile, his sons were exposed to the German educational system. The three eldest were first sent to a boarding school in Gütersloh. They did not like it at all. They were used to having much more personal freedom and found the atmosphere oppressive. The chief opponent of the system was Alexander Jr., the oldest of the three. Eventually the experiment was abandoned and the children were brought home to their parents' home in Berlin-Moabit. Then they were sent to the Luisenstädtische Gymnasium in Moabit for the remainder of their secondary schooling. Hans Merensky was not a brilliant scholar, but he also never did particularly poorly. Generally, he preferred to perform at an unobtrusively average level. His father was occasionally really worried about this. He felt that his son "lacked bite". When he began working towards his *Abitur* (his senior and 13th school year), his parents made another attempt to turn him into an actively engaged pupil. They hoped that a new environment, and perhaps some new friends, might make a difference, and so the boy was sent to a school in Gartz an der Oder. And indeed things did change, but not quite in the way that his parents had hoped. With the approval of the school's directors, Hans Merensky established a rowing club. Thanks to his organisational talent and his gift for persuasion, he was soon able to attract active members from among his school fellows and after some training the club soon had its first sporting successes. Alas – it comes as no surprise – these successes were accompanied by even poorer scholastic performance, not only by Hans Merensky, but also by some of his fellow pupils. Fortunately, the situation was not so bad that it seriously endangered his completion of his *Abitur*.

Nevertheless, the episode was symptomatic, and it reveals a number of the traits that Hans Merensky was to keep throughout his life. He was eloquent; he was persuasive; and, when he felt strongly about something, he was very capable of taking the lead and running a team. In addition, he was always prepared to help everyone, and was very charming. Wherever he was, he always had a large circle of friends.

Soon after completing his *Abitur*, he was called up for military service. He served with the Rifle Guards, which were garrisoned in Berlin-Lichterfelde. He ended his military service as a Reserve Lieutenant.

An episode from this period of his life shows that, when push came to shove, Hans Merensky could act very decisively and was courageous, even cold blooded. He was an enthusiastic hunter and a very good shot. One of the hunting opportunities open to him at any time, was one offered on the von Thaer family's estate in Silesia. The family were old friends of the Merenskys'. The father of the family was a general, and his son, Albrecht von Thaer, was Hans Merensky's best friend from an early age.

At some point, while he was still serving in the military, he visited the estate for a weekend. One evening he went out alone to stalk some game, when, suddenly, he was confronted by four armed men. From behind some trees about 30 or 40 metres away from him, they ordered him to drop his weapon and surrender. They were Polish poachers who had crossed the nearby border (this kind of incursion happened quite frequently). Merensky instantly took refuge behind a tree himself and ordered the poachers to surrender. He had barely shouted his command when one of the men took aim and fired. Merensky shot back at virtually the same moment. There was a scream and the man disappeared into the underbrush. Seconds later, another man appeared from behind another tree and took aim. Merensky shot again and the man fell down and lay still. Then came the sound of branches breaking and a few muffled words, and then there was silence.

Merensky waited for more than a quarter of an hour to be certain that the men had left. Then he slipped over, very cautiously, to the man lying on the ground. He had been hit between the eyes and was dead. Where the first shooter had stood, there was a bloody trail through the woods. The situation was awkward. He had shot the man in self-defence, but there were no witnesses and therefore he was afraid that he would get into some trouble.

Fortunately, old Mr von Thaer, who knew how dangerous these poachers were, took the matter in hand. The police were informed, but at the same time, it was made clear that Merensky was a soldier and that therefore the military authorities would have to be involved. Back at the garrison, Merensky waited anxiously to see how things would develop. Some time later, he was ordered to go to see his Commander, who told him that the matter had been resolved. The dead man had been identified as a wanted gang-leader, and the Royal Commission of Hunting and Forests had recommended that Merensky be decorated for his bravery.

The von Thaer family and their estate Pawonkau played an important role in the development of the young Hans Merensky in several ways. When he was still at school, he spent large parts of his holidays with Albrecht, this friend of his youth; and later, when he was in the army and when he began to study, he was a frequent weekend guest. Old Mr von Thaer was a wise and far-sighted man. He was a dedicated and enthusiastic soldier, but at the same time, it was completely clear to him that the estate was the focal point of the family, and he did all he could to preserve it for his family for the future. That meant that his son Albrecht had to learn all he needed to know about forestry and agricultural activities from the bottom up early on. Later, he was inducted into the business management side of the running of the estate. That was often very hard work, but it was also highly instructive, because the estate was run as a model estate. Whenever Hans Merensky visited Pawonkau, he was integrated into the same educational programme as his friend. He participated gladly, because he had grown up on a farm and these things interested him. This was where he learnt a great deal about agriculture and forestry in passing. Forty years later the experience he had picked up in Silesia would be very useful to him.

While he was performing his military service, he came to a decision about his career. Hans Merensky's military record was without blemish, but he felt almost unbearably hemmed in, and so he wanted a career in which he could work independently. He often discussed the problem with his friend Albrecht von Thaer. Albrecht's personal future was laid out very clearly for him. He wanted to become an officer, as had been a tradition in his family for generations, and, after all, Pawonkau was his home and main concern. For Hans Merensky things were different. For a while, he considered taking up an old family tradition. His paternal grandfather, who had died early, had been a fourth generation forester in Silesia, and hence he briefly played with the idea of becoming a forester too. He loved the forest and the work in it, and, of course, hunting. But then he began to recognise that even in this job, all his life he would have to work for someone else, and would always be dependent on someone else. Once he had come to this insight, by a kind of process of elimination he eventually settled on a career as geologist and miner, because he believed that this career would give him the greatest possible personal liberty.

His studies for this career began, as prescribed for mining students, with one year of practical training underground. So he worked as *Bergbaubeflissener* (a mining student trainee doing his compulsory year of underground training) in a coal mine in Upper Silesia. Then Merensky went to Breslau, which was the perfect city in which to study geology. The university was a good one, and a mere 90 kilometres away was the Riesengebirge, the Eulengebirge and the remaining Sudetes, in which in those days there were still numerous active ore pits. Moreover, in the lower reaches of the mountains was the lone peak called the Zobten, a mountain with exceptionally interesting geological formations and deposits of semi-precious stones, including the famous Silesian Chrysoprase. This offered the young student the possibility of excursions to find lots of study material. As a result, he thoroughly enjoyed his studies in Breslau. Even then, his professors certified his noticeably good ability to observe detail during practical work in the field.

Merensky left Breslau after two and a half years. Initially he again worked for another half year in a coal mine in the Saarland, this time as an overseer. Then he went to Berlin for the technical part of his mining studies. After another six semesters, he sat for his first State Examination and thus became a *Preußischer Bergreferendar* (in the Prussian system, a mining graduate became a *Referendar* after passing the first State Examination while undergoing preliminary in-service training before attempting the second State Examination to become a fully-fledged assessor) for three years. This period was exceptionally important to him because he had an opportunity, which he took with great enthusiasm, to study practically all the mining districts in the German Empire. He went into the pits in the Erzgebirge, into the lead and zinc mines in the Harz

Mountains, into the most famous and oldest German ore mine, the Rammelsberg near Goslar, and the coal mines in the Ruhrgebiet. But he was not only fascinated by the study of mineral deposits. During his time as a *Referendar*, he also acquired the business management skills connected with the proper submission of accounts for mining and acquired particularly excellent technical training. Eventually, he completed his second state examination, and at the age of 33 he was pronounced a Prussian mining assessor.

He barely had his certificate of appointment in his hand when he took an option open to him to take one year's temporary leave from state service. All the young men who did their examination with him did so. They took a sabbatical and took a year to work in private industry to see whether they could pursue a career there. The government tolerated this migration of young mining assessors, and indeed even promoted it, because the practice ensured that the German mining industry got well-trained successors for its top functions later. So Hans Merensky claimed his right to such a sabbatical, but his application and the permission granted to him looked somewhat different from that granted to his fellow students, namely: *Genehmigt. Studienurlaub in Südafrika zwecks Berichterstattung über die Grubentätigkeit in Südafrika* [Granted. Sabbatical in South Africa to report on mining activity in South Africa].

CHAPTER 4

# Consulting geologist in South Africa

Hans Merensky arrived in South Africa at the start of 1904. He was 33 years old – for an immigrant (for such he was) who was to become a multi-millionaire, this was quite old. At least he did not start as a dishwasher, but arrived in South Africa with excellent double professional qualifications. When it came to geology and the study of mineral deposits, he was at the very forefront of scientific knowledge, and the training he had completed in Berlin as a mining engineer was then regarded as the best in the world. Moreover, he spoke the two languages of the country, Afrikaans and English. He did not know very much about the country, because he had been too young to see much before he went to Germany with his parents in 1882. But he was to prove to have something far more important, namely a special feeling for the peculiar mentality of the Boer farmers. This was to prove vital, because the farmers formed part of his clientele. He was familiar with their way of life from his childhood. The friendship that he encountered on many farms made his work in the field much easier and in this way contributed to his successes. And it was the Boer farmers who raised him up at the lowest point in his career, when he was physically in a terrible shape, and who literally put him back on his feet and helped him to get back to work again. It was also the farmers who asked him to lead the prospecting campaign for platinum, which was to become one of his biggest successes.

But there was something else that was even more important than these personal traits: Merensky came back to South Africa with a very clear idea of what he wanted to do over here, or rather, of what he was certainly not prepared to do. He wanted to be independent and he wanted to work as a freelance geologist. He clung to this ideal for the rest of his life. It became the basis of his success.

There are no reliable reports about the first few weeks he spent back in the country. We also do not know who the first people were that he made contact with. We do know with certainty, however, that he never tried to get a job as a geologist at any mining company.

Two months after he arrived, he was in Johannesburg. He had rented a small office, not exactly in the city centre, but not too far away from it. The furniture was simple: a table, two chairs, a bookcase and a hat stand. He had a small side room in which he could store his rock samples and do simple analyses. On the door there was a proud sign, which read:

Hans Merensky
Consulting Geologist and Mining Engineer
(Previously of the Prussian Mines Department)

Such a description of the professional background of a person on his firm's sign or business card would seem strange in Germany, but in South Africa at that time it was quite normal. Moreover, Hans Merensky knew that if he wanted to have any business success he would have to advertise; and so, he did not hide away modestly. Indeed, he did not hide his light under a bushel, and advertised his good training and origins clearly.

So, what did a consulting geologist do in South Africa in those days? To understand that, one has to understand the mining legislation in the Transvaal. It was phrased in such a way that the owner of a piece of land owned all the minerals found on his land, irrespective of what they were. The finds could be coal, gold or any other kind of mineral, or even diamonds. Whoever owned the land could give people options and thus permission to dig or pan on his land.

If a prospector found anything, he could exchange his options for concessions. These then gave him the right to mine the mineral resources.

The land people owned in the Transvaal consisted mainly of scattered farms, large and small, of which there were over 4000. Many of these belonged to the farmers themselves; others were owned by large companies that rented out the land. Beside Pretoria, named after President Andries Pretorius and already founded in 1855, there were no large cities other than Johannesburg, which had begun from a gold diggers' settlement in 1886, but then grew very quickly. By 1887 Johannesburg already had a stock exchange; and now, a mere 20 years later, it was rapidly becoming a large city. For the rest, there were only a number of smallish settlements. At that stage quite a number of significant mineral deposits had already been discovered in the country. In 1869, the first large diamond finds had been made in Kimberley. These were soon followed by more. By the start of the 1880s, the first gold mines had begun to operate on the Witwatersrand. Several coal deposits and deposits of various ores had also been identified.

The farmers and the townspeople of South Africa at that time shared a sense of living in a country in which there were still many hidden treasures and where, with a bit of luck, anyone could get rich if he found precious stones, gold or a useful ore. People acted accordingly. There were countless numbers of gold and ore prospectors, trekking through the land, panning here and there or moving from one gold-field to the next. Even if one had a solid job and a fixed abode, one was always thinking and wondering whether there would not be a big find waiting out there. Many farmers panned and dug as a hobby. When they rode out into the veld, they often took along panning equipment, dangling from their saddle, and when, after a shower of rain, they came across a large puddle, they quickly panned a few pans full of soil or sand around it, to see whether it did not contain a few flakes of gold or anything else that was of interest. And so every stone that looked a bit different or was heavier than others was taken home and then taken to an expert for appraisal.

This meant that consulting geologists had a lot to do. From all corners of the country, rock and soil samples were sent to Johannesburg for expert appraisal and analysis. These were not large jobs. A single analysis cost only about one pound, but it brought in a small income.

There were a few large commissions, because, if any ore concentrations had been found anywhere that looked promising, consortiums were quickly formed that were interested in exploiting the resources and acquiring a concession. And that was when the problems started. To start a mine, no matter how small, one needed capital, and that was not freely available. The concessionaires were often farmers. As farmers on their own land, they were self-sufficient and had everything they needed to survive, but they had no cash. Even the prospectors looking for ore throughout the country tended to live from hand to mouth. This implied that to get money, people had to issue share certificates which could be traded on the stock exchange in Johannesburg. However, to be able to do so, the potential mineral deposit had to be thoroughly examined and a genuine geological expert opinion had to be presented. This was the consulting geologists' sphere of activity, and preparing such a "bank document" in preparation for shares being released on the stock exchange was generally also financially quite worthwhile.

Even more lucrative were commissions from the large finance houses or private financiers. By this time, all the large European banks had branches in the Transvaal, particularly in Johannesburg. They followed the ups and downs of the raw materials markets and waited for an opportunity to get a stake in the financial development of new mining enterprises. The condition on which they would do so was that there was proof that the project would be profitable. And since these backers often wanted to invest considerable sums, they set great store by the relevant expert opinions. Thus only the very best consulting geologists could count on being commissioned for that kind of work.

At that time, there were quite a number of such consulting geologists in Johannesburg; or at least, this seems to have been the case from the number of names that appear with Merensky's in various publications or documents. There were old, experienced geologists who had worked in the country for many years, some of whom had had great successes. And then there were young mining engineers or geologists like Merensky who were just starting to establish themselves. They came from mining schools in England, the Netherlands,

Austria and Germany and were familiar with state-of-the-art mining techniques and with the newest developments in geology as a science.

There were others who had never even seen the inside of an auditorium in a mining school or university, but who were top rate practitioners. There were men who had panned for gold and who had been working in the gold-fields in South Africa and neighbouring countries for 30 or more years, and there were men who had panned for diamonds and who had taken part in every diamond rush since the discovery at Kimberley. These were men with a good "nose" and an enormous amount of experience. The theoretical basis of geology as a science did not concern them. On the other hand, they knew how to evaluate an ore find, how to put together a prospecting project and what material was needed. More importantly, they knew what one had to do when one had made a major discovery and how to prevent speculators from robbing one of one's hard-earned living. Now that they were old, they advised farmers who had found something on their farms, or passed their knowledge down to young men who wanted to learn the craft of prospecting.

Then there were others who were only interested in certain parts of the country, for example, the north or the Bushveld or the Orange Free State to the south. They too managed to earn a living.

The young Merensky moved effortlessly among all these specialists, some of whom were still surrounded by the glamorous aura of their earlier successes. Thanks to his genial nature and his charm he soon made friends in this circle. From the start, he had no problem getting jobs, even though in the beginning only smaller jobs were passed on to him.

In the year after his arrival, Merensky experienced the big tin rush of 1905. At that time, tin was found in the granite hills of the Bushveld to the north of Pretoria. There were several deposits. Some of these finds were based on the rediscovery of ancient diggings from pre-European times, others were new discoveries. The deposits stretched over many kilometres, and at some of the places where the ore was discovered the geologists noted exceptionally high ore concentrations. The level of excitement in Johannesburg about the finds was correspondingly high. The prices of tin shares shot up dramatically; and soon the whole stock exchange was buzzing with rumours of tin. Then some reports placed in question the real extent of the mineral deposits and described the possible ore reserves as much more modest than had initially been estimated. Subsequently, the share prices fell between 40% and 50% within two days, only to rise again a week later, when different news came in. The new report was only a "preliminary" one, but speculators claimed that the report was extremely positive and were able to mislead other investors. This game was repeated several times. For two months the prices of tin shares were characterised by wild fluctuations. By the time the price stabilised at a more moderate level, some speculators had made good profits, but many investors had lost vast sums.

For Merensky the tin rush and the related stock exchange speculations were important experiences. He was shocked at the rashness with which preliminary geological reports that, from a specialist point of view, actually had very little substance, were made public. He was horrified that the authors of such reports apparently knowingly accepted that their reports created upsets in the stock exchange or were even abused by speculators. These shenanigans taught him a lesson and showed him what not to do. In his later professional life, Merensky never compiled a prospecting report without ensuring that the results and overall judgement were underpinned by very thorough investigation. Consequently, he never had to withdraw or rescind a report because of incorrect projections.

Of course, in his long professional career, Merensky did not only deliver positive expert opinions. To protect those who employed him from making investments that would result in losses, he was often forced to evaluate a potentially good deposit negatively. It was one particular negative evaluation that gave him his big breakthrough.

---

**Textbox 4 – What is the difference between prospecting and exploration?**
These two terms are not used consistently by internationally active mining companies, oil companies and the Geological Services in various countries.
　　According to American usage, **prospecting** refers to the search for usable mineral deposits by **individual** geologists or prospectors based on their personal observations and the samples they take in the field.

By contrast, **exploration** is a systematic search for viable mineral deposits by mining firms, Geological Services or other international organisations. In exploration, a broad spectrum of instruments and geophysical and geochemical investigative methods are used, and this implies **teamwork**.

In the German use of the terms, the term **exploration** is used to refer to the quest for oil and gas fields, while the term **prospecting** is used almost exclusively to refer to the quest for viable deposits of ores or industrial minerals.

The **methods** used in prospecting by an individual prospector who works for himself are relatively simple and limited in terms of their scope. A thorough knowledge of the rock formations and the minerals or ores that may be expected in individual formations remains the basic requirement for this type of work. A "feel" for the ways in which different types of rock weather and for the shape of the landscape is vital, because outcropping ore bodies are often visible in the landscape if the prospector or geologist knows what morphological details to look for. So, for example, iron ore deposits in the tropics are often covered by hard iron ore crusts. That is how they resist erosion and then create mighty mountain ranges. Other mineralisations are connected to quartz dikes or veins that can be seen clearly in the landscape because they are so hard and do not weather away as easily as surrounding soil or some other types of rock.

Basically, a prospector needs to notice any deviations from the norm, because it is precisely such deviations that may indicate the presence of a mineral beneath the surface. That is why an ability to spot detail and register everything is so important. While it is relatively rare for a prospector to find pieces of ore in the gravel or even tiny pieces of coal in the bed of a stream or in the scree on a slope, it does occasionally happen. But a prospector far more frequently comes across less unambiguous signs, such as rust-brown oxidation zones or ochre deposits around springs. A prospector must be wide awake when he encounters unusual colours. Only seldom do these take the shape of lovely crystals, such as those one sees in mineralogical collections. Far more frequently, they take the shape of microcrystalline masses visible as encrustations on bedding planes and in open cracks in rocks. They could appear as mere colour variations in the soil or in the rock. So, for example, mauve patches in the soil could indicate the presence of lithium ore, blue or dark green stainings could point to the presence of copper oxides, pale green crystals could point to the presence of nickel and amorphous yellow masses could reveal molybdenum ochre. A prospector must follow up every indication he finds. This also applies to variations in the vegetation. So, for example, stunted vegetation could be caused by a body of ore that does not lie too far below the surface.

Otherwise prospectors have to rely on simple analyses and methods to determine particular types of rock. There are also various kinds of mechanical tasks that a prospector can perform himself, or with the assistance of helpers he can engage locally where he is working. These include washing sand and soil samples in a pan (a perfectly effective instrument to prove the presence of gold, platinum, tin or diamonds), digging test trenches or sinking small shafts and also drilling smaller holes by hand. All in all, this is a very modest bag of tricks, and the most important of the "tools" at the disposal of a prospector is the individual prospector's "nose".

This kind of prospecting by an individual has become quite rare. Only occasionally does one still encounter such an independent prospector or digger in Namibia, South Africa or Australia. The seekers of valuable ores and precious stones that are found in the Andes countries or in the Brazilian jungle, looking for gold, emeralds and diamonds, or the hobby prospectors that one occasionally comes across in Alaska and the Rocky Mountains, also belong to this group.

Modern exploration as practised by the large firms or geological survey services is quite different. Right at the start of a prospecting campaign, while they are collecting data on the region they are interested in, they tap any imaginable sources of information. Sometimes they harness the expertise of widely divergent branches of science. This sounds very abstract, but it can be explained by means of two examples:

In the 1950s, in Mauritania in the vicinity of Fort Gouraud, one of the most significant iron ore deposits in Africa was discovered. By then, the pointers to the possible existence of this deposit were already 25 years old. Famous French postal pilots Jean Mermoz (1901–1936), Antoine de Saint-Exupéry (1900–1944) and others had first reported the indicators. At the end of the 1920s, these mail pilots were flying some of the first flights from Marseilles to Rio, with a stopover in Dakar (Senegal). They reported that when they flew from Marseilles, after they had crossed the Atlas Mountains and the Mauritanian Desert, they experienced some difficulty in keeping their south-westerly course toward Dakar, because their compasses sometimes went crazy.

The suspicion that this magnetic anomaly could be caused by a magnetite-bearing iron ore deposit obviously arose. But at that stage, there was little interest in investigating whether this suspicion was correct. At that time, an iron ore deposit in the dessert, far from any port, would not have been economically viable. At that stage, the only prospecting that was done in francophone West Africa was for gold, and that only in areas where there was a lot of water and where people had been panning for gold long before the arrival of any Europeans, for example, in Guinea and in the Ivory Coast. When large-scale geological exploration of West Africa took off after the Second World War, one of the first prospecting campaigns followed up on the clues left behind by the mail pilots, and this soon led to the discovery of the iron ore deposit near Fort Gouraud. By then, the two pilots had already died – Mermoz in 1936 on his 24th flight over the South Atlantic, Saint-Exupéry in 1944 on a military reconnaissance flight over the Mediterranean.

But there is another story to tell where the first clues are even more unusual. In developing countries, it is an accepted geological practice to interview local people in the bush or jungle and, if possible, to show them samples of the ores or types of rock that the geologists are looking for. Because these people are so close to nature and because they often have amazingly accurate powers of observation, they have been able to give geologists in many countries valuable pointers towards viable mineral occurrences. In the 1960s, the directorate of the French Bureau de Recherches Géologiques et Minières responsible for West Africa went one step further, and decided to go through all the literary sources they could get hold of. Since most African peoples tend to have a rich oral culture, but did not develop writing, one might suppose that written testimonies about West Africa would be rare and would only start around the middle of the 19th century with reports written by the first European explorers in Africa. But that is not the case. Five hundred years before, the entire Sahara had been part of the Arabic Muslim cultural sphere of influence. Since the climate then was not quite as arid as it is now, at that time the Sahara was often crossed by travellers, geographers and writers from East to West and back again. Among them was Ibn Battuta (1304–1377), who had trained in law and who is regarded as one of the most outstanding world travellers ever. He travelled in the Orient as far as China, and reached Timbuktu in the western Sahara.

When the Arabic texts on West Africa were studied, it was found that three springs whose Arabic names contained the word "copper" were mentioned in the vicinity of Agadez, which is in the north of what is today the Republic of Niger. Alas, in this region no Arabic place names survive today. When the French arrived in the central Sahara around 1900, the Tuareg lived there, and all places had Tuareg names.

This implied that the problem could not be solved by studying maps, and so it was decided to send geologists into the area around Agadez to prospect for copper. In the young sandstone formations that surround the much older Aïr Mountains, they found numerous thin coverings of malachite in rock clefts and bedding planes relatively quickly. Malachite is a copper carbonate that is often found in the oxidation zone of copper deposits. This was a good start. But they noticed something else in the rock clefts – a mineralization in shades between the colour of sulphur and lemon yellow. This indicated the presence of uranium.

The rest of the story can be quickly told. The French Commissariat à l'Energie Atomique (CEA) was informed. The CEA geologists were flown in, and swarmed over the region. In the desert along the western edges of the

Aïr Mountains, they found further signs of uranium mineralization. They stopped prospecting for copper, the CEA took over, and soon the uranium deposit at Arlit, 60 kilometres to the north west of Agadez, was found. It is the fourth largest such deposit in the world.

Coincidence played a role in this discovery in two ways. Firstly, the fact that the initial hints of the mineral riches near Agadez came from Arabic texts, was unusual. Secondly, it was unusual for uranium minerals to be immediately identified in the field, because there are only a few geologists who would be able to do so on first sight. But in the group of geologists who had come to prospect for copper and who did not have a Geiger counter with them, there was a young Hungarian geologist called Imreh, who had fled from Budapest in 1956 and who had been in the Belgian Congo since then. There he had worked in what was then Katanga, in Shinkolobwe, and had encountered uranium minerals. If he had not been one of the team at Agadez, the uranium mineralization there would probably have been overlooked.

The examples above illustrate the comprehensive preparation that precedes actual prospecting. The subsequent **main prospecting** process is no less detailed and comprehensive. Aerial surveys play a large role in the main prospecting activities. **Satellite images** reveal large geological structures and help geologists to narrow the areas to be investigated. **Aerial photographs** can replace topographic maps in remote areas. They also show details that enable the geologists to focus their work on certain places. Inspection of such photographs is followed by **geophysical** prospecting, done partially from the air and partially on the ground. In this process, various physical parameters of the types of rocks below the surface are measured and mineral occurrences are identified where the parameters of one type of rock is clearly different from that of the surrounding type of rock. Here are a few examples: Since the density of deep-seated salt plugs is lower than that of the surrounding rocks, salt plugs can be identified by measuring the specific gravity. Ore occurrences can be identified in the same way. In this case rocks containing ores have a greater density than the surrounding rock. The De Beers company employed this principle in the eastern Kalahari, where they used a low-flying Zeppelin to do gravity measures. The purpose of such measurements is to identify diamond-bearing kimberlite pipes under the desert sand (see Textbox 7). Magnetic measurements have been used to locate iron ore deposits (see above) and electromagnetic measurements have helped identify sulphide deposits with a good conductivity. If one is prospecting for radioactive materials, radiometric apparatus (such as a beryllometer and a scintillometer) are used. Once an area has been classified as promising based on such measurements, **geochemical** prospecting begins. Today, prospecting companies no longer analyse a few isolated ore or rock samples, but hundreds or thousands of soil samples. They are taken in the form of longitudinal lines or in grid patterns and are tested for the percentage of two or three, sometimes up to twenty, elements they contain.

All this can only be touched on briefly here. What is important is that modern prospecting involves the simultaneous or co-ordinated input and work of many specialists. This implies that today, with a few rare exceptions, deposits are no longer discovered by individuals. Maintaining geophysical apparatus, field laboratories, the vehicles used in what is often rough terrain, etc. requires the kind of logistic expenditure that only organisations with a number of specialists can provide; and the team members need to complement each other.

CHAPTER 5

# The Madagascar gold

During the first few months of 1905, reports reached Johannesburg about significant gold finds in Madagascar. Initially people were somewhat surprised, because Madagascar was not noted for being a land rich in gold deposits. There were known to be rock series that were believed to be very ancient, but, at that stage, no one knew whether their age and origins were anything like those of the known gold-bearing formations in South Africa. Generally, little was known about the geology of the country. At that point only the Madagascan semi-precious stones had a worldwide reputation. French seafarer Captain Jean Fonteneau wrote about these finds as early as 1547, but they only began to be mined properly in 1895. In the years after that, the famous geologist and mineralogist Alfred Lacroix, secretary for life of the French Academy of Sciences, had had semi-precious stones from Madagascar cut and had exhibited them at the Paris World Exhibition in 1900. The tourmalines displayed in the French Africa pavilion, particularly the breathtakingly lovely pigeon blood red variety, rubellite, became one of the sensations of the Exhibition. But that was all people knew about deposits in Madagascar. Gold had so far played no role in that country. Here and there natives had found gold in alluvial placer deposits, but the official statistics quantified the production at a mere few kilograms.

Now a mining engineer called J.E. Jones had returned from Madagascar and reported that he had made some magnificent gold finds. He claimed that they had been in very generously staked-out concession areas held by a Monsieur Louis Lecomte. Jones, who had already acquired 14 of the 32 claims from Lecomte, reported that there were ore reserves of 25 million tons with an average gold content of 10 ounces (311 gram) per ton. That was indeed sensational, because this calculation implied that the concessions Jones had acquired would yield 7775 tons of gold. Jones, who had meanwhile started the Lecomte Madagascar Gold Concession, took on a string of renowned financiers in his company and this gave him access to a considerable amount of capital. The large South African mining companies and finance houses therefore quickly took up options on the remaining 18 claims. This rapid action by the mining companies was both understandable and necessary, because, if the figures proved to be correct, they faced the threat that the Madagascar gold would provide real competition for what had thus far been the most significant gold deposit in the world – the Witwatersrand. No bank and no large mining company could afford to ignore this threat or miss such an opportunity.

The next logical step was to check the deposits. The banks and mining companies engaged the services of the best geologists they could find. Merensky was engaged to undertake this task for Friedlaender & Co., a Rothschild subsidiary. By then, the Rothschild group had already been involved in raw materials projects throughout the world for decades. So, for example, the group had financed the drilling of the first European oil fields at Baku, on the Caspian Sea, a few years earlier. Naturally, the group also wanted a share of any new Eldorado that was possibly to be mined in Madagascar.

In the end, 21 geologists gathered in Durban, each working for one or another company or interested party. Since no scheduled steamship was departing for Madagascar, a ship on its way to Mauritius, the *Comrie Castle*, was chartered to make the detour to Madagascar. The group of geologists sailed on board this ship on 20 July 1905.

The experts disembarked on Madagascar's hot and humid east coast, on the beach at Mananjary, and they were then quickly transported from the mosquito-infested coastal region to the highlands, to Fianarantsoa, 150 kilometres away. There the party split into two groups. One team went to Anjeva, where some options had been taken up; the other, among them Merensky, travelled toward Anosivola, where Lecomte's concessions were situated.

Close to the areas where the gold had reportedly been found, a large camp had been prepared for them in which a round hut stood ready for each of them. There was also a large roofed area where they could eat together and where they spent their evenings talking. Immediately after their arrival, the various mining specialists began to work on the respective strips they had been allocated or which had already been taken. The area Merensky was to examine was traversed by a long crystalline lime ridge in which there were several bands of gneiss, a coarse-grained metamorphic rock type. Its original mineral composition was not obvious at first glance. The gold mineralisation was supposed to be found in these irregularly distributed gneiss bands. This was in principle not the kind of geological environment in which one would expect this type of mineralisation, but this question was not particularly important at this stage.

Merensky had been given a rudimentary sketch of the terrain. The map showed the range of hills, a small stream that ran behind these hills and beyond a number of hills dissected by side valleys. All the points where rock samples had been collected and analysed were also marked on the map. Using this information, Merensky started his work. He started with the bands of gneiss in the prominent limestone ridge. He soon found the places in which the various samples had been taken, because in an area where no one had prospected before (virgin territory, as it were), the traces left by a geologist taking rock samples are visible for years afterwards. This may seem unbelievable to a layman, but it is indeed so. A site where hand-sized pieces of samples have been removed from certain easily accessible parts of a rock face and, after examination by the geologist with the help of a magnifying glass, have been discarded in the field, will definitely be noticed by any geologist passing through the same area later. After all, there is no reason why any animals or members of a local population would remove such samples, and it takes years for a rock that has been struck by a hammer to weather enough for the tool marks to be indistinguishable. So, Merensky speedily found the sampling spots used by his predecessors, and took rock samples at exactly the same places. Then he inspected the whole ridge very thoroughly and returned to the camp.

The next day he prepared his samples and panned the material he had crushed. He was amazed to find that the very first sample already revealed clear traces of gold. He had not expected this, at least not in these concentrations. He tested the other samples one by one, and believe it or not, all of them had a highly acceptable gold content. This was a good start indeed!

But a professional prospecting geologist does not only need to be knowledgeable about minerals and ores. In addition he needs to know in what kinds of rock series one can expect a certain type of mineralisation. As important are the technique used to take samples, the way in which the samples are transported, the nature of the analyses and finally the behaviour of the geologist when he has found something interesting. As a matter of course, the results of any analysis that could lead to economic activity are rechecked. If the project will require large investments, the results may have to be retested and rechecked, and normally, in such a case, it is appropriate to use the services of a neutral third laboratory. When samples are sent to such a laboratory for testing, their origins are not revealed. Instead, each specimen is marked solely by a number. It is quite customary to send the samples to the laboratory in leaded metal containers or at least in sealed packets. All that was not possible in Madagascar at that stage, but Merensky did a routine second round of sampling. The next day he returned to the same profile he had looked at on the previous day, took samples at the same places, crossed the hill, prepared his own samples at the edge of the little stream behind the hill and panned them. None of the samples contained any sign of gold.

Along the stream itself, there were a few places at which there were clear traces that river sand and gravel had been panned, and these places had been marked as gold-bearing in the sketch of the area. So, Merensky panned some of the material lying along the stream. And again he found nothing, not even the tiniest flake of gold. This answered the mystery of the alleged gold mineralisation of the lime ridge and its bands of gneiss. Merensky had long mastered sampling techniques and he knew everything there was to know about preparing and panning a sample. He was sure he had not made any mistake. And hence, he did not hesitate for a second in reaching a conclusion: there was no primary mineralisation in the solid rock, and therefore there was also no secondary gold concentration in the sand and gravel in the stream.

Back in the camp, he re-examined the gold that he had panned from crushed rock samples he had taken the previous day under a strong magnifying glass. He recognised that among the gold particles he had found, there were also rolled gold particles that had clearly been washed down in a river or stream. However, he knew very well that they should not be there, as he had himself taken the rock samples from the solid rock.

But that meant that the samples taken the previous day had been "salted", in other words, gold had been added to the samples after they had been taken. Merensky had a strong suspicion that it might have happened when he had briefly left his hut to join the other geologists for their communal meal. The how and when was clear; and who had done this did not matter much at that moment.

What he wanted to know immediately was whether it was only the samples from the lime ridge (which was close to the camp) that had been spiked with gold, or whether the entire concession area was worthless. The next day, he went to investigate the hills on the other side of the stream. While he was on his way there, he remembered a student joke from his time at the University of Breslau. At the time, a list of trick examination questions was circulated among the students (similar jokes still do the rounds today), to which students then gave ridiculous answers. One of these questions was: "What is a gold mine?" One student answered: "A gold mine is a hole in the ground next to which a geologist sits and lies!"

How true this light-hearted student quip was Merensky realised an hour later, when he walked through the said hilly section of the concession. To his amazement, he discovered that these hills had not been prospected by any geologist. Different points at which samples had allegedly been taken had indeed been entered on the map sketch, but the traces typical of any prospecting were completely absent. Nowhere was there any freshly chipped rock, no samples had been struck from the rocks, and the sand and gravel lying in small side valleys were untouched.

In this situation, he did not know whether to be indignant or to laugh. There was reason enough to be indignant: fraudsters had been at work. They had entered sampling points randomly in the map and believed that that would be enough to fool the representatives of the large mining companies or international banks. That was enough to be very annoyed about. After all, the mining companies had sent the very best South African geologists to Madagascar. The fraudsters should have known that that would happen, because the financial implications of the prospective gold sales would have been huge. It was indeed shocking that the fraudsters had actually believed that this high-powered team of experts could be fooled. But apparently, it had never entered their minds that if they wanted to be successful in their scam, they would also have to fake the traces of prospecting activity. One could really only laugh at such bungling!

Merensky was neither indignant nor amused. He rushed back to camp immediately. The whole "Enterprise Lecomte" was clearly a fraud that had been planned long beforehand, but had been badly prepared. The most important thing now was to warn his client.

Merensky acted quickly. An hour later a messenger was on his way to the nearest telegraph station. The warning he sent to Friedlaender & Co. was weighty, if concise. It consisted of only one word.

That evening Sir Aubrey Wools-Sampson arrived. He had been in Anjeva with the second team of experts to investigate the options there. He had also begun to suspect that samples may have been artificially "enriched". But he was not yet quite sure of his facts. He and Merensky exchanged information and now the full extent of the affair became clear. It was a gigantic fraudulent manoeuvre that did not affect only one or two of the option areas on offer, but probably the entire concession held by Lecomte. (This suspicion was later confirmed.) It was hard to believe. The plan was clearly not just to rook a single financial institution or a single mining company by ten or twenty thousand pounds. No. The plan was to cheat the entire South African gold mining industry. Neither Sir Aubrey nor Merensky could imagine that such a plan could have succeeded, because the irregularities in this supposed gold mineralisation were too obvious. They were sure that in a few days the other experts who had come to Madagascar would recognise the deception too. But still – both men shuddered at the idea of what could have happened if this fraud had not been uncovered in time. The number of investors who would have been fooled was large, and the sums at stake were vast. But more than that: if a large number of investors had suffered such dramatic losses because of fraud, there would have been a crisis, in that confidence in the South African gold mining industry would wane. This crisis might well have affected other mining branches in South Africa. It was high time to end this little confidence game.

It was barely dawn before a second messenger was on his way to the telegraph station. The second warning to Friedlaender & Co. was even clearer, but it was just as short. Then Merensky left for home.

Meanwhile, in Johannesburg, there had been some turbulent scenes. While the group of experts were on their way to Durban and while they were waiting for a ship to Madagascar, trading in options and concession shares continued for a while. Some speculators became worried when they realised what a high-powered group of experts was going to Madagascar. Had they missed anything? If the big mining firms were sending the best geologists in the country to Madagascar, it seemed logical that there was more to be had than had been officially admitted. They also tried to get into the business, even though the prices of the Lecomte shares were already very high. Then there were others who grasped the opportunity to make a profit when the prices rose again, and who got rid of their shares. At last, there was a hiatus. The market heard that the specialists had left the Madagascan coast and had started for the interior. Everybody waited eagerly for the first news to come back from them.

Then Merensky's first telegram arrived. At Friedlaender & Co., everybody was stunned at the short message. The text consisted of one German word: "*Faul*!" ["Fishy!"] Was this a code word? No, it was not! It was a warning! At Friedlaender & Co. there were enough employees who knew German trading jargon. "Dud credits", "shady business" and now "fishy mining speculation" – that was the very last thing they wanted to be involved in. At this point, Friedlaender & Co. was in the process of extending the company's engagement in Madagascar substantially. A number of options were just running out and either had to be allowed to lapse or had to be extended at considerable expense. A number of concessions had also been acquired that either had to be paid or would revert to the seller if they were not paid. At Friedlaender & Co., there was much guessing about what could have led to this telegram, but the message was clear enough, and there was no hesitation in putting a hold on the immanent transactions.

In Johannesburg's financial circles people began to prick up their ears. What did Friedlaender & Co. know that others did not? Rumours flew and the prices of Lecomte shares began to drop. The situation became even more confusing when, soon thereafter, a first telegram arrived from the consulting mining engineer working for Lecomte's company. He reported excellent prospecting results, which – so he said – justified the most sanguine hopes. A frantic exchange of telegrams ensued between Johannesburg and the bush post office in Madagascar, which received more telegrams in two weeks than it would normally receive in five years. Lecomte's managers in Johannesburg demanded that the company's representatives in Madagascar discover the reason for Friedlaender & Co.'s withdrawal from the Madagascar business on the spot and immediately, and that they recheck their own prospecting results and then, depending on the situation, either confirm their initial results or refute them. Friedlaender & Co. asked Merensky for clarification as to whether or not they should give up their engagement in Madagascar altogether. The latter telegram was never delivered, because by then Merensky had already started on his return journey.

Then the second telegram from Merensky arrived. This time it was twice as long, but just as concise. It consisted of one word: "*Oberfaul!*" ["Superfishy!"]. Nothing can be more damaging for a financial institution than being connected to shady speculations and so Friedlaender & Co. did not hesitate for an instant. They announced their complete withdrawal from the Madagascan business, and this time they made it public. Almost simultaneously news came from Sir Aubrey Wools-Sampson, who expressed his personal doubt about the Madagascan gold. Now even the most trusting of investors began to feel some doubt and tried to sell their shares to whatever buyers they could still find. But many more telegrams were needed for the mystery to be resolved in the second half of August. Alarmed by the urgent queries from Johannesburg, the experts had retested the spots where they had had such positive results the first time and had examined the material themselves, on the spot – and everywhere they had the same results: there was no gold. Thereupon the local employees of Lecomte's company were interrogated individually, and finally two of them confessed to having "salted" the samples after they had been taken. The dream of a large Madagascan gold find was over. There was no second Witwatersrand deposit. What remained was the bitter aftertaste of a rather clumsy attempt to commit fraud. However, the Johannesburg Stock Exchange jargon was enriched by the concepts of *"Faul"* and *"Oberfaul"*.

Merensky had disappeared for that entire period. He reappeared in Johannesburg two months later, pale and physically much weakened. He had suffered a severe attack of malaria on the journey back and when he had landed at Durban, he had been taken to hospital straight from the ship.

Malaria is a treacherous illness. The patient is not only weakened by the bouts of high fever, but every bout of fever destroys thousands of blood cells and then it takes months for the blood cell levels to normalise. The patient stays weak for a long time. That was what happened to Merensky. But despite the fact that he could barely stand, when he arrived in Johannesburg, he was greeted with great joy and praise. He was the man of the hour, the man who had uncovered the Madagascan gold scam.

Merensky knew that this was not strictly true. He had only been the person who had reported on it first. He had little doubt that each of the gold experts gathered in Madagascar would have noticed the scam within a few days, even without his assistance. He said so repeatedly, but this was regarded as false modesty.

In any case, it was a fact that, after this gold-related scandal, Merensky was counted among the top cadre of South African geologists. This dramatically changed the commissions he received as a consulting geologist. From then on, the big mining firms engaged Merensky more and more frequently. His opinion was highly valued, because, in addition to his considerable geological expertise, he also had the ability to make rapid, accurate decisions at the right time, to the benefit of the enterprise that had engaged his services. He had made the professional breakthrough he had worked so hard for.

> **Textbox 5 – "Primary" and "secondary" deposits**
> 
> Concentrations of metals or precious stones can come about in many different ways. Depending on which natural processes played a role in their formation, experts refer to this or that type of deposit. It is very important to establish the type of deposit in each case, both for the course of the prospecting process (the search for continuations of the deposit or for sim-

ilar occurrences in the wider area) and for planning the actual mining and the preliminary calculation of the costs involved in such mining operations.

This is not the place to explain the large number of known types of deposits. In the text, the terms "primary deposit" and "secondary deposit" are frequently mentioned. These terms distinguish broadly between two large groups of occurrences.

"Primary" deposits refer to deposits in which the ores or precious stones are still in the original rocks in which they were first formed. In South Africa this group of deposits plays a prominent role. The platinum of the Merensky Reef, the chromite deposits in the Bushveld and the diamond-bearing kimberlite pipes are but a few examples.

However, "secondary deposits" are even more important in this subcontinent. These come about when an older rock formation or deposit is mechanically destroyed (weathering) and/or subject to chemical leaching and when the valuable minerals contained are transported to a new environment and become more concentrated in that new position. The resulting ("secondary") deposits are called alluvial deposits or placers.

When alluvial deposits are formed, the specific gravity of a mineral or precious metal that concentrates in a particular location is the governing factor. So, for example, gold is transported as the tiniest gold flakes by the water that carries away the eroded material. But, because gold is seven times heavier than the silicates and carbonates that are carried away with the gold, the gold flakes are obviously transported more slowly and when the water flow slows down, these flakes are left behind. Some of the places where these flakes are often deposited include the shallow inner curves in bends in streams and rivers, potholes and areas behind large rock barriers where the water tends to stand. "Secondary" gold deposits are formed in such places. The gold tends to settle in the deepest part of the sand or gravel profile, that is, immediately above the bedrock which forms the true bed or floor of the stream bed or valley. The gold flakes also often stick together while they are being transported in the water, or are "hammered together" by the constant motion, creating so-called "nuggets", which can reach a remarkable size.

The resistance of the minerals to the stresses of being transported in the water or in a mudflow is the second determining factor in the development of a stream placer. While they are being swept along, some minerals (such as cassiterite, the most common tin ore), which are in principle quite hard, but which are also brittle, tend to break along existing lines of discontinuity. The small pieces of cassiterite are then quickly crushed and that means that they would clearly not be carried as far as gold or even diamonds. So, when a prospector finds cassiterite in the bed of a stream, he can be reasonably certain that he is only about 10 kilometres away from the original source of the tin. He can then work his way back to the source quite easily.

The technique of tracing a find back to its original deposit by panning sand and gravel is one of the classic prospecting methods. Not only tin deposits, but also many of the large gold deposits have been traced in this way. The identification of primary gold occurrences has almost always been preceded by the discovery of alluvial deposits of gold. That was the case both in the discovery of gold in California in the 1850s and in the gold rush in Alaska forty years later. (The occurrences that were found first were often very rich, but often also relatively short-lived. In the first phase of mining, great fortunes were often made. But, in many cases, this phase lasted no more than 10 years. Then the large mining companies took over and mined the primary deposits, where the gold concentrations were clearly lower, but allowed mining to continue for much longer.) It would be wrong to believe that another gold rush would be impossible today. In largely unexplored regions gold fever could break out again, especially if the rights of landowners are not decidedly defended by the State. A fairly recent example of this was seen around 1985 in the Serra Pelada in the Brazilian Amazon.

When valuable minerals are swept downriver into the sea and are then thrown back against the coast, selected and washed together, one finds beach placers. This would obviously only apply to the types of mineral that can survive being transported over long distances. Every summer visitor to the seaside has seen the fine lines of black sand along the edges of the high water marks. They contain high density minerals such as ilmenite (an iron titanium mineral), monacite (a thorium cerium-bearing mineral), zirconium and magnetite. These black lines are created in much the same way as the beach placers and in some other places in the world they occur in sufficiently large masses to form deposits that can be mined for many thousands of tons of the minerals concerned.

Along the South African and Namibian Atlantic coast diamond-bearing beach placers play a significant role. The precondition for the formation of these occurrences is the great hardness and resistance of diamonds. Probably the pipes from which the stones originally came were somewhere in the interior. The stones were swept downriver to the ocean over long distances and then the surf threw them back on land. However, they show barely any signs of being worn down. Nevertheless, selection has occurred in the process of their being transported over such distances. Most stones that had flaws or inclusions seem to have been destroyed. At any rate, it is noticeable that some of the beach placers, for example, the Oyster Line that Merensky discovered, contain mainly particularly lovely, flawless stones. Otherwise what was said about alluvial gold deposits also applies to alluvial deposits of diamonds: they are often rich, sometimes even extremely rich, but their life is noticeably shorter than that of the mines in kimberlite pipes and from which, in the end, more carats are extracted.

Secondary mineral concentrations can also come about when a less interesting adjacent type of rock is eroded, leaving behind a greater concentration of the valuable minerals in their original site. This phenomenon is called residual placers. The weathered components of the host rock can be swept away by water or by wind ("aeolian placers"). The diamond deposits that Merensky examined at Kolmanskop, near Lüderitz (previously Lüderitzbucht), were formed by a combination of these two mechanisms. The stones were originally carried toward the sea by rivers; then they were thrown back on land by the surf; and finally they were exposed in the beach placers by wind. Finally, the diamonds lay loose in the dune sand.

Of course, there are also placers that were formed in prehistoric times, millions and in some cases billions of years ago. The erosion of mountains and therefore also of mineral deposits and the resulting possibility of a subsequent concentration of valuable minerals have always existed. In such cases, we speak of "paleoplacers" or "fossil placers". Such placers tend to look somewhat different from more recent placers. The originally loosely aggregated sand, gravel and valuable minerals have recompacted in the long time that has passed since they were first formed and they have again become a hard rock. Some very famous deposits belong to this group. So, for example, in Brazil, loose diamonds were initially found in river gravel, but later a very hard, ancient conglomerate was identified as the source rock of these diamonds.

In South Africa, the gold in the Witwatersrand formation also seems to have originated from an ancient placer formation. In any case, in the hard, quartzite rock in which the gold is found today, there are clear indications of the outlines of ancient pebbles that have been rolled out and stretched. It is widely supposed that these pebbles were originally swept along by rivers and were deposited in an intramontane basin which was probably about 300 kilometres long and about 120 kilometres wide. The gold which came down as a result of the erosion of the surrounding mountains ended up in the sand and gravel deltas of the river mouth. The Witwatersrand gold is therefore found in a secondary deposit and came from a much older geological system. However, this interpretation is sometimes rejected (as with many very ancient deposits). Some experts believe that the gold was not deposited at the same time as the gravel and the sand, but was only introduced later, via hydrothermal solutions which penetrated the Witwatersrand sequence.

CHAPTER 6

# Bankruptcy

In the following years, Merensky was constantly on the road. He travelled throughout the subcontinent, crossing it in all directions, from north to south and vice versa, from the Atlantic coast to the Indian Ocean and back again. He worked in every part of South Africa and in all the neighbouring countries. He worked in what is today Namibia and Zimbabwe particularly often, but he also wrote investigative reports about areas in Bechuanaland (today Botswana), Swaziland and Mozambique. Wherever some new prospecting possibility arose, Merensky was on the spot.

At that time there was a particular interest in any potential gold and diamond occurrences. He prospected the ancient gold-fields in what was then Southern Rhodesia. Some of these occurrences had been discovered 40 years earlier by Carl Mauch, his father's friend. The parts of these deposits that were close to the surface had long since been mined, and in many places mining operations had ground to a halt. Now Merensky's work gave gold mining in Southern Rhodesia a new lease of life. Often he did these investigations in a kind of circular tour, so that he might look at eight or nine gold deposits in Southern Rhodesia in a row. For each one, he would write its own detailed report, because each of these deposits represented a separate concession. He would write a draft in the field or while he was staying overnight at one of the nearby farms. Then he would add the analysis data and his final conclusions back in Johannesburg. His output in those years was phenomenal. It was made possible by his highly concentrated working style.

Merensky played a particularly important role in the expert appraisal of the Voorspoed diamond occurrences. He was consulted soon after the first diamonds had been found there, and his various appraisals contributed materially to the rapid development leading to the mining of this deposit.

In 1908, when diamonds were found in German South-West Africa (today Namibia), just inland from Lüderitz in the dune sand at Kolmanskop, he hurried there to examine the area. The concessions were firmly in German hands. Nevertheless, he looked very carefully at the occurrences. He did not only look at those parts of the deposit that were being mined at the time, but also paid a lot of attention to areas where mining had already been abandoned. He spent days in the dunes and looked at many hundreds of sand and soil samples under his magnifying glass. He also set aside time to talk to those who had discovered the deposit and those who had worked there first. What did the terrain look like before it had been affected by prospecting activities? What was the exact position of the first diamonds that were found in the context of the dunes? Once he had found the answers to such questions, he acquired a horse, and widened the radius of his investigations. Initially, he looked at the dunes around Kolmanskop. Then he followed the mighty chain of dunes running parallel to the coast all the way to the Orange River southward for quite a distance. As he rode, he continued to take and analyse soil and sand samples. He dismounted, walked up the dune ridge and, as he climbed, he studied the profile he saw metre by metre. Before his eyes, a clearer picture of the formation of the diamond deposit at Kolmanskop gradually began to unfold. His observations led him to conclusions that differed radically from those of other geologists. But more than that: it was even more important that he developed a clear idea of where this diamond deposit might continue. The insights he gained on this trip were eventually, 20 years later, to lead to what was probably his most spectacular prospecting success.

Then he travelled back from the South Atlantic coast to the other side of the continent, to Mozambique, to devote himself again to the investigation of a gold find. But in those years he was by no means interested only in gold and diamonds. Indeed, he prospected for every possible mineral. He studied tin deposits in the Bushveld and in Namibia; he searched for tungsten and tantalite; he did an expert appraisal of molybdenum occurrences in Natal; and, again and again, he examined coal deposits.

Even though Merensky did many expert appraisals for large mining companies at this time, he did not neglect his original business, which had been to provide consultation services to individuals and small enterprises. As he had done in the beginning, he regularly checked and analysed the many individual samples that farmers sent him for testing. His office in Johannesburg had become bigger – he had increased the size of the office and had employed some staff. Since he was often away for weeks at a time, he now had a permanent assistant to help him. His assistant dealt with his mail, completed the draft reports and sent them off and regularly kept him informed per letter or telegram of any new developments – or even just rumours – while he was away.

When Merensky was in Johannesburg, he stayed at the Rand Club. This was the ideal solution for him as a bachelor. He did not have to worry about any domestic details and lived in the very spot in which all mining information and news about any newly discovered deposits was discussed. At the Rand Club one could count on meeting both eminent mining magnates and elegant bankers, and active gold diggers and ore seekers fresh from the veld, weather-beaten and sometimes rather tatty-looking. The former met at the Club to sniff out useful business opportunities on neutral ground, the latter, who had spent weeks or months in the bush, came to meet old friends and to exchange news – sometimes a rather noisy affair. Some fixtures were the now ageing discoverers who told stories about the 1880s, when gold was first discovered on the Witwatersrand. The Rand Club was always a hive of activity, humming with news, rumours and gossip. Not everything one heard there was true. There were fantastic stories and hoary tales about the old days, but if one listened carefully and took the tale from whence it came, one could glean some very useful information.

The Rand Club was an important source of professional information for Merensky, and he moved effortlessly in the heterogeneous circle of the guests. But it has to be said that in his heart of hearts he did not feel that he belonged there, because, however well Merensky might be integrated in the social mix at the Rand Club, he was not a city person. He felt happiest out in the veld. He slept over on all kinds of farms and had become friends with most of the owners. Later that would benefit him greatly. He loved life on the farms, and he was not at all bothered by the fact that time had stood still on most of them. He himself came from his father's mission station where he had spent a happy childhood.

When he was out in the veld alone with his horse and his tent, he felt completely free. He loved the quiet hours at his camp fire, in the cool evenings, after the heat of the day. And even more beautiful were the cool morning hours, when after a fresh night, dawn broke quickly and the beams of the rapidly rising sun changed the play of colour in nature minute by minute. He loved these moments.

Merensky was riding the wave of his success – not undeservedly so. He worked hard. He had an astounding sense for a find, phenomenal powers of observation and considerable experience. He was not in the least lazy, and he avoided all excesses. He was also gifted with enormous personal charm, which drew many friends to him. He was not only successful, but also a contented, yes, happy person.

His financial situation had changed very positively. His expert appraisals brought him an income of about £2000 per year. For those days, that was an exceptionally high sum. But that was not all: because he was earning more than he could spend in the few short weeks that he was actually in town, he bought shares. He tended to prefer shares in mining enterprises for which he had just prospected. And since he was generally aware quite early on which mining projects were likely to produce above average profits, his investments were almost always well placed. So, for example, he bought shares in the Voorspoed diamond mine and did very well. The firms valued this type of engagement, because there are few better recommendations for a new share issue on the stock exchange than the consulting geologist buying shares for himself. In the end, he doubled his annual income from consulting fees every year through his investments on the stock market.

People soon heard about his good sense with regard to business on the stock exchange, and friends also began to ask his advice on where they should invest their money. In the end, to simplify matters, many entrusted their money to him to invest it as he saw fit. In the beginning, he was happy to oblige, and many of his friends made a quick profit. His reputation spread to the extent that soon acquaintances of acquaintances wanted him to invest their money for them. This became so onerous that in the end he had to refuse to perform such favours, including an offer from the Deutsche Bank, which wanted him to invest 5 million gold marks (£250 000) on its behalf.

Anyone who knows the stock market knows that this could not continue indefinitely. One often hears the saying "nobody is perfect". When people use this expression, they do not intend to blame someone for a mishap, but they are looking for an excuse for a misfortune which could have been avoided if that person had acted or reacted differently in a certain situation.

One should perhaps excuse Merensky on those grounds. He made no professional errors, but his thinking was not focused on the global intricacies of the raw materials industry. He prospected and appraised ore deposits. That was his job and that was where his skill lay. When his assessment showed that a deposit was of above average quality and could be profitably mined, he recommended that his client develop it. His expert appraisal supported the issue of shares, and often he also bought some of these shares for friends and acquaintances and for himself. However, he appears to have completely overlooked the fact that the prices of the shares of a mining company depend on a great many parameters. The quality of the deposit is only one of them. The price is even more dependent on the prices that raw materials can be sold for, which in turn depends on demand. However, the decisions about demand and supply were not made in South Africa, but on other continents and often on the basis of reasons that were not yet known in South Africa at that time.

Then came 1911, which was a difficult year for the world economy. In Europe several well-known banks collapsed, the stock market was shaky and there was trouble in the Balkans – again. The causes of the resulting effects are debatable. However, one of the clear results was that the demand for metals went down worldwide and that the value of South African mining shares decreased.

This trend started with the tin shares with which Merensky and his friends had speculated successfully in previous years. The market crashed, and Merensky lost considerable sums, both on his own shares and on those that he had bought for his friends. He tried to save what he could. He sold out at a loss and invested the sums he had been able to salvage in gold shares, which had thus far been fairly stable. And then the usual scenario repeated itself in a lengthy bear market, which the shareholders (including Merensky) did not recognise in time. The bear market eventually affected every single branch of the mining industry, even the diamond market. Merensky, who had changed his investments several times, lost almost everything he had – and, worse than that, he got into debt. In the hope that he would be able to balance out his losses, he continued to buy shares, and that in the midst of dropping share prices and on credit. Each time he bought, he was firmly convinced that the market had reached its lowest point and that things could only get better – and every time, he was wrong.

His greatest error was not to have clearly told his friends, when they entrusted their money to him, that buying shares was always a risk, and that they had to accept this risk themselves. Indeed, he had even promised some of his friends certain sums if they invested. Now he felt himself to be responsible for their losses and tried to make up for his friends' losses by reinvesting his own money, and so his losses became greater and greater. In the beginning, he had unlimited credit with the banks. But when his losses got bigger, the banks became more cautious. In the end, he took a mortgage on his father's farm, which he was managing. The bank gave him £10 000, which was only a fraction of the amount he needed.

As Merensky had also borrowed various sums from many private individuals to cover his daily expenses, his situation became less and less clear. Eventually, he no longer knew how high his total debts were, and, above all, whom he owed money. It became clear that he was not only having a lot of bad luck, but that he was not able to keep his books in order or to manage money. In the end, he himself recognised that without expert assistance he would not be able to resolve the problem, and so, in 1913, he handed over the management of his debt load to a lawyer. He hoped that such an expert would be able to bring some order to his finances and would be able to work out a plan to repay his debts. But this was not to be. The lawyer spent two whole days on his paperwork, but had to declare Merensky bankrupt. This was a huge shock to Merensky. The worst was that from this moment on, no further credit of any kind would be forthcoming from any financial institution.

Throughout this period, Merensky continued with his work as a geologist, because he was still getting commissions. But it became more and more difficult for him to do his work. The difficulties of his situation affected him emotionally. He did not know how he would ever be able to repay his debts. He could see that even if he earned well consistently, he would only be able to pay off his mountain of debt in decades. This thought wore him down.

CHAPTER 7

# Interned

Things got worse.

In July 1914 Merensky was out in the veld. It was winter and that made working in the veld easier. He had only noted the events that were causing turmoil in Europe in passing, and he had never dreamt that what was brewing there could have any consequences for South Africa. Who could have guessed that the European conflict would escalate to a world war?

Europe seemed very far away to him. He had already been in South Africa for ten years and, except for his parents and siblings, with whom he maintained regular contact, he no longer had any personal links to his old fatherland. In the first year after his arrival he was still a Prussian official on leave and that meant that he could theoretically return to Germany. In 1905 he applied for an extension of his leave, which was granted. One year later he submitted a second request, to be released from the civil service to the Ministry in Berlin. He definitely wanted to stay in South Africa. The reasons were obvious: nowhere else in the world would he face such interesting geological tasks as in this country. Nowhere else in the world was the mining industry booming as much as it was in South Africa at that time. The reason for that was that after the end of the Second

Anglo-Boer War, the country experienced an unprecedented amount of investment. In South Africa – he was convinced of it – there was a real chance to make his fortune. He also felt happy in South Africa. The people in the country suited him. Irrespective of whether he was in the hurly-burly of Johannesburg, with its immigrants from all the countries across the world, or out in the veld, where he was dealing with the Boers who had settled there, he got along with everyone. He liked the feel of the land itself. Thus he felt extremely positive about South Africa. Even his current financial crisis could not change that. Hence what was about to happen to him was all the more of a shock.

Some time in the first days in August, Merensky was back in Johannesburg. He had barely arrived at the Rand Club when two British officers appeared and politely asked him to accompany them. It came as a double surprise when they announced that they were sorry to have to tell him that they had come to take him to an internment camp. He protested vehemently. After all, he had been born in South Africa, and had lived in the country for quite a long time. But the authorities did not see things that way. Merensky was not only a German citizen, but also a Prussian reserve officer. There was no chance whatsoever that he could avoid internment.

The period during which he was interned was a tale of woe for Merensky. He, who had specifically chosen his career as a geologist because he detested any coercion, was now suddenly a prisoner behind barbed wire. He, who was uncomfortable in mass quarters and who was used to living in the open and to seeing only the wide horizon, was suddenly crammed up into what he felt to be the tiniest of spaces with thousands of fellow internees. He suffered enormously from this loss of his liberty. The lack of any sensible activity, together with uncertainty about the duration of this internship and the even bigger anxiety about what would happen afterwards, tortured him continuously. His health was affected by this suffering.

To be fair, though, the conditions in the internment camp were not unbearable. They could not be compared in any way to the conditions endured by prisoners of war in Europe, irrespective of the uniforms worn by their guards. The South African internment camp was very large and was situated in Natal, at Fort Napier in Pietermaritzburg, 50 kilometres to the west of Durban. The guards were British, and they treated the prisoners fairly. However, they did take their task seriously, and hence contact with the outside world was very limited. On the other hand, the percentage of Boers in the general population was very high – and they were not necessarily on friendly terms with the British. This was understandable, since memories of the Anglo-Boer Wars and the British concentration camps used to intern Boer women and children were still too fresh. This meant that the camp fence was permeable to a degree, at least from the outside to the inside. This proved to be very useful, particularly during the first year, when the camp was not yet completed. Everything that was necessary to make camp life bearable managed to find its way in. In addition, the internees were a highly active, innovative and gifted group. The percentage of young people was high, and many of them were technicians and artisans. There was practically no profession or craft that was not represented, and soon the camp not only had every essential installation and facility, but also an exercise yard, a swimming pool and tennis courts. Physical needs were met – even some Schnapps was made. Various cultural activities developed. The internees painted and sang; amateur dramatic groups performed plays. Cultural and technical themes were covered in a series of lectures. Overall, the guards were surprisingly generous with regard to the independent organisation of camp life. At any rate, they had no problem with the fact that the German camp inmates held a parade on the Emperor's birthday (27 January), admittedly not in uniform, but all dressed in white shirts and black trousers, and that afterwards the inmates held a large gymnastic festival. Several photographs in the Merensky Archive testify to these events.

Merensky himself held back from these activities and remained a loner. Every day, he walked for hours along the inside of the barbed wire fence, but he kept to himself. Only occasionally could he be persuaded to present a talk. Then he would speak about the geology and deposits in South Africa and describe the vast unexploited potential of the country. These talks were fascinating, and nobody had the least doubt that he was highly competent in his field. Anywhere else, and at any other time, these would have been rousing speeches, but here his passion was not quite as infectious. The barbed wire fence was more than a fence: it was a wall that separated the camp inmates' minds from the world outside the camp.

Ten years later, when Merensky celebrated the most spectacular of his successes after he had discovered diamonds in Namaqualand, some of his erstwhile fellow camp inmates recalled that he had spoken about the diamond fields near Lüderitz several times, as well as the likelihood that further diamond occurrences could be found on the Atlantic coast. He presented a complicated scientific theory with great enthusiasm, but his audience was the wrong one. To people locked away from the outside world for years, focused on the tiny universe of life inside the camp, such visions meant nothing. Such dreams could not move them.

Time passed. At last, the war ended in Europe, but it took several months before the camp was dissolved. In his last year in the camp, Merensky had become seriously ill, probably for psychological reasons. For many weeks he was bedridden, and lay in a darkened room for much of that time.

Finally, he was released. He had both longed for and feared his release. His future was completely uncertain. He had serious doubts about whether he would be able to set himself up as a consultant again, and he still had no idea how he would be able to repay all his debts. Other than the clothes he wore, he had nothing. The last bit of money he had still had left in Johannesburg had long since been claimed by his lawyers as consultation fees. Merensky had absolutely nothing. In his pocket he had £15 – borrowed money. His creditor was Sir George Albu, one of his many friends from the time when things were better, before the war.

Merensky felt as if the best years of his life were behind him. In another two years, he would be fifty. At that age, one could no longer travel through the bush on foot or on horseback for days on end. At that age, one could no longer work in just any temperature. These thoughts tortured him, and he lacked the strength and perhaps also the courage to return to Johannesburg immediately. Instead, he accepted one of the many invitations he had received to visit a Boer farm. In the years before the war, he had often been a guest on many of the farms, had advised the owners, and usually he had left a firm friend of the farmer and his family. Now he found refuge in the rural areas. Here he felt at home – after all, he had spent his early childhood on a farm. Here he felt happy and hoped to find new strength. He was to succeed, but it was to take him a very long time.

Merensky spent many months in the rural areas with various families. He was familiar with their simple rural lifestyle and particularly their honest life, which reminded him of his youth, and this contact did him a lot of good. Whenever he could do so, he was outside. At some point, he rode out into the veld again for the first time, and literally breathed free air. Over time, his body and spirit healed. As he began to recuperate, his desire to make a fresh start began to grow. He knew that he had to return to Johannesburg. He knew the ropes there, and he believed that that was the only place in which he would be able to restart as a consulting geologist. That became his goal: he wanted to earn back his erstwhile position in the mining world.

CHAPTER 8

# The art of getting into debt

It was 1920. Merensky was back in Johannesburg, but starting over again was proving to be difficult. The city was no longer the same as it had been before the war. When he had arrived in Johannesburg 16 years earlier, he had found a young, vibrant town to which young people from many countries across the world came to seek their fortunes. Anyone who had good ideas, who was capable and who was not put off by hard work could go far.

Now things were different. The mood was sombre. No matter whom one spoke to, business was looking bad. The reasons for this could be found in the economic structure of the city, or, to be more precise, in the city's dependence on mining: All the money earned in Johannesburg was in some way related to local mining, or was obtained from abroad via the banks and mining companies in the form of investments. For about 40 years, these had been the two largest streams of money that provided the city's economic lifeblood. By comparison, economically speaking, the agriculture in the surrounding Transvaal had always played a subordinate role.

Now these two sources of money had not dried up completely, but they had become more of a trickle. As before, the causes for this state of affairs were elsewhere and South Africa could do nothing to influence these. The war was over, and the prices of metals dropped on a broad front. Globally, the effect of the war could be felt. Huge stockpiles of raw materials had been created by the war economy. Now these were being sold off and began to flood the market. That depressed prices. In addition, in the countries that had lost the war – among which there were a number of important consumers of raw materials – economic growth had been slowed for years to come. Entire markets fell away. Profits for producers of raw materials shrank, and soon more and more companies were in the red. But the large mining firms did not panic. Economic ups and downs in ore mining and the metal industry had always been cyclical. In boom times, the industry did well; and when the demand for raw materials dropped and the proceeds were not large enough to cover costs, the industry had to get by. The mining companies realised that and knew exactly what to do. Their strategy now was to save costs and rationalise where they could. So they acted accordingly.

However, it meant for Johannesburg and for everyone who was involved in the mining industry in some or other way – business people, suppliers to the mines and consulting geologists – that they received barely any commissions or orders (and those they did receive, where certainly not large ones). There was no exploration. Nobody was prepared to finance a detailed investigation programme even when there was an indication of a potentially promising mineral occurrence at this or that location deserving to be taken seriously. In these difficult times, no mining company was prepared to purchase ore reserves that they would only need in five or ten years' time. Instead, the companies focused on rationalising their mines, both in terms of the mining techniques they used and in terms of their selection of the parts of the deposits they wanted to mine.

For Merensky, this meant that he was neither able to get larger prospecting commissions nor asked to do expert appraisals. These two activities had previously been his main sources of income. That left the small sums that he occasionally received from farmers for appraisals of ore or rock samples. This source of income was barely enough to live on. Even worse, these small commissions often led to awkward situations: when one of these samples tested positive (in other words, the concentrations of chrome, tin or gold were good), the farmers would ask whether the areas where the sample had been taken, or even better, the entire farm, could not be examined more thoroughly. And since they themselves did not really have much cash, they would ask Merensky to find backing. Merensky would then be forced to undertake the thankless task of disillusioning the farmers and explaining to them that at that time there was no funding to be had for any prospecting work, not even if the indications were very promising.

One ray of hope in these difficult times was that Merensky was requested to join large mining companies as a resident geologist on a number of occasions. Although some of these offers were financially quite attractive, Merensky refused all of them. However depressing his personal situation might be, he did not want to relinquish his professional independence under any circumstances. Nevertheless, at this dark time, it provided some solace that his geological successes before the war had not been forgotten. Thus he still had a sense of belonging to the ranks of the top South African geologists, even though he had no significant commissions at this stage.

Since the income from the small jobs he received from the farmers was barely enough to cover his living expenses, he was forced to borrow money again and again. These were never large sums – after all, he had had no credit with any bank for a long time – but sums between £5 and £10 that he borrowed sometimes from this or that old friend or acquaintance. It was perhaps surprising that he could always find someone who was prepared to lend him some money. Ultimately, this has to be a sign of how much his friends liked him and trusted him, despite everything. No one who lent him money had a sense of just giving away his money or feared that he would never get it back. Quite the contrary – people lent him money because they were firmly convinced that one day he would have a big breakthrough and would then repay all his debts with interest.

Even though he constantly needed to borrow money, Merensky never lost his sense of humour or his inborn sense of hospitality. One anecdote (reported similarly by various sources) tells of how Merensky had just borrowed £5 and immediately invited the rather stunned lender for a lavish meal at the Carlton Hotel. And since a good meal had to be washed down by a decent Rhine wine, soon only a few shillings of the £5 were left!

Given his persistent financial embarrassments, it was inevitable that Merensky had to change his personal lifestyle. Living at the Rand Club as he had done before the war was no longer an option, as he simply could not afford to do so. First he took a room in a small boarding house that belonged to an Austrian couple. A number of representatives of some large German firms that manufactured machinery also lived there. Like Merensky, they had fallen victim to the reluctance of mining companies to invest. To make their situation worse, German industrial firms in general experienced some difficulty in attracting any business in English-speaking countries after Germany had lost the war. Hence the financial problems experienced by these German tradesmen were acute, something everyone in this circle had in common. This led to many close friendships. Since the Austrian couple themselves got into financial difficulties, the German group eventually moved out and rented a small house that they shared. But this bachelor establishment lacked a feminine touch, and the arrangement was not a permanent solution. In the end, Merensky found a small room in one of the suburbs, in the house of a Fräulein Linhardt, a retired German teacher. Although the monthly rent was modest, the day when Merensky had to confess to her that he could not pay it, soon arrived. Fräulein Linhardt took the news calmly, since she too had long succumbed to Merensky's personal charm. "It does not matter, dear Mr Merensky," she said, smiling. "One of these days you will discover a big gold-bearing vein, and then you will pay me everything that you owe me." The old lady did not say this just to be polite or to comfort him, no, although it sounded very unlikely, she was firmly convinced that what she said was true. She was sure that one day this nice and charming Mr Merensky would make a very successful find.

Fräulein Linhardt was not the only one whose faith in Merensky was unshaken and who was prepared to take a financial risk on his behalf. Merensky had employed a permanent co-worker, an Austrian called Wipplinger. He was a merchant by trade and took care of Merensky's correspondence and represented him when he was not in Johannesburg. Wipplinger then sent his employer letters and telegrams to keep him up to date with the most current news and rumours from the mining world. No matter how badly Merensky's business was going, he could not do without such a pair of eyes and ears in Johannesburg to monitor the situation, unless he was prepared to lose contact with the mining scene while he was away from town. Moreover, Merensky had long been accustomed to delegating any kind of office work and all technical tasks. It was part of his effective working style. He wanted to keep his head clear to solve geological or mining problems, and this was his priority. However, the problem with his one and only employee was that soon Merensky could no longer afford to pay him. It was fortunate for Merensky that Wipplinger was not without means and did not insist on being paid punctually every month. Because he too had firm faith in Merensky's future successes, he stayed undismayed and continued to work for Merensky for many months without regular pay.

CHAPTER 9

# Light at the end of the tunnel

Every bear market has to end sometime, and the depression after the war was no exception. It is typical that one cannot pinpoint the exact turning point at which things began to improve, and that the increase in economic activity was initially very gradual. Nevertheless, from 1921 onward, commissions for initial investigations were again given to geologists, and the trend strengthened in the next two years. It was symptomatic that the first commissions did not come from the big mining companies, which were still being very cautious, but from private financiers. The latter were clearly more flexible and they were already reacting to the first barely noticeable signs of a future reanimation of the raw materials markets.

There were new developments in respect of the raw materials that the markets were interested in too. Among the large number of prospecting reports that Merensky left behind, for the first time there were now reports on investigations focusing on small occurrences of bitumen, asphalt and oil shale. Most of these were found in what is today Namibia, in the Fish River region and in the Gibeon district. Unfortunately, none of these occurrences was extensive enough to warrant further investigation.

Merensky's efforts in this regard were in line with the trends at the time. The rapid motorisation of the country and the country's experiences during the war had alerted South Africans to the fact that the lack of local oil reserves could create considerable problems for the economy at critical times. Hence, Merensky did not limit himself to prospecting, but spent some time in the early 1920s on a detailed study of the problem of coal liquefaction. He compiled several reports on this matter and corresponded widely on the issue with relevant German firms and university institutes. Merensky saw the liquefaction of coal as the real solution to South African energy problems. Given the enormous capital injection that would have been necessary to undertake such a project, it was not possible to realise this dream at the time. But the fact remains that Merensky's ideas were a precursor to the later superb development of SASOL.

The second raw material for which more and more prospecting was done from the 1920s onward, was phosphates. Merensky was also repeatedly and actively involved in this arena, including some work in Mozambique. There he was still held in high esteem because of his gold prospecting before the war, and so, in time, he was given a commission to examine coal occurrences in that region. The first reports of coal finds went back to Livingstone. Now, about 65 years later, a number of outcropping seams had already been identified. The coal was exploited locally on a modest scale, using somewhat primitive methods. However, thus far, there was no overview of these deposits, nor any clear idea of whether and how these individual occurrences were related to one another. No proper geological and mining study had been undertaken, because the local demand was too limited. Also, there was no real infrastructure to enable the coal to be transported to the coast. Based on his intimate knowledge of the stratigraphic sequence of the Karoo system in the Transvaal and in Southern Rhodesia, Merensky had no difficulty classifying the scattered coal outcroppings with regard to their relative age and working out how they were related to one another. In a subsequent much broader and comprehensive prospecting campaign, he was able to reveal the existence of connected and significant coal deposits that covered large areas. However, these deposits only began to be mined on a large scale 20 years later, when a railway line had been built.

It was interesting that at this time South-West Africa also began to attract the attention of several financiers. The erstwhile German Protectorate had been fairly well studied from a geological point of view even before the First World War, and the techniques used in the mines there were quite up to date. Two deposits, namely the copper, lead and zinc mine at Tsumeb in the northern part of the country, and the diamond deposit at Lüderitz, were world famous. There were also a number of other smaller ore mines that were being quite economically mined. When South-West Africa became a South African mandate after the end of the war, the ownership of the mines and concessions changed. These changes had barely been effected when investors began to question whether the Germans had in fact examined all the deposits as fully as possible, and whether, here and there, new mining possibilities could be opened up using improved methods and more modern techniques.

Hence, in the early 1920s, Merensky was repeatedly sent on field trips in South-West Africa to give an expert appraisal of the local gold, copper, lead, zinc and particularly tin occurrences. One of the first to commission his services was Sir George Albu, who had been the first to assist him financially when he had just been released from his war internment.

By the middle of 1923, Merensky was again on the road in South West Africa for several months. He was accompanied by a good acquaintance, Carl von Roeder. Their primary focus was the tin deposits in the Erongo massif in southern Damaraland, to the north of the road between Windhoek and Swakopmund. By then, Merensky was using a car to reach remote areas more rapidly and to transport his bulky materials, but for the field work itself he still often travelled on foot or on horseback. This was particularly necessary in a place such as the Erongo massif, which is situated in an inhospitable, inaccessible and particularly arid region. The Erongo, which gave the area its name, is a very old volcano, elevated above the surrounding landscape to a height of 2200 metres, with a diameter of almost 40 kilometres. The surrounding plateau is characterised by vast granite block fields and isolated mountain massifs, the most famous of which is probably the Spitzkoppe, probably the best-known mountain in Namibia today and a kind of an icon for the country. These granites are linked to pegmatites – igneous rocks containing sometimes giant crystals that solidified last from rest magma when it cooled down. Such rest magma tends to be rich in volatile ingredients. Pegmatites therefore often contain minerals such as apatite, beryl, cassiterite, columbite-tantalite, garnets and all kinds of semi-precious stones. This is also true of the Erongo massif. At that time, there were a number of small tin mines, but mining conditions were very difficult, because there was virtually no water for mining activities.

But there were also many local indigenous tin collectors. They roamed through the massifs and tried to pick cassiterite from the weathered pegmatite rubble. It is fascinating to watch such cassiterite gatherers at work. Since the open sandy plains have usually been searched and depleted long ago, they investigate every crack or fissure in the rock that is filled with sand. Often they push an arm into such a fissure, right up to the shoulder. Their fingers are so sensitive that they can sort the small pieces of cassiterite or even other interesting minerals from the coarse pegmatite sand without seeing them. The only problem is that such fissures or overhanging rocks under which they want to probe the sand may well hide a snake. Since snakes are very sensitive to sound and immediately react to it and tend to flee when they detect any vibration of the soil or rock where they are hiding, before they investigate such a fissure, the tin gatherers announce their presence by beating the rock with a stick and probe the fissure with their stick first.

Thus the pegmatite fields of the Erongo massif were one of the areas to be prospected on this field trip. Merensky was asked to clarify whether the mining of the tin ores in the various scattered mines could be coordinated in any way and could then perhaps be rationalised. It was even more important to see whether there was any chance of setting up a central processing plant. Since tin ore is not marketable in the form in which it is extracted, it must first be separated from the accompanying waste rock. This has to be done in a processing plant by submitting the finely ground tin ore to a hydro-chemical process, which separates the cassiterite from the slime of the waste rock. At the end of this process, one has a cassiterite concentrate with a specific degree of purity which can then be sold to a smelter. The tin smelter who buys the concentrated ore can be quite some distance away. The problem that beset the tin mines in the

Erongo was that, because there was no water, the cassiterite could only be separated from country rock by means of dry sieving and hand sorting. This had two great disadvantages: many very small cassiterite pieces were overlooked and thus lost; and the concentrate that was obtained in this way was not very pure. This implied that the yield was far from optimal. In addition, penalties had to be paid on these impurities. The smelter paid a considerably reduced price as the delivered ore yielded less tin. This meant that the viability of these tin mines was constantly under threat.

Unfortunately, Merensky had to conclude that the prevailing conditions precluded setting up a central processing plant in the Erongo. There was not enough water, and the infrastructure in general was so inadequate that building a new plant would have been disproportionately expensive. Merensky, who was, after all, not only a geologist, but also a mining engineer – and an experienced one at that – calculated that even once the full yield of the entire deposit in the whole area had been taken into account, given the maximum price that could be achieved for the tin concentrates produced, such a facility could never be viable. This concluded his task, even though the results were not what the people who had commissioned him and he himself had hoped for.

Merensky had already prepared himself to stop his work in the Erongo, but wanted to complete one or two things before he left. He and von Roeder still had to go to Usakos, a small place on the road between Windhoek and Swakopmund with a train station. They wanted to top up their food and fresh water supplies and pick up their mail. There was a whole stack of letters waiting for Merensky, including one from Wipplinger from Johannesburg. "One of the usual reports on the mining situation," Merensky thought. This was true, but this letter was a little different from Wipplinger's other letters. He reported that in the Transvaal, near the Waterberg, some platinum had been found. The report was quite detailed. The discoverer was a man called Adolphe Erasmus. The platinum occurred in a brecciated quartz vein which was situated in a deep fault zone that traversed the Karoo formation, and was therefore younger than the Karoo sediments. The metal concentrations that had been observed appeared to be considerable, and it was hoped that the deposit would turn out to be quite large. The news was arousing great interest in

Johannesburg's expert circles, and various financiers seemed to be quite ready to fund further investigations of the occurrence. Merensky understood this interest by the financiers very well. At this time, platinum had become a much sought-after metal in the global market. Traders paid five times more for platinum than for gold.

"I must go," was his first thought. He did not doubt for a second that the news was essentially correct. If the discovery was indeed the indication for a larger platinum deposit, then that would bring about an upswing in South Africa's fortunes in a still weak mining cycle. Moreover, he was certain that that would mean excellent work opportunities for him.

Within minutes, Merensky made up his mind to set off for Johannesburg that very evening. Fortunately, that was the day on which the one weekly train passed through Usakos. Von Roeder was not nearly as excited by the news as Merensky was. After all, traces of platinum had already been found in the Union of South Africa three or four times in the past. Each time the discovery had caused great excitement, and then it had been found that the amounts of platinum in these occurrences were too small to warrant further investigation. Von Roeder therefore saw no reason for such a hurried return to Johannesburg, but he did not hinder Merensky from leaving.

In those days the train trip from Windhoek to Johannesburg was still a long and arduous journey. When Merensky eventually arrived, he was very tired, but he was also anxious about what the next few weeks would bring. Wipplinger's first words already disappointed him. Once again, it had turned out not to be a large deposit. For Merensky this was a heavy blow. However, he was not the kind of person who gave up hope easily. He was an experienced geologist, and his experience told him that in this country, in which small amounts of platinum had been found in various places, there had to be a larger platinum occurrence somewhere. All he had to do, was to find it. The time was ripe – and he wanted to be involved in this adventure.

---

**Textbox 6 – The history of platinum**

Platinum was unknown in ancient times. It was occasionally found in Egypt, but it seems that then it was believed to be a special kind of silver. In Thebes, in Upper Egypt, a metal casket found in the sarcophagus of the priestess Queen Shepenupet was decorated with gold and platinum.

It probably once contained documents. Today the casket can be admired in the Louvre. The casket has been dated back to the 7th century bc. Since Egyptologists have fairly accurate information on the gold that was worked in Upper Egypt – the gold comes from alluvial deposits from the rivers on the western slopes of the Ethiopian Plateau – the geologists who were working there looked carefully for any signs of platinum. And indeed, around 1925, a Russian mining engineer called Kurmakoff found that in the province of Ouallaga, about 600 kilometres to the west of Addis Abeba, members of the local population (which has been panning for gold there for centuries) secretly added heavy silvery-grey grains of metal to their gold before selling it. These were platinum grains. They occurred in the river sands of the Birbir, together with gold flakes. This observation led Ethiopia to become a small platinum producer for more than 30 years, even though its production was insignificant by world standards.

Such platinum occurrences in rivers were apparently also found in the Andes. There the Indians already mined this metal in pre-Columbian times and processed it, in the shape of platinum-gold alloys, into necklaces and nose rings. These ornamental fineries, which date back to 100 bc, are today among the most valuable items displayed at the Museum of Indian Art in New York.

Probably the first written mention of platinum was noted by the Italian doctor and humanist Julius Caesar Scaliger (1484–1558). He described a mysterious white metal that resisted all attempts to melt it down.

However, Europeans only really became aware of platinum around 1590 or 1600; and that in much the same way in which 325 years later it would be discovered in the Birbir valley in Ethiopia. In those days, in the Spanish territories in South America, gold was panned in many places, sometimes by Spanish adventurers, but more frequently by the indigenous Indian population, who then sold the gold they produced to the Spaniards. This was also the case in Columbia. There the Indians panned for gold in the Rio Pinto valley and occasionally they found some platinum grains among the gold. Since they were paid for their gold per weight, it is not surprising that they repeatedly tried to slip some heavy platinum grains in with the gold. The Spaniards did not appreciate this kind of deceit at all. They beat the fraudsters and strictly prohibited any further panning or sale of this silvery-grey metal. When the authorities got hold of any of this material, it was immediately thrown into the sea. In the end, the Indians who were panning for gold became accustomed to picking out any platinum grains that they found in their pans and they threw them away to avoid any trouble with their Spanish overlords.

It was at this time that this silvery metal got the name "Platina del Pinto". "Pinto" was the name of the river where it was found, and "platina" is the diminutive of "plata", the Spanish word for silver. In the Spanish, the use of the diminutive can mean one of two things. In some cases, for example with children's names, it implies affection and is a cute form of the name; so, for example, "Juan" becomes "Juanito" or "Carmen" becomes "Carmencita". In other cases, it has derogatory implications; so, in this case, for example, "plata", silver, becomes "platina", or "little silver", in other words, a worthless metal. It is thus from the Spanish "platina" that the modern name "platinum" was derived. How much the meaning of the concept has changed in a mere 300 years! But this shift reflects the changes in the economic valuation of this metal away from being an undesirable admixture in a pan of gold to a sought-after precious metal used for jewellery and as a raw material with industrial applications.

We do not know for how many years the Spanish colonial officials maintained their refusal to take note of the existence of this silvery-grey metal. It may have been decades or even 100 years, and in all that time any platinum export was prevented. The first person to report on the South American platinum was the Spanish naval officer Antonio de Ulloa y García de la Torre, in 1735. He mentions in his travel accounts that in the gold-bearing sands that are found in the Columbian rivers there is occasionally also a silvery-grey heavy metal. Six years later an English prospector called Charles Wood, who had just come from Jamaica, brought a platinum sample that he had acquired in Cartagena, in Columbia, home to England. There the material was first known as "white gold". But the English metallurgists soon realised that this was, in many ways, a very special material which differed from all metals known thus far. They were particularly amazed that, unlike gold, which has a melting point of 1068 °C, they could not get this metal to melt. It was no wonder, because platinum only melts at 1769 °C, a temperature that even the most sophisticated smelting furnaces could not reach at that time. Otherwise, the metal was good to work with. It was highly pliable and could be stretched; and it could be rolled into wire and small plates. Platinum was also even more indestructible and less sensitive than gold: even concentrated acids could do nothing to it. This led platinum to be grouped with the so-called "noble" or precious metals. This term was only used later, though. It was finally classified as an independent chemical element by a Swedish researcher, Heinrich Theophilus Scheffer, in 1751.

The epithets "precious" or "noble" in the language of chemists implies inertness. Among the precious metals, the degree of inertness increases from silver to gold to platinum and further to the remaining platinum metals. Silver does not oxidise, but it is affected by sulphurous compounds (it tarnishes) and it can be dissolved in nitric acid and concentrated sulphuric acid. Gold, platinum and palladium (which is closely related to platinum) can only be affected by aqua regia, a mixture of three parts concentrated hydrochloric acid and one part of concentrated nitric acid, while the other platinum metals, namely osmium, ruthenium, rhodium and iridium, which have even higher melting points, are immune even to aqua regia.

In the last third of the 18th century there were already some attempts to launch platinum in the world markets as a metal to be used in jewellery. So, for example, Parisian jewellers made a platinum item for Louis XVI in 1780. However, platinum was hardly known in middle-class circles.

This changed in the first quarter of the 19th century. First, in 1803, Englishman William H. Wollaston succeeded in developing an improved way to forge and process platinum. At the same time, he discovered the closely related metals palladium and rhodium. Soon thereafter, in 1819, the first platinum occurrences were discovered in the Urals, followed by many others in the course of the next 30 years. Initially only secondary deposits were found in the forms of riverine alluvial deposits; later primary mineralisations were also found in basic rocks. Consequently platinum lost its rarity value. For a while, Russia could even use platinum to mint coins: From 1828 to 1846, platinum roubles were in circulation.

It was the German chemist Wilhelm Carl Heraeus (1824–1904) who succeeded in solving the problem of how to smelt platinum in the middle of the 19th century. That in turn made it possible for jewellers to use more platinum in the manufacture of jewellery after 1870. It was around that time that the diamond deposits were discovered at Kimberley, and over time diamonds became the favoured gemstone in middle-class circles, and diamonds were often set in platinum. Parisian jeweller Louis Cartier played a large part in this development soon after 1900, as he understood better than anyone else how to intensify the brilliance of diamonds by means of setting them in platinum. Simultanously, platinum was also used in extravagant valuables, for example, in the world-famous jewelled eggs that the imperial jeweller Peter Carl Fabergé made for the Tsar's family for Easter, year after year, between 1880 and 1900.

At the same time people also remembered the special physical characteristics of platinum, for example, the fact that it is practically inert. In 1875, an international agreement was reached in Paris about the metric system that the French had already tried to introduce in 1795, during the French Revolution. Now, a Bureau International des Poids et Mesures (International Bureau of Weights and Measures) was founded, and its headquarters were in the Parisian suburb Sèvres. There, in the park of St Cloud, in the Pavillon de Breteuil, the normative standard metre and the standard kilogram are kept. Both are made of a platinum-iridium alloy. Many unprepared visitors are surprised at how small the standard kilogram looks. Given the high specific density of platinum (21,45) and of iridium (22,48) the one kilogram precious metal cylinder is only 3,9 centimetres high and has a volume of only 47 cubic centimetres.

The world demand for platinum grew slowly in these early years between 1870 and 1900, but it grew steadily. Around 1885, one ounce of platinum (31,1 gram) cost about £2.

Another 30 years on, at the start of the First World War, the other physical and chemical characteristics of platinum attracted the attention of technicians. The metal became interesting in terms of warfare. Platinum's suitability for ignition magnets, for contact points in ignition systems in aeroplane engines, for any kind of electro-motor, for electrodes and as catalysts made platinum a much sought-after industrial metal, which it has since remained.

Soon after the First World War there were dramatic changes in the world platinum market. In hindsight, the developments at that time are a textbook example of what happens in raw materials markets. At that time, 90% of the world production still came from Russia, 7 to 8% from Columbia and the small remainder from the USA, Canada and a few other countries. Russia dominated the world market, and not only that – since the mines in the Urals had been taken over by the State after the October Revolution, there was practically only one large supplier, namely the Russian Foreign Trade Bureau, in other words, a monopolist. This is the kind of situation which traders in raw materials have always seen as a particular threat. They were not only afraid because of their dependence on this supplier (a monopoly can set any prices it wants), but because they were concerned that there could be shortages caused by mere political decisions. But that was not the case. The Russian mines did have some problems delivering at times, but these were not the result of political manipulation, but rather the result of unrest caused by the Revolution. There was never any question about the willingness of the Russians to deliver platinum, and the shortage in the markets was never so severe that it seriously threatened economic development in the industrial nations.

In this rather tense situation, which the buyers probably saw as more threatening than it really was, the Russian Foreign Trade Bureau made an error that was to have serious consequences. Because the Russians hoped to earn more money from the sale of platinum, they asked their sales agent in the United States to sound out whether the market would accept an increase in the platinum price. Unfortunately, this enquiry was done so clumsily that a rumour spread like wildfire that Russia was about to increase the platinum selling price. Of course, what happened next was exactly what usually happens when price hikes are known in advance: the traders held back their platinum, or sold at a higher price to cover their possible restocking costs. There was a sudden shortage of immediately available platinum, even though Russia had not yet increased its selling prices. If the platinum price had been increased moderately, without any preliminary enquiry or pre-announcement, the matter would have been forgotten in a few days. But now the market had been destabilised.

But that was not all: in every such situation, there is always someone who is unwise enough to add fuel to the fire. In England various industrial enterprises that were dependent on regular platinum supplies expressed concern about the possibility that there might be an extended shortage of platinum. The British government addressed the problem by announcing a rigorous state monopoly of the platinum trade in 1923. Free trade in platinum was prohibited. Traders, metallurgists, jewellers and anyone else who had any platinum was ordered to make available their platinum reserves for sale. The entire market was to be taken over by government agents immediately. The result of the announcement was dramatic, because it was interpreted as an official government confirmation of a shortage in the platinum market. Anyone who could possibly do so, began to hoard platinum. The prices of this precious metal rose quickly and reached a high of £25 per ounce (31,1 gram) – an exorbitant price for those days, five times the price of gold.

This distortion in the ratio between the prices of gold and platinum also had some benefits though, since, when a raw material has become so overpriced, the market tends to try to regain some balance. This happens when new producers who want to profit from the high prices enter the market. In the case of platinum this was not yet possible, since no other deposits had, as yet, been discovered. But it made geologists everywhere think hard about where they might find new platinum deposits. One country in which the geologists were certain from the start that they would be successful, was South Africa. The leading geologists in the country were familiar with the Russian publications about the platinum finds in the Urals, and they agreed that in their country there were similar geological formations in some places. After all, if the same formations are present, there is a good chance that the same kinds of ore deposit may exist. There were no guarantees, but the quest for platinum deposits in South Africa had begun, at least in the minds of the geologists.

Hans Merensky was the person who found the first platinum occurrences in solid rock outside Russia in the Bushveld in 1924. But more than that – it was the largest platinum deposit in the world. Today, this deposit bears the name of its discoverer: the Merensky Reef. Of the ten platinum mines that are operating in the Bushveld today, eight draw on this reef.

After a number of years in which prices fluctuated, South Africa became the world's platinum market leader. According to the statistics in the U.S. Geological Survey of January 2005, in the previous year 74,8% (163 tons) of the world's annual platinum production came from South Africa and 16,5% (36 tons) from Russia. The world market shares of South Africa and Russia for palladium, which is in just as much demand in industry, are around 41,2% and 40% respectively. South Africa's lead in the world reserves for metals belonging to the platinum group is enormous. They are estimated at 174 times the annual production of 2004. That means that the South African Bushveld boasts 88,7% of the world's reserves, while by comparison, Russia has 8,7% of the world's reserves.

CHAPTER 10

# Platinum in the Bushveld

At this point something needs to be said about prospecting for platinum. A layman could ask, if the leading geologists in South Africa at that time agreed in general that a good chance existed to find platinum in their country, why did they not simply go out into the field and look for it? After all, the geological formations that were likely to be the parent rock for platinum mineralisation were apparently known. The answer to such a question would be that taking this route was not possible. Platinum, when it is present, is found in conjunction with magmatic, basic to ultrabasic types of rock. This fact was known. Such types of rock are found in South Africa in areas of many thousands of square kilometres. From the descriptions of the occurrences in the Urals, one also knew, additionally, that the platinum mineralisations found there never involve the entire ultrabasic rock complex, but are always restricted to small, highly limited areas, and that the platinum content in these places is normally only between 2,5 and 25 grams per ton of rock. That is not very much. Moreover, platinum occurs in a variety of chemical compounds. Only in very rare cases it can be recognised with the naked eye in its pure form. To find a platinum mineralisation in South

Africa, it would have been necessary to analyse all occurrences of basic and ultrabasic rock in a metre by metre grid. That was clearly not possible.

What remained, was the hope that one would find platinum in river sands or in a similar environment, in other words, weathered out of its original parent rock, from where it would then perhaps be possible to trace it back to the primary deposit. But that was only a faint hope. After this introduction, we can return to Merensky's story.

The deciding moment in Hans Merensky's life came in May 1924.

Merensky was back in Johannesburg from South-West Africa and he had returned to his dreary everyday work. Now and then some smallish commissions came in, but nothing big. In between he constantly received letters from his creditor, asking whether he was not ready to start repaying his debts. His answer was always polite, but always the same: "I regret that at the moment it is not possible for me to do so … business is still very bad … however, we sincerely hope that soon …" etc.

This hope of a better future was not a mere white lie. Merensky was sincerely convinced that the mining economy would improve sometime and that consulting geologists like him then would get plenty of new commissions.

On that day in May 1924, Merensky received a small parcel in the morning mail. It came from Lydenburg (today Mashishing), the town where his father, the missionary, had first found a refuge after fleeing from King Sekhukhune. That was 59 years ago. The person who had sent him the parcel was a lawyer called H.C. Dunne, an old acquaintance. When Merensky opened the parcel, a small translucent medicine bottle rolled out. He grabbed it and immediately felt that it was heavy – very heavy. And then he saw the contents: a silvery-grey metal. "Platinum!" he thought. Very carefully, he poured the contents of the small bottle out onto a piece of white paper, and even more carefully he pulled the sample apart with a pair of tweezers and looked at it under his magnifying glass. The sample consisted of tiny grains of a silvery-grey metal. It was platinum, of that he was certain. But the sample was not pure. All kinds of debris was mixed into the sample – typical for a concentrate that had been panned by someone who was not very skilled in panning. A practised panner would have washed the concentrate to absolute purity, while an unpractised panner tends to avoid to remove the last bits of impurities because he is scared of losing any of the metal concentrate by doing so. The accompanying letter from the lawyer was concise and matter-of-fact: "Could this be platinum? The sample comes from the Lulu Mountains, from an erosion channel on Maandagshoek, in the area of Lombaard's farm ..."

Merensky took a deep breath. Could this be the tip of the platinum deposit of which he had dreamed for so long? Probably not. Such deposits were not usually presented to geologists on a platter. Nevertheless, the sample had to be analysed immediately. A little later Wipplinger, carefully carrying the little bottle, was wending his way to a chemical specialist laboratory. There were several of these in Johannesburg. They worked reliably and, when necessary, very quickly and, in special cases such as this, also very discreetly.

The results came that very afternoon. The silvery-grey metal was indeed platinum, as Merensky had suspected. In addition, traces of rhodium and iridium, two other rare metals from the platinum group that commonly occur with platinum, were present. The impurities that Merensky had already noted in the sample were iron oxides.

The same afternoon Wipplinger wrote to the lawyer in Lydenburg and informed him of the results of the analysis. At Merensky's express command he added an urgent warning to be very careful and under no circumstances to tell anyone about the find until the rights of the discoverer had been officially confirmed. From years of experience, Merensky knew that many discoverers who told others about their finds too early in the process lost their rights to the deposit.

Two days later Dunne was in Merensky's office. He asked the geologist to come to Maandagshoek and to inspect the place where the find had been made. Andries Lombaard and two cousins of his wife wanted to take a closer look at the area. The only problem was that they did not know where to begin. They all had often panned for minerals, but they knew little more than that. So they asked Merensky to join them and asked him to lead the prospecting work. This was another of the tricky situations of the kind that Merensky had experienced several times in the last few years. There was an interesting indication that could be the key to a discovery of an important deposit and he was supposed to organise the prospecting operation. He would be delighted to do so, but that also meant that he had to find funding for the investigation, because – he could take that for granted – cash was not something these farmers had. In fact, they would need a lot of money. There were tools to be bought, and they would need transport and supplies for the weeks in the veld. It was even more important to have ready enough money for what happened afterwards. If they did indeed find a significant mineral occurrence, they would have to act quickly. Without any delay, options and concessions would have to be taken on areas as large as possible around the find. This meant that they would need capital with a large "C". Once news of the mineral find had got out, the discoverers would not have any time to look for funding. Speculators would buy up digging rights for all the adjacent pieces of land with lightning speed. Whatever the discoverers did not own, and had in black and white, was lost to them.

Merensky was caught between a rock and a hard place. He wanted to take the commission – but where would he find the money he needed? In his mind's eye he reviewed the list of potential backers. He had no credit with the banks any longer. There were a number of private financiers who were interested in mining projects, but, as a rule, they only got involved once a known mineral occurrence was actually to be mined. They were generally not interested in the kind of prospecting Merensky was about to do. It would have been nice if he could have found some funding in the circle of his German acquaintances. There were people in that circle that he knew well, people whom he trusted and who trusted him. Sadly, many of them were in much the same financial straits as he was, and the ones who were a little better off had committed their money to longer-term projects. Then there were his many acquaintances in mining circles, but he was not sure that he could rely on their discretion. The risk that his project would soon be common knowledge if he told anyone connected to the Rand Club was simply too big. The only other option was to find a backer from a completely different field. It would be best to find a merchant or trader who was not in mining circles and who had some cash available and was not afraid to take a certain amount of risk. Merensky began to investigate matters and eventually found a merchant called Schlimmer who was prepared to invest up to £5000 in the project. For Schlimmer this was purely a business venture. He hoped that he would be able to make a good profit without too much effort. Fortunately, for reasons of self-interest, he would also keep the information completely confidential.

It took four weeks before everything was ready and Merensky left for Maandagshoek, accompanied by Wipplinger and Schlimmer. They travelled to Lydenburg by train. Then they rented a car to get to the farm, over 65 kilometres of bumpy and bad roads. In many places there was only a track consisting of deep ruts cut by wagon wheels – originally in damp soil but now dried to rock-hard consistency. The area was very lonely. The fact that Schlimmer had no idea about mining and prospecting showed at this point to be a drawback. On the trip to Lydenburg, the mood among the travelling companions had been cheerful, but now Schlimmer became increasingly quiet and withdrawn. Instead of becoming excited by the possibility of a big find, he was rapidly developing an aversion to the venture. Merensky could feel this instinctively. Clearly this potential financier lacked the imagination needed to recognise that a significant find was possible in this isolated spot.

When they arrived on Maandagshoek, the farmer Lombaard and his wife's cousins Schalk and Willem Schoeman welcomed them. The place of discovery was quite near the farm house. As Dunne had already told Merensky, the soil sample had been taken from a fissure-like depression at the foot of a rock massif. Merensky took a good look at the area. Below the area where the sample originated, there was a very wide, flat valley. On the opposite slope, quite a distance away, one could see a number of rocks. Directly above the spot where the find had been made, the rocks climbed slowly. These were dark basic rocks of the type that belonged to the very old formations of the Bushveld. Between the large rocks there was barely any soil, only scree and rubble. All in all, the location of the spot from which the sample came was very interesting. It seemed quite possible that the platinum that Lombaard had found and panned in the watercourse could indeed have originated from the jumble of rocks of the Lulu Mountains rising up behind the spot. If this assumption were to prove correct, then they would have found the first platinum occurrence in basic rock outside Russia; and if one thought about the masses of basic rock in the Bushveld, this would probably not be the only occurrence. Merensky took it for granted that they should get to work and put in all the effort necessary. Hence he did not hesitate to convey to those present what his impressions were, and he did so most persuasively.

Lombaard and the two Schoemans, who tended to be men of few words, just nodded. What Merensky said about Russia meant little to them, but if he thought that this might be the tip of a big deposit, they were happy to hear it. But it was more difficult to convince Schlimmer. He had imagined that he would be shown a body of ore that he would be able to recognise as such, but what he saw here told him that all that had been found was enough platinum to fill half of a small medicine bottle – no more. Looming above the sampling spot, there was a rock massif which Merensky believed "might" contain platinum, but this was not certain; and even if his intuition was correct, who could predict how long it would take before the platinum deposit would be developed and mined? There was no a guarantee of a risk-free investment that would make a quick profit. He thought that investing money here would be like betting on a payday far in the future. More than that, it was an incalculable risk. In the end, he said that he had to think things over calmly.

Merensky sensed that Schlimmer was not prepared to provide the start-up funds they needed. It was a rather depressed group that decided that they would return to Johannesburg. Before he left, Merensky took the two Schoemans and Lombaard aside and promised them to find another backer. At the same time, he gave them instructions about where they should take more samples and to pan them until his return to the farm.

They were barely back in Johannesburg when Schlimmer telephoned Merensky and definitely withdrew from the platinum project. He repeated the reservations he had expressed the day before. It was a double mistake. It was perhaps understandable that he did not want to take a risk on the basis of what Merensky merely suspected, namely that there could be platinum in a particular rock massif, but his second argument, namely that even if platinum was found, it would perhaps take a very long time before the deposit could be mined, was a cardinal error from a business point of view. In the future, it would become clear that as soon as platinum had been found, vast streams of capital could be mustered very rapidly.

Merensky was surprisingly unconcerned about Schlimmer's withdrawal. After the discussion out in the field, he had expected this about-turn, and he was already trying to find other backers. He was even more enthusiastic than before, because he had now seen the place where the sample had been taken, and had very high hopes of prospecting successfully for platinum there.

The quest for a backer had, however, not become any easier, since Merensky was determined not to mention platinum. Merensky spoke to anyone that he hoped might have some money available. He even wrote to some friends in Portuguese East Africa, where he had a good reputation since he had prospected for coal in that region. Alas, it was all in vain. He went back to his old bank, to which he owed large sums, but whose directors knew him and valued his geological intuition. Again he came up empty-handed. Given his debt load, the bankers could not overcome their reluctance. In the end, he fell back on his circle of German friends. They were stunned by how much he wanted to borrow – at least £2000, he said, but preferably £5000. This was a vast sum. They knew him well enough to realise that he must be pursuing a project that was quite different from anything else he had undertaken in the past few years; and, so, they tried to help him. Two of his friends, Gustav Becker, who represented several German firms, and Otto Baerecke, the local Krupp representative, were prepared to raise £500 each. In return, he told them that the project involved platinum. These two friends managed to find two more men to participate in the project, M. Elkan and P.C. Baerveldt. All four had a sense of getting involved in a risky adventure, but in the end, they succumbed to Merensky's eloquent arguments about the project's prospects.

At last everything was ready, and the first syndicate to exploit the Bushveld platinum was founded. What a moment in South Africa's history! And yet, how transient such moments are! A year later there were about fifty platinum syndicates in the Transvaal, some of them with a starting capital of half to one million pounds.

The external circumstances of the founding meeting were odd since there was something secretive about it. The newly established syndicate was called the L.P. Syndicate, but it was decided at once that the members of the syndicate would tell no one else what the letters "L.P." actually stood for – namely for Lydenburg Platinum.

The place where the syndicate started was just as unusual and modest. Today many well-known American technology firms are proud to say that the company started in a small garage. Why do global firms stress this aspect of their founding history? Perhaps it is not enough to be able to claim that one has a leading firm in one's industry, but it is also important to prove that one has started from scratch. This was certainly true with regard to the place where the L.P. Syndicate was established, so this tendency can perhaps be understood. Of course, the syndicate was not founded in a garage, nor in Merensky's office. No, it was among the lace doilies in the best parlour in the little house of Fräulein Linhardt, in suburban Yeoville. Fräulein Linhardt was the old lady who had given Merensky a temporary extension on his rent because he was "such a nice young man". She had little clue of minerals and ores, but she was convinced earlier than most other people that Merensky's quest for precious metals would one day lead to a very big find. The fact that instead of a rich gold vein he might find "only" platinum, did not matter to her in the end.

Merensky was back at Maandagshoek by the start of August. Two and a half months had passed since the parcel from Dunne containing the little medicine bottle with the platinum sample had arrived. Then he had been interested, but sceptical. Now his mood can best be described as "wildly determined".

For Lombaard and the two Schoemans, things were different. In the meantime, they had taken multiple samples along the prospecting lines Merensky had asked them to investigate, and had panned the samples, but they were not certain that what they were doing was advancing the project much. They were noticeably relieved to hand the project over to Merensky. The farmers were particularly frustrated by the fact that the soil samples that they had taken right around the spot where the original sample had been found had not contained any traces of platinum whatsoever. Subsequently, based on Merensky's recommendation, they had extended their sampling down the slope. There too, they had initially found nothing until, at last, almost in the centre of the valley, three or four of the samples had revealed some very weak traces of platinum in the pan. But even this platinum appeared to be completely isolated. At any rate, they had been unable to trace any continuation in any direction.

Merensky was now faced by a basic decision. Should he continue prospecting in the valley? The platinum traces that had been found there were weak and were probably not connected to the platinum Lombaard had first found at all. The prospecting method that was most likely to be successful seemed to be to work slowly, starting in the valley, panning soil samples, toward a primary mineralisation in solid rock. The alternative was to climb up into the jumble of rocks above the place where the first sample had been found and to test every rock there, metre by metre. The latter method meant an "either-or": either one struck a rock and found platinum – or one did not and then had no further clue as to whether one was any nearer the source of the platinum or not. Merensky was hesitant about working in the rocks because of the huge effort required. In a few weeks they would only be able to explore perhaps three or four kilometres, but no more. The primary source of the platinum could be further away, who knew?

Based on this argument, Merensky decided to start by following up the weak platinum traces in the centre of the valley. Starting from the place where the Schoeman brothers had found the second set of samples, they laid out prospecting lines in all directions, took samples and panned them. Nothing!

That day and the next passed, and then the third. The three amateurs were becoming increasingly uncertain. What if these platinum traces were after all just isolated occurrences, without any continuation? Merensky reconsidered. Should he shift the focus of the work and start prospecting in the rocks after all? In the end, the uneasy sense that his fellow prospectors would become even more frustrated up there deterred him.

The fourth day dawned. Merensky did not despair, but his mood was subdued. He felt that they had undertaken a long and arduous task. He was concerned about his assistants, and was not sure that they had enough nerve to keep going. There was nothing to indicate that this would be the decisive day for the platinum project.

Merensky tried again. He took a sample on the opposite slope, quite a distance from the indicators the Schoemans had found. Wonder of wonders – he did indeed find weak traces of platinum in his pan! And he found more in the next pan. Thirty metres on, the traces had disappeared again. But Merensky worked on, undeterred. His prospecting line was now aimed at a group of rocks that he could see in the distance on the slope. Again and again, he lost the traces, but every now and again, there was a sample that contained some platinum. It was already dusk when he reached the last few metres before the group of rocks he was aiming for. He was exhausted. Standing bent over for hours while panning had tired him. He took his last sample and set off for the centre of the valley, where he panned the sample in a puddle of water. The light was fading so rapidly that he could not see clearly whether there were any platinum flakes in the bottom of the pan or not. In any case, the flakes would be tiny. Despite the gathering darkness he stumbled back to the rocks. He took one last soil sample directly under the rock and put it into a small linen bag. When he stood up, he supported himself against the weathered rock, and almost without thinking about it, scraped off some of the weathered surface grit and put it into his jacket pocket with a small piece of the rock.

The next morning, the first thing he did was to pan the soil sample he had taken in the dark. It did indeed contain platinum flakes. The trace was intact, nothing had been lost; the day's work could start. Then he realised that he was still carrying about some rock from the previous evening in his jacket pocket. He put it in the pan and crushed it lightly. He panned the material, and suddenly saw platinum flakes in the bottom of the pan.

Wow! Merensky stood up and took a deep breath. For him as a geologist this was an unbelievable moment. For the first time a basic platinum parent rock had been identified outside Russia! He looked around the valley. Would this be the site for the first platinum mine in South Africa? He did not know. But he did know that from this moment on, things would be hectic. He and his people would have to work in a very focused way from now on.

He waved and called to his fellow prospectors, who were scattered throughout the valley, and gathered them. The whole day long all four worked around the rock where he had found the sample. Metre by metre, they took samples, panned them and tried to ascertain what kind of mineralisation they were dealing with. A reef? There was no indication of one so far. Was it only an enrichment of platinum particles spread in the surface area of the rock? No, apparently not, since there were some rocks close to the place where Merensky had taken the sample that contained absolutely no platinum. By nightfall, they had clarified the matter. They had gradually "looked into" the rock. What had initially looked like a uniform mass of rocks displayed obviously certain diversities. They could identify a zone several metres wide that was a fraction paler than the surrounding rock. This zone, which ran diagonally into the ground, contained the mineralisation. This was the most exciting day of Merensky's life. Later he wrote about it: "This night I did not sleep!"

Merensky knew exactly what to do next. The place where the platinum occurrence had been found was not on Lombaard's farm, but on the next farm, Mooihoek. Early the next morning, he went to the Mining Commissioner in Pilgrim's Rest to report his finders' rights. The Commissioner knew the farm. "Yes, on Mooihoek there are many small chromite occurrences," he said, picking up his pen. Then he asked again: "Chromite?" This was not really a question, but merely a confirmation. Merensky shook his head: "No, not chromite, platinum." The Mining Commissioner's expression was disbelieving and Merensky repeated: "Yes, platinum, on Mooihoek."

Unfortunately, this conversation was overheard. Some of the Commissioner's assistants who were in the big office had only listened with half an ear so far. Small chromite occurrences were nothing new in the Bushveld. But when they heard the word platinum, they pricked up their ears. Merensky knew that from this moment on he would have to change his tactics. In a few days, the news that he had found platinum on Mooihoek would spread like wildfire. He was now in a race against time.

Back at Maandagshoek, he held a war council with his fellow prospectors and explained what would happen next. In a very short while, the area would be swarming with strangers who would try to get options on all the surrounding farms. Now there was no more time for detailed prospecting. Merensky and his friends had to try to secure as many large surface areas in the area as possible. Clearing up whether there was indeed platinum-bearing rock there would have to be left until later.

Then Merensky asked whether Lombaard or the Schoemans had seen any rock anywhere in the area that was similar to the rock they had found the day before. Willem Schoeman nodded. He thought that was quite possible. He recalled seeing some at a hill called Kuwetshwane. The next day he drove there and collected some samples. By evening they knew that the rock contained platinum. This showed that the platinum on Mooihoek was not an isolated occurrence!

Merensky was already thinking of the next steps. They had found two platinum occurrences. More would follow, of that he was certain. Now the enterprise had to expand, and what they needed was a lot more capital. That would be forthcoming, he knew, because now the situation was quite different from what it had been a few weeks before. Nevertheless, if one wanted to attract new capital, one needed to be able to offer something attractive. But what? The platinum occurrences were present, but to attract investors, the finds had to be documented better. What was needed immediately were exact analysis results.

Once more, Merensky carefully took rock samples at the places were platinum had been observed, and then he set off for Johannesburg. Before he left, he gave his fellow prospectors some precise instructions. Every basic rock that was a little paler than the others had to be studied closely. They were not to waste time on other rocks. They should also take samples on the slopes at the same heights as the places where Lombaard had taken the first sample and where the two subsequent occurrences had been found.

Back in Johannesburg, Merensky got Wipplinger to crush the samples he had brought with him. Then they were taken to a chemical laboratory for analysis, marked only with letters and numbers, without any indications of their origin. The results were better than expected. The best average values were those of the occurrences on Mooihoek, namely 6,53 to 7,77 grams per ton, which was an interesting value for platinum.

Meanwhile, Merensky had called together the members of the syndicate and had explained the financial considerations that resulted from the finds to his friends. The two known platinum occurences had to be followed up. The next goal would be to prove that there was a coherent and continuous deposit that could be mined. That was only possible if they had a lot more money. They agreed to try to get four times the starting capital. The members of the syndicate managed to raise a further £6000.

They also agreed that now there was little point in continuing to be secretive about the purpose of the syndicate. On the contrary, it was now important to attract the interest of potential new backers. Their platinum prospecting was no longer a secret. Henceforth, they acted as Lydenburg Platinum Ltd.

By the time Merensky returned to Maandagshoek, it was already September. Lombaard and the two Schoemans had used their time well and had continued their work with good results. Andries Lombaard had just identified a further platinum occurrence on his own land. It was a rock layer 12 metres long. He had found it by working along the slope at the same height as his original find and starting from the point where he had first found platinum. The whole team rushed over to look, and Merensky gave a cry of amazement. This was a completely different type of rock from what they had found on Mooihoek and at Kuwetshwane. Here the rock was dark and it contained all kinds of sulphide minerals, such as phyrrotite, chalcopyrite, pyrite and pentlandite. Merensky thought that the rock was a pyroxenite. Later, when the rock was examined under a microscope, that suspicion was found to be correct. The most noteworthy thing about this find was, however, that the rock displayed a type of layering or stratification that could be followed along the slope. The group got to work immediately. Indeed, the band of rock could be followed, with only a few breaks, right across the farm, to the north, into the neighbouring farm and then further across various farms. Merensky could hardly believe it. They had found a continuous platinum-bearing layer that was freely accessible at almost all points and dipped into the mountain at a slight incline. This was the continuous deposit that he had mentioned so hopefully in the meeting with the syndicate! He sensed that this layer of rock was actually the large platinum deposit he had sought, and that the occurrences on Mooihoek and Kuwetshwane in their tubular or vein form were the exceptions.

He was to be proven right. The prospectors had discovered a vast platinum deposit. But, at that time, they were not to know that they were about to set off the discovery of one of the most important platinum deposits worldwide. Likewise, they could not guess at that moment, a detail they were only to learn much later, what a great stroke of luck discovering this platinum-bearing layer in that place was. In fact, this layer does not show itself as clearly in other places in the Bushveld, as it is overgrown or covered with rubble, which means that it could easily be overlooked when one is prospecting. The stratification of the layer which enabled them to trace the deposit so rapidly was also a local phenomenon which is much less noticeable in other parts of the Bushveld.

All this did not concern Merensky at that stage. He was already a step ahead. What could be found in the north could also be found to the south, where the Steelpoort River formed a natural barrier. Therefore he sent Willem and Schalk Schoeman into the area on the other side of the river to check whether the platinum-bearing layer continued there.

Then came a setback. What Merensky had long feared, happened. The competition became active, or, to be more precise, free loaders entered the scene. Lombaard remembered that he had seen similar rock formations to that found on Mooihoek on a neighbouring farm called Onverwacht. He rode over to discuss an option with the owner, only to find that the Transvaal Land and Exploration Company had already taken an option on the farm. For Merensky this was a severe blow. Later they would find that this was also a financial loss, because Onverwacht was to prove to contain particularly rich platinum deposits.

Then something worse happened. Merensky had a bad accident. It was only thanks to his unbelievable tenacity that the entire platinum project did not collapse at that time. The accident was caused by something small, as it so often is. Merensky was on the road with a wagon and a team of mules and was transporting some rock samples. Somehow one wheel got stuck in a deep rut. The wagon tilted, tipped over and flung Merensky out. When he hauled himself to his feet, he felt a stabbing pain in his chest, so severe that he could barely breathe. The terrified mules somehow managed to get out of the traces and ran off. Despite his pain, with some difficulty, Merensky managed to capture the team. He drove directly to a doctor who he knew he could find on a neighbouring farm. The doctor found that Merensky had two broken ribs and one cracked rib, as well as a number of painful bruises. The doctor bandaged Merensky's chest and ordered several days strict bed-rest. Of course, Merensky had no intention of following these instructions. He worked on, despite almost unbearable pain. His fellow prospectors did not even guess that anything was wrong. In the end, they only heard about the accident because the doctor came around to the Lombaards' house to ask how his patient was doing. The patient was out in the veld. Merensky's argument was simple: the competition was already busy. He and his friends therefore had to use every minute available to them to continue to prospect and to secure as many options as they could. If he took a breather now, he risked losing the best parts of the deposit to others. His farmer friends and his friends in the syndicate had entrusted him with leading the prospecting process. He could not and would not leave them in the lurch.

He was also worried about the Schoeman brothers. They had left for the southern banks of the Steelpoort River days ago and he had heard nothing from them. At last they sent word. They had taken some time to pick up the platinum "spoor" on the other side of the river. They had almost despaired, but now they had again found platinum flakes in their pans. Despite his pain, Merensky hurried to the other side of the river. There was no doubt – it was indeed the same platinum-bearing layer as the one that they had identified to the north of the Lombaard farm. And once again they could track the layer quickly across several farms. Then the layer ended, apparently finally. Merensky was still not prepared to give up. They worked along the ranges of hills and, after a break of 32 kilometres, they found another piece of the platinum-bearing layer and could again follow it for kilometres. They had discovered a vast occurrence. The layer that they had discovered ran, from its northernmost to its southernmost spur, for almost 160 kilometres.

Merensky was at last satisfied. Now it was high time for him to seek medical care. He went back to Johannesburg, where the doctors were horrified to discover how long he had avoided proper medical treatment. They took their task seriously. He was put into bed and was barely allowed to move. It seemed that the chapter in his life entitled "prospecting for platinum" was definitely over.

CHAPTER 11

# Platinum, platinum without end

It was late in the year when the doctors let Merensky out of their care. His friends on Maandagshoek greeted him enthusiastically. On the first evening, they sat together in a companionable circle and exchanged news: what did people in Johannesburg say about the future of platinum in South Africa? What had happened on the stock exchange? What were the latest analysis values? What news was there about the other syndicates? It was late in the night when the conversation turned to the fact that it really was time to give this platinum occurrence a name. This was customary among miners and prospectors. In Europe everyone knows the names that pious miners gave their mines in the Middle Ages, for example, the Barbara-Stollen (called after the patron saint of miners), the Marien-Stollen and so forth. In South Africa occurrences tend to be named after their discoverers. Therefore, Merensky thought that it was appropriate to call the reef the Lombaard Reef. His companions did not agree. Lombaard had admittedly found the first traces of platinum and the platinum-bearing layer that was to become the main deposit. No one could argue that. But his friends also agreed that without Merensky they would not even have known where to start prospecting. Lombaard would probably never have had his second find if Merensky had not driven them all so hard the previous few weeks, and had always encouraged them. Without Merensky they would not have been able to trace the platinum layer, and without the money he had raised – and the farmers knew how difficult that had been – the work would have had to stop very quickly. They decided to call the platinum-bearing layer the Merensky Reef.

Merensky demurred, but his objections were ignored. He was outvoted and so the name stuck. Merensky was honoured many times in his life (and posthumously): with honorary memberships and medals from academies of science, with more than one honorary doctorate, with the dedications of famous subject specialist authors and symposia that were named after him. But probably the honour he valued most of all was the fact that these farmers, who had worked in the blazing sun with him until they were all at the point of exhaustion, in the end honoured him, without envy and with great gratitude, as the one without whom nothing would have happened as it did, by naming the Merensky Reef after him. This is the best known of all the honours that came to him, and the one that will be remembered longest. In the past 80 years and more there is not a single textbook on mineralogy or mineral resources, no matter in what language in the world, that does not mention and describe the Merensky Reef. Every mineralogist knows about it, and there is every likelihood that this will still be true in another 100 years.

The situation on Maandagshoek had changed radically during his absence. The phase of rough surveying was nearly over. The location and extent of the platinum-bearing layer at Lydenburg were now more or less known. Now they were starting to test the metal concentrations of the layer systematically.

The predicted rush of platinum diggers had begun. The government had opened up a number of farms for prospecting, and the region had been flooded by a large stream of platinum seekers. They came on foot or on horseback, in carriages and cars. In Lydenburg there were no lodgings available, and the roads to the farms were choked with vehicles. Among those who had come to try to find more platinum, there were some experienced prospectors, but many more "wannabe" diggers who knew neither what platinum looked like nor how to find it. They pegged out claims anywhere they liked, ignoring the fact that most of the pieces of land had long since been claimed. By this time there were already fifty syndicates. Some had very small capital amounts available; some of the bigger ones had already issued shares which were being traded on the stock exchange. No one knew any details about the size and extent of the deposit concerned, but the public was eager to snap up any platinum shares that were issued.

Merensky's personal circumstances had also changed. Once again, he was in great demand, even more so than in the years before the war. Mining companies that he had once worked for suddenly remembered him, and financiers asked him for advice. This was surpassed by the number of people that he had never met before and who wanted him to tell them where and how they could get into the platinum business. It was ridiculous. Five months earlier he had battled to raise £5000 to get his platinum project off the ground. Now he met people every day who just happened to have £10 000 or £20 000 lying about and who desperately wanted to invest it in platinum.

Despite all the brouhaha, Merensky kept his head. In the weeks when the doctors forced him to rest, he had had a lot of time to think about the platinum mineralisation of the Bushveld. Now he analysed the prospecting situation again. Then he prepared his next coup, which was to be a big one. So far he had only used some of his considerable range of skills. He had used his unbelievable geological intuition, his tenacity during the search, his ability to motivate his companions and to keep them going even when the prospecting was going badly, and, of course, one of his most important gifts – the charm needed to persuade his friends to trust him and to raise money. So far, he had not drawn on his knowledge of the country and his familiarity with the geology of the Bushveld. After all, he had spent 15 years – excluding the war years – prospecting throughout the Transvaal.

At this point, it may be helpful to pause briefly to note the geological characteristics of the Bushveld. The Bushveld covers an area of approximately 480 kilometres from east to west, and 120 kilometres from north to south. Basic rocks play a large role in the region. They were deposited by several distinct magmatic intrusions, with longer periods in between. The chemical composition of the individual layers changed gradually due to this process. Today one can compare this sequence of layers with a giant stack of pancakes. This may not sound very scientific, but a stack of pancakes has two characteristics that are shared by basic rock strata in the Bushveld. First, pancakes are very thin. This also applies to the rock layers in the Bushveld. The individual layers are seldom very thick in any place – more often less than ten metres and sometimes as little as one metre. Second, when one looks at a stack of pancakes, one can only see the edges of the pancakes below the overlying ones. This also applies to the rock layers in the Bushveld. The platinum-bearing layer is situated in the lower part of the Bushveld sequence and what Merensky and his fellow prospectors had found at Lydenburg (what would now be called the Merensky Reef) was the eastern edge of such a thin rock layer. Everywhere Merensky had identified this layer, it dipped or inclined slightly to the west or north-west, so that the layer went underneath the rest of the Bushveld sequence that lay above it.

Back then, more than 80 years ago, the Bushveld had not yet been studied in as much detail as it has been today. Not much drilling had been done, as it was very difficult to drill into these very hard old rock series. Nevertheless, Merensky knew that the individual rock layers were plate-shaped. Hence, it was obvious that he would want to check whether the Merensky Reef was not visible at other places along the edge of the Bushveld, emerging from below the layers of basic rock above it. In other words, he wanted to ride around the entire Bushveld.

While Merensky was still contriving ways and means of doing this, a coincidence showed him a possible way to organise it. One morning late in 1924 he had barely walked into his office when Wipplinger came to tell him that Gustav Troye had tried to see him the previous evening. Troye was an old acquaintance, a prospector who owned a farm near Potgietersrus (now called Mokopane), and who worked as a farmer or as a prospector, depending on how things went. Merensky valued him and sent for him immediately. They had barely greeted each other, when Troye complained that Merensky had not involved him in his platinum venture. Merensky took his reproaches calmly and said: "Dear Troye, I was looking for partners with a sore heart. If I had met you then, you may be sure that you would not have escaped! I would have involved you in the business, but then I had already bled you of your last penny. But forget about that – there are more important things to worry about now!" He told Troye how things stood, and Troye left the very next morning for Potgietersrus to look for the reef in this area, which he knew very well. Just one week later, he let Merensky know that he could not follow Merensky's geological indicators. The sequence of the rock layers was different from what Merensky had described and there were no signs of a platinum-bearing reef.

Merensky left at once. He travelled unobtrusively. He took the train north, then drove part of the way in a rented car, and finally hired a horse in Potgietersrus. In Johannesburg his sudden disappearance was noticed immediately, because potential investors asked to see him almost every day. No one knew where he was, and Wipplinger would not say a word.

Merensky did not carry a pan with him, and his geologists' hammer was tucked away in his luggage. When anyone asked him what the purpose of his journey was, he said that he wanted to visit some farms, which he did. This was not a problem, since he knew many farmers in the region.

Potgietersrus is situated on the northern edge of the Bushveld. He did not think it should be very difficult to find the platinum-bearing layer, considering what he knew. Theoretically, all he had to do was to ride up a profile perpendicular to the layers. If the platinum-bearing layer was there, he would have to cross it sooner or later. Soon, however, he realised that it would not be that simple. The area was partly rocky, partly covered in loose gravel, and he was forced to take many detours and often had to dismount. Countless times he struck off pieces of rock with his hammer to examine the rock under his magnifying glass. He realised that in this area the layer sequence did indeed differ from that in Lydenburg. It was particularly the chromite layers, which in Lydenburg lay under the platinum-bearing reef and served as an orientation point, that were absent or not developed at Potgietersrus. It was no wonder that Troye had not managed very well. Nevertheless, Merensky continued the search, and after several days, he found the platinum-bearing layer he was looking for, although not as clearly defined or stratified as at Lydenburg. The next day, he rode along another profile for a distance of more than 15 kilometres and here too, he was able to identify the platinum-bearing layer. Since he was fairly certain that there was a connection between the two points, he was convinced that the Merensky Reef could be followed for longer distances in the Potgietersrus area, just as it could near Lydenburg. That was enough for now. In the meantime, he approached two experts he knew, a prospector called Busschau and a geologist, Dr I. Celliers, and informed them of the geological situation. He left the detailed prospecting to them. Then he left the area and without hesitation travelled quickly to Rustenburg, about 300 kilometres away, at the western end of the Bushveld.

There, the terrain made the process even more difficult than at either of the two other locations. Merensky soon realised that he would not succeed in locating the exact position of the platinum reef in two or three days. He had a good idea of where he had to search for it, but he did not get much further in the rush. The real problem was that option hunters were already gathering in Rustenburg. They had barely any idea of what a platinum mineralisation looked like and they knew nothing about the plate-like structure of the Bushveld, but they were determined to get options in the western Transvaal and hoped to get lucky in some way. This posed a threat, and Merensky had to act quickly.

He returned to Johannesburg in great haste. His feelings were ambivalent. On the one hand, he was pleased with what he had found at Potgietersrus. On the other hand, he was under enormous pressure. Once again, even half a day could make a difference. It was vital that he managed to buy as many options in the Rustenburg area as he could. This had to be done very quickly, and the process needed to be undertaken unobtrusively by someone he trusted. He could not act in the matter himself, because he was too well known. He chose a good acquaintance, Hans von Gernet, who involved his friend Schreiner Cooper. Their orders were to buy any options available in the area that Merensky had indicated, immediately. There was no time to investigate the terrain in detail. They had to be faster than the other option hunters.

The hunt for options in Rustenburg became quite an adventure. There were real races to get to one or other farm first. False manoeuvres to mislead the competition were part of the daily game. So, for example, if they planned to go to a farm to the north of Rustenburg, they would order a taxi from the hotel the previous evening, saying that the taxi was needed for a trip south. The call was put through on the one telephone in the hotel, and was made in such a way that whoever was eavesdropping – and there was always someone – would overhear the ostensible destination. The next day, they would leave, driving south, but then turn and, driving around the town, would go north, to the real destination.

The hunt for options was made more difficult by the fact that large parts of the area were reserved for indigenous groups. These areas were under the protection of the Native Affairs Department, who were suspicious of any kind of negotiation or trade with the inhabitants of the reserves and who had to authorise the option agreements. Communication with the chieftains and elders was also extremely difficult. The meetings took hours. It could take half a day to get an option agreement signed with three crosses. Fortunately, von Gernet and Cooper were skilled negotiators and were able to secure huge areas. Merensky's friend Becker and his business partner H. Olthaver advanced the money used to buy these options.

At the same time, the stock exchange in Johannesburg boomed, because the circles interested in platinum shares were getting wider and wider. This meant that the stock exchange was experiencing an influx of investments. Just before the end of 1924 – about half a year after the first platinum finds – the total value of the platinum shares traded in Johannesburg was already £13 million. This was remarkable, since the mining of these platinum occurrences had not even begun. There had been some analyses of samples taken at various points, but no systematic studies had as yet been undertaken. There was neither a grid of diggings or trenches, nor pits or shafts to follow the platinum layer into the mountain. All this did not concern the stock exchange. As always, the exchange was far ahead of the actual economic development.

The biggest profits at this time were, however, not being made on the stock exchange, but by companies that owned large amounts of land. There were a number of these: African and European Investment Corporation, South African Townships, the Mining and Finance Corporation and the Transvaal Land and Exploration Company, which was already mentioned above. They owned large pieces of the country, divided into farms which they rented out. (Only some of the over 4000 farmers who lived in the Transvaal in those days lived on their own land. The rest were tenant farmers.) Since the platinum reef ran right across the country, the farming land of many companies was affected. Without doing any prospecting themselves, they benefited from the platinum boom, as many pieces of land increased enormously in value. Occasionally, Merensky himself showed the members of other companies in the field where the Merensky Reef was to be accessed on the land they held options on.

Some of the people who did particularly good business in those months were Merensky's friend Becker and his business partner, Olthaver. When Lydenburg Platinum Ltd was founded, Becker still had trouble getting his capital share together, because his means were tied up elsewhere. Meanwhile he and his partner had read the signs of the times and had regrouped their activities in such a way that they were now more liquid. This meant that there was a good capital injection for Lydenburg Platinum Ltd. They also became strongly involved in the Potgietersrus area, where they began to buy up options.

Then 1925 dawned. The platinum scene was now constantly changing. Out in the veld, the rough investigation of the terrain was now more or less concluded. The outline and shape of the platinum reef was now known. There were also some early signs of consolidation among the platinum companies. Several smaller syndicates that had not managed to secure interesting option areas gave up. Others, whose options looked promising, accepted offers from bigger syndicates and were absorbed by them. This meant that the number of companies active in the Bushveld dropped. Accordingly, the remaining companies became financially stronger, and they did not hesitate to involve new partners that could bring in more money.

The stock market was extremely volatile at this stage. Prices rose repeatedly. Some of the increases were sparked by the wealth of rumours circulating in the market. Others were based on real reasons, such as a new valuation of a particular part of the reef, or a change in the business strategy of one of the big companies. So, for example, the announcement that Anglo American, the biggest South African gold mining company, would enter the platinum mining business led to a jump in the prices of all platinum shares. There was another jump when Johannesburg Consolidated Investments announced its intention to become involved in the platinum business. In between, there were a number of setbacks on the exchange.

Initially, the platinum boom was limited to the Johannesburg Stock Exchange. The London Stock Exchange remained sceptical for a long time. The finance magnates believed that this was merely a local South African phenomenon which would not affect the world markets. The turning point was the visit of the British Commissioner, Mr Farquharson, to the platinum fields, and his positive report to London. The British press took note of the government report, and soon every paper was reporting that South Africa was about to become the world's biggest platinum producer. The spell was broken. From now on there was international interest in South African platinum.

However, platinum speculation could not continue unchecked. The London stockbrokers had just begun to warm up to South African platinum when, in June 1925, there was a stock market crash in Johannesburg. The platinum shares quickly lost about a third of their value. This led to consolidation across a wide front. Many syndicates with inadequate financial resources collapsed. From then on, the big firms took the lead.

In the first half of 1925, detailed investigations of the platinum reefs had advanced considerably. There had been some surprises: at Potgietersrus the reef was not just visible as a narrow strip, but was quite broad in some places. It was also discovered that the platinum there is found not only in pyroxenites (as native platinum with the other platinum compounds admixed), but also mixed with finely distributed sulphides which occur in the nearby norite bands. (Norites, like pyroxenites, are basic plutonic rocks.) More than that: the analyses indicated excellent platinum concentrations. It was clear that the area around Potgietersrus could become the richest platinum deposit in the world. Merensky had not expected this, but he was also not really very surprised, because in his experience one seldom found the heart of a deposit with the first find of a mineral. That was one reason why he had insisted from the start that his companions should secure options over as large an area as possible.

Becker and Olthaver were among those who benefited most from this development. They had funded almost all the prospecting in the Potgietersrus area and had managed to secure options on a strip of

48 kilometres during the first half of 1925. This strip ran across several farms. When eventually really big mining companies entered the arena, Becker and Olthaver were quite happy, since they had never intended to get involved in the mining operations of a platinum mine. In July 1925, one of the genuinely big syndicates, Potgietersrus Platinum Mines Ltd, was launched. It had three important partners: Becker and Olthaver, South African Townships and Anglo American. The start-up capital was £500 000. A few months later another partner joined them, the even more powerful Barnato group, one of the old diamond companies. The group brought a capital injection of £700 000 with it and took over the management.

But that was not the only surprise. In the first half of 1925, in the Rustenburg district, Merensky located the platinum-bearing layer and was able to follow it over long distances with the help of some assistants. By the end of the year, it had become clear that the platinum occurrences in the Rustenburg area were even more plentiful than the ones at Potgietersrus. The options that Hans von Gernet and Cooper had acquired, proved to have the highest analytical values. They became the richest platinum fields in the world.

The prospecting phase was now concluded. Only slightly more than one and a half years had passed since Merensky had first held the little medicine bottle in his hands. Now platinum deposits all round the Bushveld across an area of almost 2000 square kilometres were known. In the east and south-east, where the first platinum had been found, there was a narrow belt about 160 kilometres long. In the north, at Potgietersrus, there was a noticeably wider belt, just over 75 kilometres long. In the west, at Rustenburg, the reef could be followed for nearly 300 kilometres. Merensky's work as a prospecting geologist was done. Now the initiative passed to the miners. Mining could begin.

The completion of the exploratory phase and the establishment of operational mining companies ran parallel to the scientific study of the Bushveld platinum. This scientific study had a first important impact in 1929.

It was quite understandable that the discovery of a deposit of this magnitude attracted scientists from across the world. Year by year, a large number of researchers came to the Transvaal. Naturally, the percentage of anglophone scientists was high, but other nations were also represented. Among the German researchers, Hans Schneiderhöhn, who already published on the Bushveld in 1929, was particularly prominent. He researched this topic his whole life long, and in 1958, then the doyen in his field, he published a summary of his own findings on the Bushveld, in his final work, *Erzlagerstätten der Erde* [Ore deposits of the earth].

The impetus for a long string of scientific publications came from Hans Merensky himself. As early as 1925, he introduced the platinum deposits of the Lydenburg and Potgietersrus areas to the scientific world by means of lectures and articles in the *South African Mining and Engineering Journal*.

The most important scientist of his time who worked on platinum was to be the South African Percy A. Wagner. This is not the place to present a history of the scientific study of the Bushveld platinum deposits, but Wagner's work is mentioned here because it documents the assessment of Merensky's work by his contemporaries.

At the time when the news of the platinum finds near Lydenburg spread throughout the country, Percy A. Wagner, who was then 40 years old, was a senior geologist with the South African Geological Survey and was regarded as one of the leading experts on deposits in the country. Since nobody in the capital knew whether the rumours had any substance, the government sent Percy Wagner to the Bushveld. Even his first visit to the terrain showed him that this platinum occurrence was something completely new for South Africa and that it might be economically very interesting indeed. He also realised that, given the vast extent of the platinum reef, there would be increasing pressure on the government and on landowners from those who sought ore to allow them to participate in this platinum boom. To prevent the rise of the irregular conditions that frequently accompany a rush, he arranged that the government open up any farms in the Lydenburg district that it had control over for prospecting and options.

In the time that followed, Percy Wagner stayed in the Bushveld and followed the course of the prospecting developments, first on behalf of the government and later of large companies. Between him, the eminent scientist, and Merensky, the field geologist with his phenomenal powers of observation, there was a lively exchange of ideas that was to continue for several years. At this time, the two of them made innumerable joint visits to the terrain in the Bushveld. This close cooperation became the basis of a deep friendship.

Over the years, Percy Wagner visited every new mine, every tiny shaft and every pit that was started in the Bushveld. He became the most knowledgeable person about these platinum occurrences and guided many researchers from abroad on their visits. From 1925, he published on the Bushveld, and it was he who introduced the name "Merensky Reef" in the scientific literature. In 1929 he published a summary and overview in the book, *The Platinum Deposits and Mines of South Africa*. Hans Schneiderhöhn contributed the chapter on ore microscopy for the book. It was a comprehensive work and, for many years, it was regarded as the most authoritative work on research on South African platinum. Its 326 pages, supplemented with numerous maps, profiles and photographs, sets out everything then known about the Bushveld platinum – even today it is still regarded as a highly instructive specialist book. Sadly, this great researcher died, only 44 years old, very soon after his book appeared.

For Percy Wagner, it was a matter of course to open his book with the following dedication to Hans Merensky:

To Dr. Hans Merensky
Mining Geologist, Super-Prospector
and best of Friends
I dedicate this book.

The heartfelt respect and affection that breathes from this dedication gives us some clue of Merensky's effect on his friends and colleagues.

Percy Wagner did not leave it at this dedication. When one opens the book, one finds another appreciative commentary on Merensky's achievements in the first few pages. This may seem surprising, since there can be almost no one among the readers of this specialist text who does not know that Merensky discovered the Bushveld platinum. It is perhaps even more surprising when one considers that by that time, Merensky had long become a South African legend, because two and a half years after he had found the platinum, he found the fantastically rich diamond deposit in Namaqualand. After that, there was no one in South Africa who did not know about Merensky.

In fact, many farm children were not playing "cops and robbers" or "Brits and Boers" any more, but "Merensky-Merensky"! The fact that Percy Wagner again highlighted Merensky's achievements shows how deeply impressed Wagner, himself a leading geologist, was with both Merensky's expert achievement and his personal attributes. This is what he wrote:

"The Transvaal, that marvellous storehouse of mineral wealth, has become in recent years an important producer of the platinum metals. She is destined to become the world's leading producer as her primary deposits of these metals are incomparably the greatest.

The sequence of events that led to their discovery has been given elsewhere. It need here only be recalled that the finding in 1923, by Adolphe Erasmus, of the remarkable lode deposits of the Waterberg district gave a great impetus to the search for platinum in South Africa. It was followed in September 1924 by the discovery of the Bushveld deposits which transcend in magnitude and importance anything that had hitherto been dreamt of in the way of primary platinum occurrences.

The story of the opening up of the deposits has often been told, but the writer feels that sufficient credit has never been given to Dr. Hans Merensky for the part he played in this epic of mineral exploration. It was he who discovered both the dunite deposits and the Merensky Reef in the Lydenburg district. It was he who located the most important deposits in the Potgietersrus area. In the end it was he who, when all hope had been abandoned of finding the Merensky Reef in the Rustenburg district, not only located it, but, with the assistance of Messrs D. McKerrell, D. Mare, J. Ellis and M. Weber traced it across scores of miles."

CHAPTER 12

# To the Adlon in Berlin and back to the Transvaal

Merensky's situation in Johannesburg had changed radically. Now, since the newspapers were constantly reporting on the events in the Bushveld, everyone in Johannesburg knew him. His picture and his life history had been printed in the newspapers several times and whatever he said about mining or raw materials issues, the journalists reported in detail.

His financial situation had also changed completely. The long drought had been broken. Now he had money and could free himself from his debts. He had been bowed under them for 14 years. Often enough he had doubted whether he would ever succeed in earning enough money to satisfy all his creditors. Now he could do so.

His main creditors were the banks. Paying them was quickly done, since the institutes knew how much he owed them down to the last penny, including interest and compound interest. They presented him with their accounts, which he paid at once. He was also able to repay some of his biggest creditors without problems. Then he sat down to check on how much of his fortune was left, and he found that what was left after paying back his biggest debts was not that much. It amounted to about £80 000. That was a lot of money, but he was still far from being one of the really rich people in the country.

Merensky's biggest problem in repaying his debts was that if he needed large sums, he needed to sell some of his platinum shares. Perforce he did so relatively early, that is, before the shares had reached their highest price. His friends and the co-founders of the syndicate were in a better position. They did not have any debts to pay off and were liquid enough to hang on to their shares long enough to achieve an increase in value. Some of his friends succeeded in building up considerable fortunes in a relatively short time.

On the other hand, Merensky's financial situation was not all that bad. The platinum finds had barely become known when he received a flood of requests to take on this and that consulting commission. He was even sent prospecting material from Sumatra to do an expert appraisal of a suspected platinum occurrence there. He corresponded about gold occurrences in the Sierra de Minas in Argentina and drilling on brine springs near Dar-es-Salaam. He was back in business and had a constant inflow of cash. It was almost as it had been before the war. But there were more debts. He had to put aside money for some of his creditors in Germany. These were people who had entrusted him with money before the war to invest it for them. This money had been lost in his stock speculations. He was determined to repay these losses. Of course, he also put aside money to pay out his brothers' and sisters' shares of his parents' farm, which he had had to sell. And then there were the innumerable small sums between £10 and £50 that he had borrowed over the years. He was horrified to find how many creditors that he had forgotten about long ago called on him, but he did his best to clear the slate.

Some problems solved themselves. He could satisfy some of his creditors by advising them on their platinum speculations, for example, when new shares came on the market. Nobody could assess better than he what the individual shares were really worth. After all, he knew the places where the platinum had been found and the metal content thereof and could thus estimate which shares could be expected to increase in value and which could not.

His assistant, Wipplinger, and his landlady, Fräulein Linhardt, also bought platinum shares. Merensky advised them but made sure that they secured their profits properly. Both were able to earn many times what Merensky owed them. This came as no surprise to Wipplinger, because he had experienced Merensky's intuitive "nose" for deposits close up. He had always had confidence in Merensky, and his trust now paid off. Fräulein Linhardt's argument was somewhat different. For her, platinum and gold came to much the same thing and she had been convinced from the start that Merensky, this "nice and charming man", would find a big gold vein. So, if he now told her that she could confidently invest her money in certain shares, then she did so with the same unshaken faith that she had always had in him.

The fact that Merensky now had some money again had its downside too. People who had lent him money years earlier now wanted him to lend them money. The sums that he owed them were generally small and he could repay them quickly. By contrast, the sums that these "old friends" wanted to borrow from him were, however, often very high. Generally they wanted several thousand pounds and sometimes they even wanted sums as high as £20 000. Each of these projects was described as a "dead certainty". He was almost never able to get the people concerned to show him the references, details and calculations. Somehow, in the back of his mind, there was always the fear that people would say that now that he had become rich, he wanted to forget his old friends. He found it extremely difficult to refuse such requests. Since most of these enterprises failed, he lost considerable amounts.

It became increasingly clear that he did not know how to manage his money. He lent people too much money, he invited too many people, and he trusted too easily. Practically speaking, at any given moment he had no clear idea of his finances. The only mistake he did not make was to speculate on the stock market again. He did learn from past mistakes. The only exception was his investments in the platinum business, which he knew better than anyone else and where – as long as the boom lasted – no problems were to be expected. His German friends, who had stuck with him throughout the lean years and who were doing well now, reproached him for his prodigal moneylending. His friend Becker in particular did not spare him some severe criticism. Merensky recognised his inability to work with money, but did not know how to change things. In a way, the situation depressed him. The freedom to do what he wanted that he had enjoyed in the first few months after first finding the platinum was gone. Now, only one and a half years after the first platinum find on Maandagshoek and after huge sums had run through his fingers, his newly won fortune was almost exhausted. He was not impoverished, but could no longer draw on abundant resources.

In this somewhat sombre mood, he at long last decided to travel back to Germany again. This was in January of 1926. After the last one and a half years, which had been hectic, he felt leeched of energy and very tired. He was also already plagued with hearing problems which were to persist for the rest of his life. These had probably been caused by a middle ear infection that he had developed at some stage while he was working out in the veld and that had not healed properly. His accident on Maandagshoek, when he had been thrown from the cart, also had a far-reaching effect. His ribs had healed well, thanks to the strict bedrest that his doctors had imposed on him, but the doctors had recommended that he should take some time off to convalesce too, and he had promptly ignored their advice. Now he noticed that his resilience was noticeably lower, and he decided to recover in Germany. He had never taken a holiday in Europe, and he had last seen his family 22 years before.

However – this was what he was like – he was afraid that he would not be able to bear being completely without anything to do in Europe, and so he agreed to have exploratory discussions in Germany on behalf of various mining companies. Unfortunately, he soon had a full programme, because the question of how to exploit the platinum resources viably and how to optimise the ore dressing had become vital in the Bushveld. The metal concentrations of the platinum ores were roughly 5 to 15 grams of platinum per ton of rock. Extracting such small quantities of a precious metal from the ore once it had been finely ground requires highly complicated extraction processes. There is no standard procedure. Every ore requires its own specialised process, which is designed to take into account the specific characteristics of the rock and particularly the presence of numerous other minerals. It is normal that the metal that has to be extracted can never be fully recovered from the finely ground platinum-bearing rock, but even a layman can see that the profit margin increases with every additional gram of platinum that one can extract per ton of rock. That was exactly the goal, since, although the deposits were good, the South African platinum mining business had to fight for its existence in the first few years. The reason for this was simple: the Soviet Union, which had previously been the incontestable world market leader, was defending its former powerful position in the platinum market with every means at its disposal, for example, by means of almost outrageous price dumping. Two or three years earlier, the Foreign Trade Bureau of the USSR had claimed that the selling price would have to be raised due to rising extraction costs. Now, suddenly, when South Africa threatened to become a serious competitor, the Soviet Union sold its platinum at rock bottom prices. The Soviets hoped that platinum mining in the Transvaal would not even get off the ground. The South African businesses, which had obviously not yet made a profit, let alone built up any reserves, were to be discouraged and driven to give up. As a state monopoly, the Soviet Union had no difficulty in selling its platinum at a price far below the actual production price. By contrast, the South African mines, which were privately owned, were forced to operate at a profit in the long term. For this reason, they were looking for ways in which to optimise the ore dressing procedures. Merensky undertook to discuss the problems these mines faced with some of the world-renowned German ore dressing firms. So, in January 1926, he left for Germany with some unusual luggage – several tons of platinum ore. The arrival of these ores at the harbour in Hamburg at the start of February and its subsequent distribution to the Humboldt AG in Cologne-Kalk, to the Krupp-Gruson works in Magdeburg and to the Erz- und Kohle-Flotation in Bochum were duly noted by the German business papers. The instruction to these three enterprises was to ascertain the most economically viable and technically simplest metal extraction procedure, both by means of conventional wet ore dressing and by means of flotation. The objective was to develop an ore dressing method that would be economically more viable than the treatment with caustic or alkaline solutions used in the Urals.

When he arrived in Germany, Merensky was surprised to find how much of a fuss was made of him. In Berlin he stayed at the Adlon. Although the big newspapers had all reported on him and his discoveries already – "the platinum king" was perhaps the most modest epithet they used – he was constantly being asked for appointments to grant interviews. He was continuously invited to give talks. No German mining company wanted to miss the opportunity to hold a reception for him. Merensky had never been unsociable, and he happily accepted these invitations, because they gave him an opportunity to meet former fellow students, some of whom were now in interesting positions. They also enabled him to build up contacts with German mining suppliers.

Some of his papers on the platinum in the Bushveld can still be read in German mining journals, such as the 1926 edition of *Metall und Erz*. The paper he presented to the Deutsche Geologische Gesellschaft in Berlin was reviewed in detail in some of the specialist journals. There were also many honours. He was particularly pleased by the fact that his former school, the Technical High School of Berlin, had recognised his work and awarded him a doctorate honoris causa. This was not the only German acknowledgement of his achievements. In 1938, the famous German geologist Hans Stille nominated him for the Leibniz silver medal *"für besondere Verdienste um die Naturwissenschaften"* [for special services to the natural sciences] from the Prussian Academy of Sciences. Although Merensky was not particularly bothered by titles and external pomp, this was an honour that he valued because of its significance. Moreover, as a Leibniz Prize Winner, he was in the illustrious company of some very interesting researchers and discoverers, such as the analytical chemist and inventor of the process to produce soda ash on an industrial scale, Ernest Solvay, the African explorer George Schweinfurth, the Zeppelin builder Hugo Eckener, and the nuclear physicist Lise Meitner.

Then he also sought out his German creditors from before the war and returned their money to them. Two of these creditors had died, so that he repaid their heirs. Most of these creditors had long before written off their loans as losses and had not counted on ever seeing their money again. Hence they were delighted, but surprised. This amazed Merensky, because he had taken it for granted that now, when he was able to do so, he would repay his debts.

Of course, he saw his family. Much had changed in the years that he had spent abroad. His parents were no longer alive. His father had died in the last year of the war, and his mother just one year later. His siblings had found their own niches. One brother had gone into law; another was a minister. The third brother, who had served as a major under Lettow-Vorbeck, had only survived the end of the war by five years. Two of his sisters were married; the third was unmarried and had taken up art as her career. The married members of his family all had children. These were large families. When he met these families, those with whom he shared the memories of his youth – his brothers and sisters – were in the minority. He still had to get to know the others, which was not very easy because he and they literally came from different worlds. The younger generation saw him as the widely travelled uncle who had had wild adventures in Africa. But he said as little as possible about that, and his brothers and sisters did not ask him much about it because of the whole episode with his parents' farm, which he had sold without his father's permission. As a missionary and as the breadwinner for a large number of children – with three sons to educate – his father had not been able to save much. For that reason he had been very proud of this farm, which President Paul Kruger had given him after the Anglo-Boer War to thank him for his services to the Boers as a doctor. He had wanted to leave this farm as his legacy to his children.

Things had turned out quite differently, and Merensky sensed that the family relations were a little chilly. No one reproached him, but he felt that the family deliberately avoided the topic. No one wanted to discuss the matter. This meant that he had no opportunity to explain what had happened or to set matters right. He never told them about the difficult years just before the war, or about the terrible time in the internment camp, or the hard times that followed after the war. It was a pity, because Merensky could well understand the dissatisfaction of his brothers and sisters about the sale of the farm. He paid out his brothers' and sisters' shares of the farm, and did what he could to make reparations. Sadly, an unspoken reproach remained.

He no longer felt at home in Germany. Life here was too busy, and he felt claustrophobic in the cities. He missed the wide open spaces, the clean, clear air and the broad vistas of the bush savannah. He missed the beautiful sunrises.

When he had been on the ship on his way to Germany, he had been filled with anticipation about what he would find there. He had wondered briefly whether he would perhaps stay in Europe. These were mere momentary speculations, far from a decision, just a playing with ideas, considering various options open to him. A man as well-known as he was, could live in Germany and work anywhere in the world. He would then be able to visit the most interesting deposits in South America or even Australia. But he had not pursued these thoughts. Now he realised that that would be quite the wrong solution for him. Europe could not become his pied-à-terre, a home he could always return to. He needed the wide open spaces of Africa to breathe and to live in and he would need them more than ever when he was exhausted after long months of hard work and needed to take a creative break. He now recognised that in his heart he had become a South African. He decided that when he returned to Johannesburg at the end of the year he would definitely stay in South Africa. The fact that he was quite positive about further travels in Europe and particularly about journeys that would give him an opportunity to study the newest technological developments did not alter his decision to make South Africa his permanent home in any way.

Merensky also used his time in Germany to build up a range of business contacts. There were many discussions and investigations that he had to complete on behalf of South African mining companies with German machinery manufacturers and chemical engineers who specialised in ore dressing, but he also met various financiers on his own behalf. Some wanted specialist geological advice; others wanted more general information about the South African mining situation. Merensky took time to build up and maintain such contacts, because he firmly believed that a relationship based on trust between potential backers and a consulting geologist had to evolve naturally and needed to be in place long before a particular project came up.

One of these contacts took him to London, where he met Ignatius Dessau, a very interesting man who had immigrated to Britain many years earlier from Hungary and now lived very elegantly in Piccadilly. He kept a large household, so that one could almost believe that he was a Hungarian magnate who had gone into exile. This was not the case. He had originally studied as an engineer, and had since become a very successful financier who was involved in both the London Stock Exchange and various mining projects. He had a passion for mining interests. He was particularly fond of getting involved in start-up operations in areas where little previous mining had been done. Merensky had already met him some time ago and had worked closely with him in the Bushveld in 1925. That was the time when the syndicate Merensky and his friends had founded, Lydenburg Platinum Ltd, had become Lydenburg Platinum Areas, and new capital investors had joined the syndicate. This transaction needed to be handled with some finesse. On the one hand, the interests of those members of the syndicate who were unable to invest more money had to be protected, and on the other hand, it was important to bear in mind the overall objective, namely to construct a financially strong company that could take rapid action. Ignatius Dessau (who was a serious, capable and purposeful man of finance) played a decisive role in the restructuring of the syndicate and in the increase of the company's capital. He was the kind of financier that Merensky liked to work with.

At this time Dessau was busy preparing to invest large sums in the lead and zinc mine at Straschimir in Bulgaria. The reports he had received indicated that the crude ore from this mine had metal concentrations of 20% lead, 30% zinc and 350 to 400 grams of silver per ton. These were exceptionally good concentrations. Nevertheless, Dessau, who considered every move very carefully, wanted the best geologist that he knew, Merensky, at his side, particularly because Merensky had considerable experience with lead and zinc deposits. Merensky for his part was happy to accept this commission, because this was the kind of expert appraisal work outside of South Africa that he had been thinking of on his trip to Germany.

The two men ate at a club and discussed the Bulgarian business. Somewhere in the conversation, Dessau mentioned something in passing, and without the least notion of the effect his words would have on Merensky: "I was briefly at the stock exchange this morning, and someone told me that some diamonds had been found in Namaqualand. He was a bit vague. Do you know anything about it? Didn't you have some special theory about diamonds in South-West Africa?"

Merensky shot up from seat as if he had a scorpion in his boot. Namaqualand ... diamonds ... South-West Africa ... he had waited for this for years; to be exact, since 1908, when he had visited the diamond occurrence at Kolmanskop, near Lüderitz. Namaqualand is the coastal strip along the Atlantic coast just south of South-West Africa, just beyond the Orange River, which forms the southern border of what is today Namibia.

Diamonds in Namaqualand. For Merensky this meant that there was a continuation further south of the diamond deposits at Kolmanskop. If there was a connection between the diamond occurrence at Kolmanskop and the diamonds found in Namaqualand, then that meant that the entire dune strip between these two areas might contain diamonds. He became almost dizzy when he thought of the length of this strip of dunes: 280 kilometres!

Merensky was as excited as a hunting dog that had taken the scent. He could barely finish his meal. His conversation was haphazard. One moment he had been interested in Bulgaria, and now he was unable to concentrate on what Dessau was telling him. He left as soon as he could do so without seeming too rude and hastened back to his hotel. From there he telegraphed Wipplinger, asking for detailed information to be sent to the Adlon. That same evening he left London for Berlin.

He had barely arrived at the Adlon when the head receptionist, murmuring apologies, handed him a telegram that had been waiting for him for six days. The Adlon was famous for its good service and had tried to reach him at three or four London hotels, and the management were very unhappy about the fact that they had not succeeded in contacting him. Merensky opened the telegram. It read: *"Prospektor namens Carstens findet in Namaqualand Diamanten, Details folgen."* ["Prospector named Carstens finds diamonds in Namaqualand. Details to follow."]

Merensky was still standing in the hotel foyer with the telegram in his hand when an old acquaintance from South-West Africa, Friedrich Knacke, came up to him. Knacke was a businessman who had several mining interests in South-West Africa and across the border in the Union of South Africa. There he had founded the Namaqualand Diamond Company, which had admittedly not yet become active in the quest for diamonds, but did own a number of option areas. He was involved in various other businesses too; he was, among other things, the London representative of Lydenburg Platinum Areas.

Friedrich Knacke had already heard the news, but did not think much of these finds so far. A few isolated diamonds had also been found in Namaqualand in the past and had made him found a firm there. But so far, no one had been able to locate larger diamond occurrences. As long as that was the case, Knacke did not see any reason to act. After all, as he put it, one could not "plough up" the whole country because of a few isolated diamonds.

Merensky did not agree. Where there was one diamond, there had to be more. There had to be some deposit from which these individual diamonds came. He did not believe that it was likely to be a diamond-bearing pipe (a primary deposit), although that was not completely impossible. It seemed to him that it was more likely that these single diamonds came from a secondary diamond concentration. Unlike Knacke and many others, he had a theory about how such secondary diamond concentrations could have come about and where they would be. That is why he was so excited – and had been so for two days, since his meal with Dessau.

Merensky decided to leave for South Africa immediately. He telegraphed Wipplinger and asked him to engage Dr Celliers and the prospector Busschau for a prospecting trip to Namaqualand. He had worked with the geologist Celliers at Potgietersrus and had approached Busschau, whom he knew very well from prospecting work they had done together over the last 20 years. A second telegram was sent to London, to Ignatius Dessau. It contained a definite refusal to participate in the Bulgarian project. However, he indicated that if his plans around the Namaqualand project were to be realised, he would be happy to involve Dessau in this venture.

Then he prepared for his departure. He still had some appointments with a few German firms. These were business obligations that he had accepted before he left from Johannesburg and that he had to honour, even though he was impatient to leave.

Then something happened that would have changed his life, if it had happened at any other time: just when all he was thinking about was "diamonds in Namaqualand", he received a thick letter with strange stamps in the morning mail – it was an offer from the Soviet Union. Written in perfect German, addressed to his current address in the Hotel Adlon, a ministry with a long name, which had to be the mining ministry, urgently requested him to do an expert appraisal of the platinum deposits in the Urals. He was offered every possible assistance. The entire trip, including supplies and accommodation, would be paid for. A car, chauffeur and interpreter would be at his disposal. He was offered a fabulous sum for his appraisal, such a sum as he had never heard having been paid for any appraisal.

It was clear what the Soviet Union was planning to do. The Russian mines were under threat from the emerging South African platinum market. They feared that the deposits in the Urals would eventually be relegated to the second rank. In this precarious situation they not only wanted to make use of Merensky's geological skills, but wanted to profit from his reputation as a platinum specialist.

What should he do? It was in the late summer of 1926. In his mind, Merensky was already on his way to Namaqualand. There was no going back. If all this had happened three years earlier, in 1923, he would probably not have hesitated for a second to embark on this adventure. But then, back in 1923, no one in Russia had even heard the name Merensky.

The offer came just at the wrong time. There is little point in speculating on how Merensky's life would have changed if he had received such an offer two or three years earlier and had accepted it. It is unlikely that he would ever have felt at home in Russia. On the other hand, one cannot deny that in Russia he would have found a largely unexplored field for geological investigations and discoveries, a field with a mineral deposit potential in some ways similar to that of South Africa. One difference would have been that in the Soviet Union there would probably have been funding for prospecting in quantities that no one in South Africa could even dream of. Be that as it may, Merensky refused the offer and never regretted this lost commission.

Merensky embarked for South Africa three weeks later. He telegraphed Dessau from the ship and sent him a detailed cooperation offer. He suggested that Dessau should finance the work in Namaqualand, where Merensky would not only plan the prospecting, but would lead the team in the field. The answer came back promptly. By return of mail, Dessau transferred £1000 as start-up capital and assured Merensky that a further £4000 would be paid as soon as the first promising reports had come in.

The way in which Merensky tackled the project was typical. By that time, diamond seekers from all parts of South Africa were on their way to Namaqualand, but that did not bother him. He did not travel directly to Namaqualand, but first made a detour to Johannesburg to access further sources of finance and to gather the kind of team that he believed he needed. It was much as it had been when he had been prospecting for platinum. First he had to find backers, then an energetic and capable crew, and only after that did he start. But above all, he was determined to prove that his theory about the origins of the diamond deposits on the Atlantic coast in Namaqualand was correct.

> **Textbox 7 – The history of diamonds**
>
> Diamonds were already known in antiquity. The name is derived from the Greek "adamas", which means "invincible". At the time, no one knew how to process or work with diamonds because they were so hard. Therefore, they were regarded as curiosities. Sometimes magical powers were attributed to them. They played no role as gems. Diamonds came from India, where the stones were probably found in river sand. The exact locations where the stones were found stayed a secret. Most of the stones that were found disappeared into the treasure troves of the Indian rulers, and probably only the bigger stones were kept. There was no real reason to collect small diamonds systematically, especially as in their rough state they generally look rather unprepossessing.
>
> The Roman emperors also knew diamonds, but for them too these stones were more of a curiosity than a true gemstone. This did not change in the early Middle Ages – at any rate, diamonds played no role in the ecclesiastical treasures collected in the early cathedrals. At this time only a few individual stones had found their way to Europe, mainly via the Venetian trade in the Levant.
>
> When the sea route to India was opened, the supply of diamonds in the European market increased. Initially, it was mainly the Portuguese traders that brought these stones to Europe and, for a short while, Lisbon became the main turnover spot in the diamond trade. Soon thereafter the Dutch began to dominate trade with India, and the centre of the diamond trade shifted to the Netherlands. It was probably in Bruges that significant advances in processing diamonds were first made. It was discovered how to polish and later also how to cleave diamonds. The main importer was eventually to be the Dutch East India Company. Particularly spectacular stones were usually sold to European royal houses, for example, the Orlov Diamond, which was a very large stone, at 199 carats. (A carat is 0,2 gram. The measure originated in the Orient and is equivalent to the weight of one dried carob seed.) This diamond was bought in Amsterdam in 1755 as a gift for Catherine the Great and was set in the Russian Imperial sceptre. In some cases, exorbitant prices were paid for diamonds, for example, for the Green Diamond, which is today in the Green Vault [Grünes Gewölbe] in Dresden and which is unique in its coloration. Elector Frederick August II acquired it in 1741 for 400 000 thaler. That was one and a half times the

building cost of the Church of Our Lady in Dresden that was just being built and that is perhaps one of the most beautiful churches in Germany.

Diamonds were discovered in Brazil in 1730. The first occurrences were found in gravel and sand. These were therefore secondary deposits. The ways in which the diamonds were extracted were extremely primitive. Some contemporary drawings in old travel accounts show a few slaves probing the soil with inadequate tools, guarded by overseers with long whips. There was no real impetus to research the origins of diamonds from Brazil, but that country soon became the leading supplier. Initially only 20 000 to 30 000 carats were brought to Europe every year, but by 1850 the supply was already 130 000 to 300 000 carats. That was 99% of the world production at the time. Even then, diamonds were bought by members of the wealthy middle classes as an investment which retained its value, and which simultaneously displayed wealth and power.

The big shift that was to change the diamond trade dramatically occurred in South Africa in 1870 to 1872. In 1869, a farm boy had been looking after some cows in the veld near Kimberley, and had seen a loose stone glint in the light of the last oblique rays of the setting sun. He had picked it up and taken it home for his little sister to play with. A few weeks later a neighbour saw the stone, noticed how hard it was and suggested that it be tested. As soon as it became known that a diamond had been found there, fortune-hunters from everywhere in South Africa streamed to Kimberley. The first run on a diamond field in South Africa had begun. This first rush was to be followed by many more.

It soon became clear that the stones occurred in a relatively limited area. They lay on and in a loamy-sandy soil which the diamond hunters called "yellow ground". The claim which each diamond digger was allowed to peg out was smaller than ten square metres. This meant that the diggers very soon had to dig deeper. The colour of the subsoil was different. It had a blue-grey or blackish-green hue and was called "blue ground". Here too, a number of isolated diamonds continued to be found. Suddenly the diggers recognised that this was not an alluvial soil formation, but a weathered outcrop of primary rock that continued deep down.

It caused a huge sensation. For the first time in the world, the parent rock of diamonds had been identified. The necessary research into the origins of diamonds rapidly followed. It became clear that the diamond-bearing rock had filled an eruption channel which went very far down. In South Africa, such channels are called pipes. The cross-section of such a feeding-pipe is round to oval in shape and the diameter can range between 30 and 900 metres. In its topmost reaches, the channel often widens into a funnel shape, but deep down it narrows into a fissure. These pipes are filled by eruptive breccia, that is, solidified rock debris that was formed of angular fragments. (The term "breccia" is derived from the Italian and was already used by Goethe.) Here, in Kimberley, the breccia consists of ultrabasic rock fragments that come from very deep down, as well as of rock fragments torn from the walls of the pipe. This type of eruptive breccia has since been called "kimberlite". The diamonds are found in the ultrabasic rock fragments, where they crystallised in the depths of the earth under high pressure and at high temperatures. The diamond concentrations in kimberlites are low – less than one carat per ton of rock.

In the period that followed, more and more kimberlite-filled pipes were found, some of which were diamond-bearing. Consequently, South Africa's diamond production rose quickly. By 1872, it had reached one million carats. This brought about the real shift in the diamond trade. Since diamonds cannot be worn down and nobody would throw away a diamond, the existing diamond holdings worldwide have continuously increased; and bigger and bigger amounts have been accumulating for the last 135 years.

Soon the many small claims, both in Kimberley and in neighbouring pipes, began to pose technical problems. The diggers dug deeper and deeper, but not all at the same pace, which resulted in flooding and rock slides from one claim into the next. The unhygienic conditions in the open cast mines became unbearable. It soon became imperative to consolidate claims and create companies that were bigger and could work more economically.

The young Cecil John Rhodes played a leading role in this process. He earned his first fortune by providing an extremely important service to the diamond diggers, namely pumping out the water from the opencast diggings. Then he and a partner began to buy up claims, and in 1880 he founded De Beers Mining Company. Seven years later he became the main shareholder of the company. Around this time he took up close business relations with Lord Nathaniel Rothschild (1840–1915, First Lord Rothschild, elevated to the House of Lords in 1885) who had been a central figure in funding the Suez Canal. Now this relation gave Cecil Rhodes access to European capital to acquire more options. In 1888 he managed to take control of the Kimberley workings and soon thereafter also of the mines at Dutoitspan and Bultfontein. He then consolidated these mines in the newly-founded De Beers Consolidated Mines, which at that time controlled 90% of the world's diamond production.

According to the current national economic theories, diamonds, as a ware of commerce that was not in short supply and the stock of which was constantly getting bigger, should have become less expensive. But that was not the case, not then and not now, because as an unopposed monopoly, De Beers dictated the worldwide supply and price of diamonds. This enterprise was supported by many traders, diamond cutters and jewellers, since they all agreed with De Beers that the prices for the final products should never drop. If prices dropped, that would imply that diamonds were no longer rare and that owning them was no longer a status symbol. At the same time, a drop in the price would probably also lead buyers to become reluctant to purchase diamonds, since potential buyers might delay their decision to purchase in the hope that the stones' price would drop even further. All this had to be prevented. To maintain an illusion of scarcity, whenever there was any threat of oversupply, diamonds had to be withdrawn from the market. De Beers bought up stones and stockpiled them. The company kept up this business strategy for decades, even though this was sometimes difficult. When, during the First World War and the big world economic crisis, for a while, buyers found themselves forced to hold back from purchasing diamonds, the difficulties of De Beers were exacerbated. It was precisely at this time that the company had to buy up vast quantities of high quality stones to prevent diamond prices from dropping. Merensky's finds at Alexander Bay also contributed to this situation. By that time diamonds had definitely lost their rarity value as a gemstone.

Such was the situation when at the end of the 1920s, Sir Ernest Oppenheimer became one of the defining personalities in the South African diamond industry. That was when a completely new chapter in the history of diamonds began: the chapter of the diamond cartel.

CHAPTER 13

# Diamonds in Namaqualand

The inner excitement which had gripped Merensky since that conversation over dinner in that distinguished London gentlemen's club was caused by events long past. In 1908, in the then German South-West Africa, in the dunes at Kolmanskop, about 10 km east of Lüderitz, diamonds had been found. Both the find itself and the nature of the place where the diamonds were found created a stir. The diamonds lay loosely scattered in the dune sand, so that it was not clear where they had come from. There was no primary rock from which they could have been weathered away, and there were no rivers that could have carried these stones into this arid region. This suggested that the stones had to have been brought there by the sea. The general idea was that these diamonds had been transported (during the Miocene period) from the interior of the continent, first down to the ocean and then northward, to Lüderitz, by currents that ran parallel to the coast. This was called the River Theory.

Hans Merensky had developed a completely different theory. He believed that the primary deposits had been situated in the Atlantic and that the stones had been cast up on the coast by ocean currents that were different from the ones found in the region today. Since

Kolmanskop is quite high above the sea level today, this had to have happened 10 million years ago, when the subcontinent was not yet lifted as far as it is today.

Merensky examined the places where the diamonds were found at Kolmanskop very carefully. He spent days sliding on his knees on the dunes, looked at hundreds of sand samples under his magnifying glass and noted that where the diamonds lay, there were minute splinters of oyster shells. These were fragments of *Ostrea prismatica*, a type of oyster that lives in warm waters, and that are still found at Durban on the Indian Ocean coastline, but that are no longer found on the Atlantic coast, where the icy temperature of the water is caused by the cold Benguela current. Therefore Merensky developed the theory that, at a time when the continent's configuration was still different from what it is now, the diamonds had been brought there by a warm ocean current and had been cast up on the coast with the oyster shells, where they formed "mussel beds". Later the beaches rose and were covered by wandering dunes. In this process, the not very resilient oyster shells were completely crushed and worn away by the movement of the grains of sand. All that remained were the hard diamonds and tiny oyster shell fragments. However, what was more important was the conclusion which he drew from these facts. He was convinced that under the dunes that ran 280 kilometres from Lüderitz to the mouth of the Orange River and further along the coast to Namaqualand, there had to be many intact mussel beds with oyster shell fragments and diamonds. It would, however, be difficult to find them, because they lay buried deep under huge masses of sand. Merensky coined the term "Oyster Line" for this confluence of diamonds and oyster shells. In January 1909, he published his theory in the *Transactions of the Geological Society of South Africa,* and thereafter he tried to tell people about this theory in personal conversations and in public talks, but nobody took him seriously.

Merensky arrived in Johannesburg at the beginning of November 1926 and immediately started to prepare for his prospecting campaign. There it turned out that about a thousand fortune-hunters had already made their way to Namaqualand, or were on their way there. That meant that it would scarcely be possible to find even a spot of land on the coast that had not yet been secured as an option. But

Merensky was not particularly concerned, since the area that he was targeting in his prospecting plan was very different from that targeted by the other diamond seekers in Namaqualand. He was fairly certain that all the claims that had been pegged so far would be close to the ocean, and that no one else had had the idea of taking options on the terraces higher up that were covered by the dunes. If there happened to be a claim or two in the dunes, it should not be difficult to buy it from the owner. From experience he knew that at the start of a rush options were quickly pegged, but that they were passed on just as quickly. As long as no diamonds had been found, the owners were happy to give up their claim if they were offered four or five or even ten times what they had paid for them.

In 1926 the price of a digging licence was modest. One could peg a claim with a radius of 500 yards (457 metres) for only two shillings and sixpence and could then dig in that area for one month. That was a surface of 0,65 square kilometres. Any finds had to be reported. That then gave the digger the right to peg 20 claims of 30 yards by 30 yards inside the original option area that he could exploit over a longer period.

Merensky was more upset by the next bit of news. Busschau was not available. Merensky would have liked to have him with him, because he was a good prospector, could organise well and could keep an overview of the whole project. Even more annoying was the news that various platinum firms had summoned him for long discussions and to report on his exploratory discussions with German machinery manufacturers and companies that specialised in ore dressing. This did not suit Merensky's plans at all, but these were obligations that he had to honour. He could be as impatient as he liked, but he was unable to escape for several weeks.

Merensky therefore decided to send some of his assistants to Namaqualand as a vanguard, with precise instructions as to what they had to do and what kind of options they should secure. He also found the ideal leader for this group. It was Dr Ernst Reuning, a geologist from the University of Gießen, Germany, with whom he had worked on the search for platinum in Potgietersrus. Reuning was an experienced diamond prospector, and in 1908 he had been one of the leading geologists involved in the research on diamond deposits above Lüderitz and elsewhere in South-West Africa. The following year, he had a commission by the Deutsche Kolonialgesellschaft to investigate the entire desert strip along the coast from Lüderitz to the mouth of the Orange River. He did so by riding on camelback and digging numerous prospection holes, but had not been able to identify any diamond occurrences. Now he wanted to leave for Europe, where he wanted to spend Christmas with his family. However, Merensky managed to persuade Dr Reuning to go to Namaqualand on his behalf for a while. Reuning was not in the least convinced by Merensky's diamond theory, because he was one of the chief proponents of the River Theory. He was certain that to find diamonds, one had to prospect on the beach, close to the waterline. Nevertheless, he agreed to participate in the campaign because he hoped to glean more information on the geological structure of Namaqualand. In Reuning, Merensky had made a good choice in terms of the organisation of the enterprise, because Reuning had excellent leadership qualities. However, given their opposing views on the origins of the diamonds on the Atlantic coast, disagreement between the two geologists was almost inevitable. This was to become an obstacle in their cooperation later.

By the start of December 1926, the team was ready to leave Johannesburg. The team consisted of the team leader, Dr Reuning, the geologist Dr Celliers, an experienced ore digger called Mare and General Manie Maritz, who had become a general in the Anglo-Boer War at the age of 24 because of his boldness and dash. He was a national hero. He knew every farmer in Namaqualand, and it was his task to make the requisite contacts and to make it easier to secure options.

Namaqualand is a desert-like, rocky and inhospitable region. Large areas appear to have no vegetation. There are only a few stunted bushes and isolated clumps of grass. At night, thick banks of fog build up over the coastline. This fog drifts inland and brings some moisture to the coastal strip. For the rest, this land lies parching under the blazing sun and very seldom gets any rain. But that is not true for the whole year. When there is a shower of rain, there is a brief spring. Then the desert becomes green, and for two or three weeks it is covered in millions of flowers in every possible colour, only to dry out again and return to its normal bleak aridity.

In those days economic activity in Namaqualand was minimal. A few farmers grazed their livestock there and battled to survive. In the hinterland there were a few old copper mines. The presence of these ore occurrences had been known since the end of the 17$^{th}$ century. Then the copper was brought to the Cape by nomadic Khoikhoi. Real mining only started in the last quarter of the 19$^{th}$ century. It brought some transient and modest wealth to the region. Then came the First World War, when these mines became very important. This made the economic decline after the war, when the demand for raw materials in the world market dropped, even more pronounced. By the start of the 1920s, Namaqualand had sunk into hopeless poverty.

One of the few tiny settlements in Namaqualand is Port Nolloth, about 50 kilometres to the south of the mouth of the Orange River. It was there that Captain Jack Carstens lived, an officer who had served in the army in India for many years. Now he was back home and he began to prospect in his free time. He and a cousin pegged out an area about 10 kilometres to the south of Port Nolloth and began to look for diamonds, first just as a weekend hobby, but gradually more intensively. The two of them had only a vague idea of how to prospect for diamonds and of what type of terrain and what kind of geological environment might have any potential. Their only source of information was *The Prospectors' Handbook*, which they took with them, but which was unable to assist them in solving the specific problems that they encountered. Irrespective of these setbacks, they sifted large amounts of gravel and sand at spots that they imagined (for no rational reason) might bring them luck. In June 1926, they did indeed discover a diamond and somewhat later some more stones. These were small stones, nothing sensational, and far from being worth a fortune. But the fact that they had found any diamonds at all was quite enough of a sensation. Because they were inexperienced, they did not keep their find a secret. It took only a few days for the news of their find to spread.

The news had barely broken when a stream of fortune-hunters began to arrive from everywhere in South Africa. There was a reason for this. Namaqualand might be very inhospitable, but Jack Carstens was not the first to draw attention to this region. Years before, Fred C. Cornell, probably the most legendary of all South African prospectors, had worked there. His book, *The Glamour of Prospecting. Wanderings of a South African Prospector in Search of Copper, Gold, Emeralds and Diamonds*, which appeared in 1920, is now regarded as a collectable and a much-sought example of early South African literature on prospecting. Originally it appeared in an edition of only 1000 copies. Fortunately, a facsimile edition is now available. Cornell had roamed through Namaqualand, the Namib and the Kalahari at the beginning of the 20$^{th}$ century, and after 1910 he had been in Alexander Bay several times. He had camped there alone for months on end, with a small tent and modest field equipment, directly at the mouth of the Orange River, and had explored the terrain. Nobody knows what he saw, but there was a lasting rumour that he had found diamonds even then. Of course, none of the diggers who streamed into the area now had ever read Cornell's book, but his name was so well known that when diamonds were found now, this was seen as confirming his ideas (which nobody knew anything about!).

Fred C. Cornell was never able to enjoy the fruits of his discoveries. In 1921 he went to England, so it was said, to find backers for a big prospecting campaign or to establish a diamond company. Soon after his arrival there, this discoverer, who had only just escaped dying of thirst on several occasions during his many wanderings through the desert areas in southern Africa, was killed in London in a freak car-accident. He took his secret to the grave. Still, his name has remained unforgotten in South Africa to this day. In the Richtersveld, the names of Cornellsberg and Cornellskop remind us of him.

Now fortune-hunters from all corners of South Africa came to Namaqualand. Many of them were put off when they realised that this region was largely desert. There was no water, nor any other resources that would make it possible to survive in this semi-arid landscape. Most had neither the equipment nor the supplies that they would need, and they soon realised that they lacked the experience to work in such terrain. Many gave up quite quickly, but they did not leave. They stayed in Port Nolloth and other small towns, which were soon hopelessly overrun.

Among the newcomers, there were some experienced diamond diggers who understood desert conditions. Among the latter group was a prospector called Kennedy, who combed the area to the north of Port Nolloth with two friends. They had a car, digging tools and enough supplies and so they were able to stay out in the field for longer periods. They worked in various places and finally began to concentrate on a cliff face some 25 kilometres to the north of Port Nolloth. It fell steeply to the ocean, and at its foot, right on the waterline, there were visible pebble and sand layers. In this spot, Kennedy found 14 diamonds in his sieve in one week. These were quite small, on average only half a carat each.

These finds excited people in Port Nolloth, and after that, all along the waterline the pebbles were dug up and sifted. More diamonds were indeed found, but they were always only small isolated stones, with no indications of a coherent larger deposit. Kennedy, who was quite a tough customer, thought long and hard. He recognised that what he had found might be interesting, but that it was too little. Three people working alone with a shovel and sieve could not get rich under these conditions. Mining companies with all the technology at their disposal would have to tackle the job to make any profit. He reached his own conclusions. A few months later, he sold his claim to Friedrich Knacke's Namaqualand Diamond Company.

Others were not discouraged and continued to look for diamonds, always in spots that for some or other reason seemed promising to them. None of the decisions made to dig in one place or another would have stood up to expert analysis. These decisions were made on the basis of a gut feeling, because nobody had any clear idea where these single diamonds might come from. Nevertheless, new finds continued to be made, and every time they were made in places nobody had thought of as likely before. One of these lucky discoverers was a shop owner called Salomon Rabinowitz, who came from Steinkopf, a small settlement 84 kilometres east of Port Nolloth, close to the main road between Windhoek and Cape Town. He had dug a test trench on the Buchuberg, eight kilometres south of Alexander Bay. Digging very deep, he had eventually taken 334 diamonds with a total of 74,5 carats from this trench. This was a large number of stones, but they were very small. Their average weight was only 0,22 carats. That was only a little less than a twentieth of a gram. Nevertheless, this find inspired the diamond hunters, and now options were also taken further inland.

Another syndicate that was formed in Port Nolloth and that went to work very purposefully consisted of the two sets of brothers Caplan and Gordon. The Caplan brothers were shop owners; the Gordons were lawyers. They joined prospectors called Coetzee, Laubscher and Louw at Alexander Bay, where they secured claims along the edge of the water. In the pebbles and coarse sand at the water's edge, they found several diamonds and therefore pegged more claims along the edge of the mouth of the Orange River.

This was more or less the situation when Merensky's vanguard, led by Dr Reuning, arrived in Namaqualand at the start of December 1926. Any land that seemed interesting had already been claimed and options had been secured. Some options had already changed hands several times. Dr Reuning had to look around for promising areas and was then to try to buy the options from their current owners or to buy shares in a syndicate. Hence, he visited the various diggings in turn. He was particularly taken by one team working on geological strata at Grootemist. These strata reminded him of the Pomona Formation in South-West Africa, in the coastal area south of Lüderitz that had proved to contain diamonds. Dr Reuning approached the members of the syndicate, and they declared themselves prepared to negotiate about options with Merensky. Discussions with Kennedy and Rabinowitz had similar results. In both cases they indicated that they would welcome a possible partnership with Merensky.

Since Dr Reuning had not been authorised to complete any further agreement negotiations, he telegraphed Merensky, urging him to come out as soon as he possibly could. Merensky arrived in Namaqualand ten days before Christmas and quickly began to visit the syndicates that Dr Reuning favoured. It was at this point that the differences between them came to the fore. Merensky was not impressed by the terrain at Grootemist. Even when Reuning pointed out the similarity between the layers there and those in the Pomona Formation in South-West Africa, Merensky was not convinced. He was not looking for such a formation; and nothing at the water's edge interested him, even if a few diamonds had been found there. He told Reuning so in no uncertain terms and refused to discuss the matter any further. What he was looking for was the Oyster Line, nothing else. When it became clear that the syndicate only wanted to give them an option for a limited time and wanted £3000 for it – considering that no diamonds whatsoever had been found in this particular claim, this was a vast sum – Merensky became quite angry. For him, a naturally amiable person, this was unusual. This indicates how annoyed he was. He regarded this offer as completely misplaced and overpriced and he told the members of the syndicate so. He was quite brusque in his refusal to continue any further discussions.

The visit to Rabinowitz was quite different. Rabinowitz was an effervescent, chatty man who loved to tell anyone who would listen every detail of his diamond find. Merensky let him talk; and he was surprised and suddenly very alert when Rabinowitz mentioned that he had found oyster shells in his trenches. Merensky did not show his excitement, but insisted that Rabinowitz climb down into the trenches with him and show him, to the nearest centimetre, where he had found the diamonds. It was a layer consisting of coarse gravel and broken oyster shells right on top of the bedrock at the bottom of the trench. Merensky found many more of these oyster shells – they were the shells of *Ostrea prismatica*!

In such situations Merensky stayed extremely calm and allowed no emotion to show. Neither Rabinowitz nor Merensky's assistants noticed that this was the deciding minute in the prospecting campaign. But that moment had arrived. At the instant when Merensky knelt in the diggings trench and Rabinowitz pointed a finger at a spot between the oyster shells protruding from the side wall of the trench, saying, "Here, this is where the diamonds were, between these shells, isn't it odd?", Merensky knew two things: first, that there were alluvial deposits combining oyster shells and diamonds and that this proved his diamond theory, and, second, that he would find diamonds in Namaqualand.

At this stage, he was unable to tell whether the place where Rabinowitz had found his diamonds would be the ideal starting point for more detailed prospecting. Quite possibly the chances of finding a longer intact strip of an Oyster Line was better at other spots. He was thinking particularly of the dune areas higher up that were closer to the sea, for example, at Alexander Bay. Therefore this became his next target area.

There, Caplan and his crew had been digging successfully near the waterline. When Merensky visited the syndicate, he was shown a yellow diamond that they had just found. It weighed four carats, but Merensky was not particularly impressed.

The team worked at the water's edge, but also owned options for areas that ran from the water's edge upstream and that they had not yet worked. Merensky asked for permission to look at the terrain and inspected the claims thoroughly, particularly those claims that lay further inland and higher above sea level. He took soil samples again and again and examined them under his magnifying glass. He repeatedly observed minute traces of crushed oyster shells in the sand. At some spots he dug a little deeper with his trowel, and was pleased to see that lower down the sand was also full of oyster shells. This showed that their presence was not a surface phenomenon. The overall situation seemed promising and so he decided to start work in this area.

They prepared an offer for the Caplan brothers to buy shares in their syndicate. The Caplans declared that they were happy to agree and they decided to sign the agreements within a few days. Once that had been decided, Merensky wanted to secure as many pieces of land on which he had observed oyster shell fragments as possible. He went back to Port Nolloth and established the current situation regarding the availability of options at Alexander Bay. On New Year's Day 1927, he was back, and he and Reuning pegged all the options that had not been secured by anyone else. Merensky spent the next few days doing a very thorough investigation of these areas. He became increasingly confident that here he would find what he had come for.

On 4 January, Merensky and Reuning met with the members of the Caplan syndicate to sign the partnership agreement that they had agreed on. But it did not get that far, because the syndicate now had different demands. These came as a complete surprise to Merensky. The demands did not affect the financial aspects of the agreement, but were directed toward the working strategy. The days Merensky had spent walking about on the inland claims and his interest in the soil samples he looked at under his magnifying glass had annoyed Caplan's co-workers and made them nervous. The members of the syndicate had quite decided ideas of why they wanted to include the Merensky group in their activities and how they intended to do so. On the one hand, the syndicate was financially weak and needed money for small machines and mechanical sieves. They also wanted an expert with Merensky's ability and experience on their team. On the other hand, they did not want to deviate from their current modus operandi in any way. Above all, they wanted to continue to work exclusively at the water's edge.

Merensky found this completely unacceptable. He repeatedly pointed out that in his opinion the inland claims were more promising. Sadly, the Caplan team's faith in Merensky's abilities did not go so far that they were prepared to change their minds. When it became clear that the negotiations had reached a stalemate, Dr Reuning, who was to prove an astute negotiator, asked for an adjournment so that both sides could think calmly about the situation. Merensky and Dr Reuning walked along the shore for a bit and discussed the matter. Merensky refused to consider any concession to the syndicate's working strategy, not even if the syndicate were to agree to give him a bit more latitude. He felt that it would be better to break off negotiations completely and to go to look for other spots to try. However, before things went that far, they should try to buy out the syndicate completely. As has already been mentioned, in the early stages of prospecting, it is often only a question of price. It was clear that the members of the syndicate had already realised that their modest financial resources were a handicap to them. Dr Reuning and Merensky therefore decided to play separate roles. Reuning would take over the negotiations. Merensky, who had once said that he was completely unable to haggle, would hold back, and would then, at a favourable moment, make a surprise take-over bid.

They proceeded according to their plan. The discussion restarted and Reuning played his part very skillfully. From the start, he made it clear that Merensky was completely against any work in the current location. This created an impasse. But Reuning did not let it come to a complete breakdown in the negotiations. He hinted that he had every sympathy for the fact that the members of the syndicate wanted to continue to work where they had already found some diamonds – only, they would need more money and better technology. The discussion kept going in circles. When everything had been said several times over, and everybody was showing signs of becoming quite tired, Merensky rejoined the discussion. In a very soft voice, as if he could not quite believe what he was hearing himself say, he said: "So, I see it would probably be best if we made you an offer to buy out the whole syndicate and paid you out." He made a vague gesture with his hand as if he wanted to take back what he had just said, because it was so illogical. Dr Reuning pretended to be very surprised and acted as if he did not know what to say. Caplan and his people were even more amazed. They had not reckoned with anything like this. When they were still speechless, Merensky added in the same doubtful voice: "We would have to take over all rights, including any diamonds that have not yet been sold, and the sieves and other equipment. Then you could compare your original start-up costs with the selling price and see whether you would be interested." Again there was the vague, self-deprecatory gesture, as if he wanted to sweep way what he had just said.

Now it was Caplan's turn to ask for a time-out. Dr Reuning and Merensky went out, leaving the members of the syndicate to discuss matters. When they came back, a decision had been taken. Caplan and his colleagues were prepared to sell the syndicate for £20 000. It was a short negotiation. Dr Reuning offered £15 000; there was some renewed discussion among the members of the syndicate and then they agreed on £17 500 for all options, for both those at the water's edge and those upstream along the Orange River. All of this went much faster and more simply than Merensky and Dr Reuning had expected. There was a sense that the members of the syndicate were suddenly quite glad to shake off the uncertainties and to go home with a not inconsiderable profit.

The agreement was drawn up and immediately signed. It covered a total of 22 options. When everything had been completed, they noticed that one option on a river terrace had been left out. Originally this area had been pegged by a digger called Van Wyk. He had paid half a crown for the option, but had passed it on to Caplan the very same day for £15. Caplan, who was very relaxed after the transaction had been completed, gave Merensky the claim for free – "a Christmas present", as he said. A few weeks later this piece of land in Merensky's hands became one of the richest diamond claims ever seen in Africa.

When Merensky signed the agreement, he was feeling a bit weak at the knees. The purchase price of £17 500 was a huge sum that he did not possess. He had one month to pay, but at that moment he did not know where he would raise the money. Some of the £1000 that he had received from Ignatius Dessau had already been used to pay for the rented car, the petrol and the prospecting equipment and for Dr Reuning and the other assistants' wages. Admittedly, Dessau had promised a further £4000, but he was only willing to make available bigger sums "when the first promising results had come in".

Merensky doubted that he could get Dessau to supply further sums at this stage and knew that he had to get back to Johannesburg with all speed to find new backers. One cannot say that he was taking a risky gamble at this stage. Since he had looked at Rabinowitz's digging trenches, he was absolutely sure that the Oyster Line really existed. That meant that he had a huge advantage over all the other diamond hunters that he could use. From his point of view the risk was limited.

Before Merensky left for Johannesburg he had to organise the work for Dr Reuning and his assistants. Two days' hard work followed. Later they were to prove to be decisive for the outcome of the diamond campaign; but not only that, they were also to change Merensky's life and were to be significant for all of South Africa. Merensky started by pegging out a line to mark out the zone in which the most oyster fragments were to be found. Then, working on his knees for two days, he tested the entire zone metre by metre. He repeatedly took soil and sand samples in his hand and looked at them with his magnifying glass. Finally he marked the spots from which he wanted to have trenches dug perpendicular to the zone.

Merensky knew that he was dealing with various unknown variables. He was convinced that somewhere under the surface there were oyster beds interspersed with diamonds – somewhere, but where? He did not know whether the tiny crushed shell fragments that he had observed near the surface were really part of a deeper oyster shell deposit. It was a risk that he had to take. However, his intuition told him that where there were big accumulations of oyster shell fragments, there had to be at least one intact oyster shell accumulation not too far away. He thought, however, that it might take some time to find the Oyster Line.

Once the various trench lines had been decided on, the working strategy was mapped out. The people who stayed with Dr Reuning were a surveying engineer, the two Coetzee brothers, Jan and Theunis, who had been taken over from the Caplan team, as well as a foreman and twelve coloured workers. The plan was that the Coetzee brothers, who were experienced diggers, would work up on the higher terrace where Merensky suspected the Oyster Line to be. In the meantime, the other man and his team would stay at the waterline. Perhaps the diamonds found there would help to cover the running expenses. Merensky would have to raise the bigger sum of £17 500 in Johannesburg. Once all this had been arranged, Merensky left for Johannesburg. That was on 7 January 1927.

At Alexander Bay the work progressed slowly. There it turned out that they had insufficient equipment and substandard sieves.

On 14 January, just before sunset, Reuning was sitting inside his tent with a few visitors when Theunis Coetzee looked in and nodded to him. After Reuning had said goodbye to his guests, Coetzee came into the tent. Reuning looked at him questioningly: "What's up?" Without a word, Coetzee pulled out an old tobacco pouch and poured the contents on the table – eight large, beautiful diamonds rolled onto the tabletop. Reuning gasped – the scene was later often sketched by Theunis Coetzee. "Oyster Line?" Reuning asked, breathing deeply. Coetzee nodded: "Oyster Line." Reuning reached for the precious stone balance and weighed the stones. The total weight was fifty carats. The biggest stone weighed 16,6 carats. It was a huge diamond. To get an idea of the size of the stone, it is important to remember that the specific mass of a diamond is 3,52. This stone therefore had a volume of almost a cubic centimetre. That is enormous. Reuning himself had never found a stone this large. But more than that – all eight stones were of exceptional beauty.

Since it was already becoming dark, Reuning decided not to investigate the trench that same evening. If they were seen working by lamplight, that would attract attention. Secrecy, as long as possible, was now imperative. The Coetzee brothers also knew this.

The next morning the three men climbed up to the high terrace to look more closely at the trench. Dr Reuning had hardly climbed into the trench when he already had a large diamond in his hand. At the bottom of the trench, the Coetzee brothers had actually come upon a thick layer of oyster shells and between these shells there were several individual diamonds. It seemed almost unreal. Dr Reuning was highly experienced in diamond prospecting, but he could never have imagined this phenomenon of fossilised oyster shells and diamonds occurring together.

The same day Dr Reuning wrote to Merensky to tell him that the Oyster Line had been found and that it was so rich in diamonds that they could be almost certain of having found enough stones by the end of the month to pay the agreed purchase price to the Caplans without any problem. As agreed, Reuning sent the letter in a double envelope. The outside one had a cover address, namely that of one of Merensky's office assistants. Unfortunately, this person was away on business, and so the letter lay unopened on the wrong desk in Merensky's office for almost two weeks. For Merensky this was a difficult time. He had hoped that he would get some positive news from Alexander Bay which would have given him some relief in his financial planning. Now nearly half the allotted month had passed and he had to look for other means of financing the purchase.

Then news came from Ignatius Dessau, to whom he had sent a telegraph about the developments and his plans. What he had feared had come to pass. Dessau regarded an asked purchase price of £17 500 for claims about which so little was known as overpriced. If he then added the running costs, travelling costs and staff costs for the next few months, he came up with figures that he was not prepared to invest. He felt that the possible profits of the Bulgarian lead zinc deposits were more attractive after all. He retracted his offer to participate in the Namaqualand project. The similarities with the situation at the start of the platinum prospecting project two and a half years previously were difficult to miss. But here the withdrawal came from a financier who was experienced in backing mining and start-up enterprises. It was difficult to understand, especially if one considered that Ignatius Dessau knew about Merensky's geological intuition.

For Merensky finding finance became urgent. One cannot say that he was really in serious trouble, because the situation differed from that at the start of the platinum project after all: everyone knew that people were looking for diamonds in Namaqualand, and so he could say what he wanted the backing for. There were also enough financially strong people who would trust Merensky at any time to have another great new prospecting success and who would therefore be prepared to make available such risk capital.

And so, at the end of January, the H.M. Association was established with a starting capital of £50 000. It had three partners. The first was Sir Julius Jeppe, who signed up with a full £12 500. His participation closed a circle for Merensky, a circle that had begun 60 years earlier, with his father and Carl Mauch. Sir Julius Jeppe was a nephew of Friedrich Heinrich Jeppe, who had been the Postmaster General of the Transvaal around 1868 and who had also worked as a cartographer. With the assistance of the missionary Alexander Merensky, he had put all Carl Mauch's place names and sketches in a map of the Transvaal. It was the first map of the country and first appeared in 1868 in *Petermanns Geographische Mitteilungen* in Gotha. This was followed by a string of new editions. Julius Jeppe, the nephew who now joined Merensky in this venture, had known Carl Mauch in his parents' home when Julius was a boy of ten. Now that he was old, he was the chairman of one of the large land-owning companies, the South African Townships, Mining and Finance Corporation, and he was a partner of Sir Abe Bailey, one of the legendary pioneers from the early period of gold discovery on the Witwatersrand. Some time later, Sir Julius Jeppe told Merensky that he had invested in his venture on behalf of and using money from Sir Abe Bailey. This was quite normal, because it was important to prevent the instability in the markets which could result if the name of a mining magnate was mentioned too early.

The second investor who also invested £12 500 was Gustav Becker. He was one of Merensky's friends from the difficult years immediately after the war and later, with Olthaver, one of the partners in the platinum deal. Becker was one of those who would trust Merensky to find new deposits at any time. It did not have to be something as spectacular as the Merensky Reef every time. Even if the project was smaller, Gustav Becker would have been involved, because he felt obliged to assist Merensky. He had earned very large sums with his platinum speculations and had been sorry that Merensky had not personally profited as much from the platinum boom as Becker had.

The third partner in the syndicate was Merensky himself. He took 20 000 shares as a discoverer's and sales premium and paid in a further £5000 cash. This was the last money Merensky had. This gave Merensky 50% of the shares in the syndicate. When he left for Alexander Bay at the beginning of February, he had £30 000 cash at his disposal, enough to pay the Caplans and to cover his running costs for quite a few months.

It is difficult to guess what would have happened if Merensky had heard about the discovery of the Oyster Line somewhat earlier than he did. It is certain that then he would not have had to rely on backing derived from including partners in the syndicate. Whether or not that would have been to his benefit is debatable. As the rest of the story will show, the syndicate was soon to be exposed to difficulties caused by the political situation, and it is unclear whether Merensky, if he had been the sole owner of the syndicate, could have dealt with these problems better on his own.

By the time Merensky finally got back to Alexander Bay, a lot of important and amazing things had happened. Dr Reuning had had the Coetzee brothers continue their work on the trench in which they had found the first diamonds. He, who had previously rejected the notion of the Oyster Line so vehemently, had crawled across the terrain, metre by metre, not out of repentance, but to seek further indications to assist him in pegging out more trenches.

It made sense that the Oyster Line, which ran high above the present coast line, would be more or less parallel to the water's edge. That implied that the trenches should be dug transversely to the waterline. A week after the first finds, Reuning was ready and pegged out a new trench line to be dug about 450 metres from the place where the first diamonds had been found. Work there began on the afternoon of 21 January 1927. By evening, they had already found 114 diamonds with a total weight of 201,4 carats. Parallel to this trench, more trenches were pegged out, and all the workers were taken off the diggings at the beach and redistributed over the new trenches. Occasionally, there was a slightly less successful day, but most days were good and they found 150 or more stones. Usually there were about ten stones or so that weighed more than ten carats each. The biggest stone that they found was no less than 71,1 carats; that is 14,2 grams!

The highlight was the find made in the small area that Caplan had given Merensky as a "Christmas present". From one of the trenches the workers hoisted a huge flat stone, which turned out to be a clump of diamonds all lumped together. There were 487 stones.

The number of stones that Reuning and his team had been able to collect in only four weeks was almost unbelievable: a total of 2762 stones weighing a total of 4308,9 carats, many of these very large, displaying the full crystalline form, not rounded by abrasion and very clearly of the highest quality.

When Merensky arrived and became aware of what had happened in his absence, he was astounded. He would never have believed anything like this to be possible. In his long career as a prospecting geologist he had never even seen such a large quantity of diamonds. He was particularly surprised by the large percentage of stones of excellent gemstone quality.

As always when he had to secure claims, Merensky was wide awake and reacted quickly. There was no more time to dig for oyster shell fragments. Once again, every hour counted, because such a find could not be kept secret for long. There would be a serious run on Alexander Bay, and since the options in the area had already been taken, the diamond hunters would peg claims on all the adjacent pieces of land that had not yet been bespoken within days. Merensky acted accordingly. Dr Reuning and another assistant, who knew the terrain well by now, were sent out to check whether in the wider environs of the Orange River there were any other spots that they had overlooked in pegging out claims. At the same time, Busschau, the prospector who had not been available at the start of December, was sent a telegraph to join them. Three days later he took over the lead in the work in these trenches, bringing to bear all his experience and care.

By this time, Merensky already knew that this was not just an isolated find of exceptionally good stones, but that his team had made an extraordinary find in the true sense of the word. A few weeks later, when the number of stones continued to rise, it became clear that this find would go down in history. The Oyster Line became the largest diamond placer ever discovered. But more than that, it was even more significant that the percentage of truly noble diamonds of gemstone quality was higher here than in any other diamond deposit in Africa.

Merensky's streak of luck was the stuff that legends are made of. Two and a half years before, he had identified the biggest platinum deposit in the world. Then his personal fortune was virtually exhausted; and now, in January 1927, he and his assistants had found the largest diamond placer in the world. To do so, he had had to assert himself against his backers and even his assistants. That was the only way that he could dig in the place which he believed would offer the best chance of success and that finally brought him what

Fig. 1  Hans Merensky, aged 17

Fig. 2  Hans Merensky as mining student trainee, doing his compulsory year of underground training in Königshütte (Upper Silesia), about 22 years old

Fig. 3  Hans Merensky when he was about 65 years old

Fig. 4   A typical South African share from the first third of the previous century

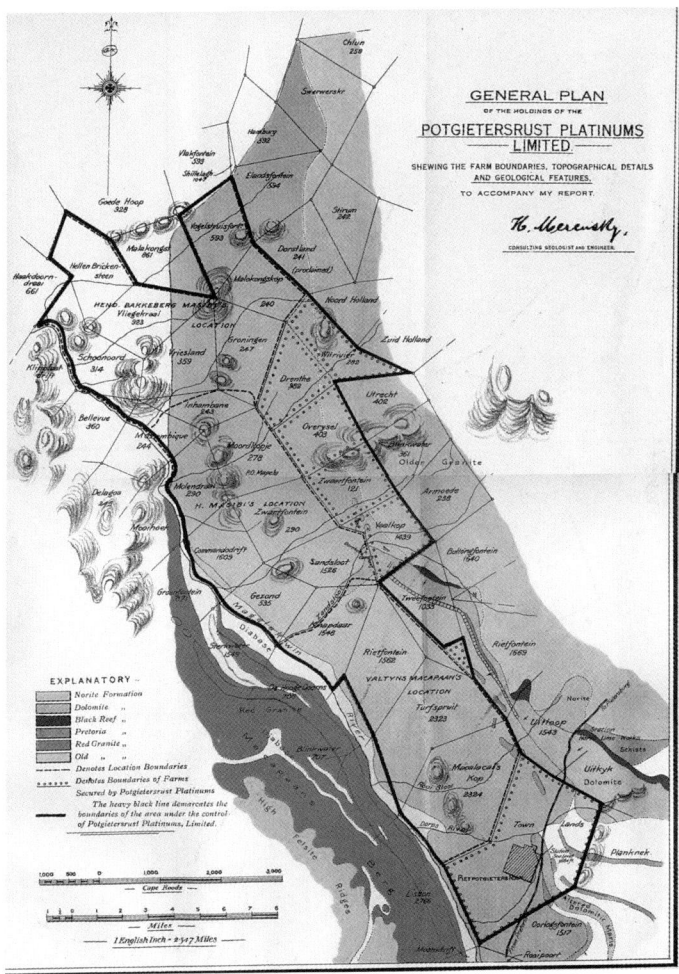

Fig. 5  The first printed geological map of the Merensky platinum concessions in the Potgietersrust area (November 1925)

Fig. 6   Percy A. Wagner, noted geologist, Merensky's friend and admirer, and the person who later best knew the Bushveld platinum.

Fig. 7   One of the modern ore dressing plants of the Impala Platinum Corporation at Rustenburg

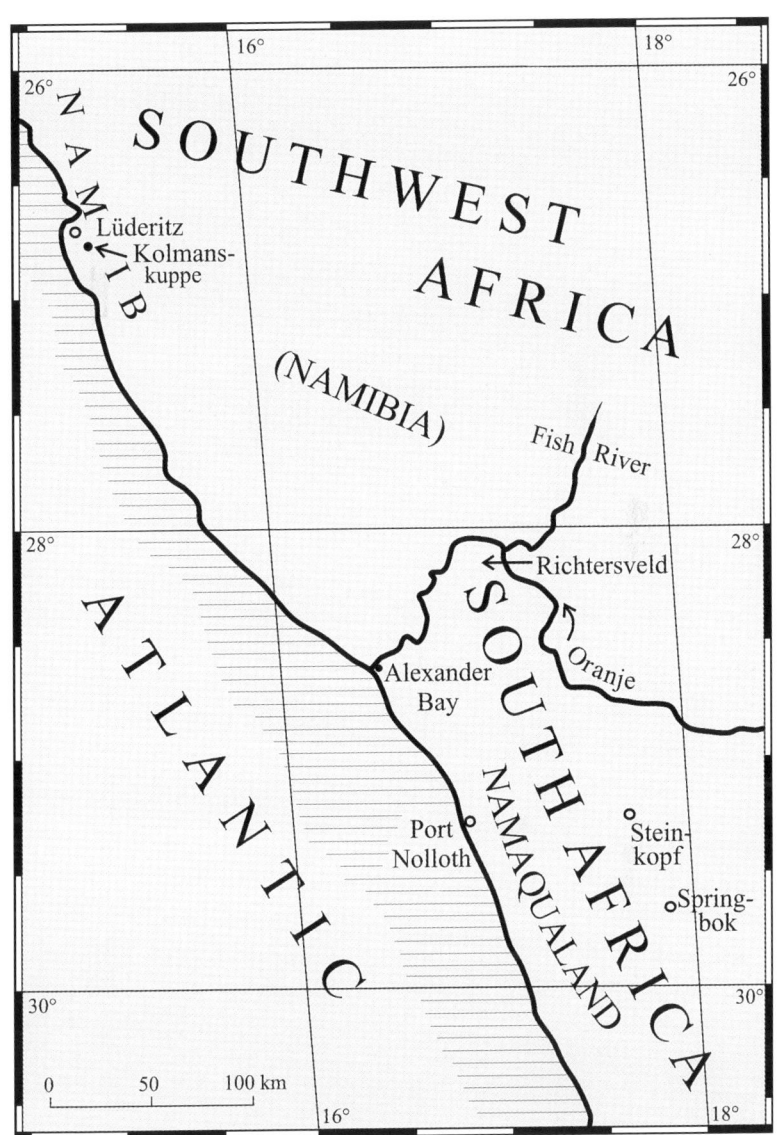

Fig. 8  Map of the Atlantic coast

Fig. 9   The first diamond hunters on Kolman's Kop (1908)

Fig. 10   In a diamond digger's camp. Contemporary wood-engraving, around 1880

Fig. 11  Oyster shells washed up together in the Oyster Line

Fig. 12  Merensky's first and still very simple diamond-sifting plant at Alexander Bay in 1927

Fig. 13  After the first restart of the diamond recovery project in May 1928, Merensky's firm installed a small but perfectly functional crusher house

Fig. 14  The very modern diamond processing plant of the NAMDEB, which operates at the other side of the border at Oranjemund

Fig. 15   Hans Merensky with a rock sample from the Oyster Line, pointing at a diamond

Fig. 16   Two discoverers who got on well – Captain Jack Carstens (left), who found the first diamonds on the Namaqualand coast in July 1926 and Hans Merensky, who discovered the Oyster Line seven months later

Fig. 17   The riverbed of the Orange River near its mouth. The pebbles and sand that originally lay on the riverbed have been dredged up in the course of the diamond mining. Today the riverbed (foreground) has been dredged down to the bedrock

Fig. 18   Hans Merensky on the steps of his house on Westfalia around 1936

Fig. 19   Top House on Westfalia

Fig. 20　Chromite seams on Jagdlust

Fig. 21　Hans Merensky inspecting one of his grass plantings

Fig. 22  Hans Merensky at the Zimbabwe Ruins (around 1935). It had been his father's dream to see these ruins 65 years before – his son was able to drive there on a three-day trip in the age of motor cars

Fig. 23 View of the forestry and avocado plantations at Westfalia

Fig. 24  The dam wall of the Merensky Dam in the valley below Westfalia

Fig. 25  Merensky Memorial above Top House

Fig. 26 The Merensky Memorial Building on Westfalia

Fig. 27 The Merensky Library at the University of Pretoria, flanked by jacaranda trees

he had dreamt of for 18 years. It was the success story of success stories.

And yet, this discovery was perhaps not as unimaginable as one might think. The story had already been written 25 years earlier, not as a factual report, but as the fantastic invention of a great writer who enriched world literature. This was the short story "Like Argus of the Ancient Times" by Jack London.

---

**Textbox 8 – "Like Argus of the Ancient Times"**

About 25 years before Merensky's amazing finds, Jack London wrote a short story about a gold digger. It was called "Like Argus of the Ancient Times". The plot of the story is surprisingly similar to the story of the discovery of platinum in the Bushveld and that of the diamonds at Alexander Bay. But this story is not a factual report. It is a fictional tale that deserves some closer reflection.

Here is a brief summary of the plot of Jack London's short story. The protagonist is old John Tarwater, who, in 1849, at the age of 22, in the grip of gold fever, travels from Michigan to California and makes his fortune there as a gold digger. Later he loses his fortune and his farm because of failed speculations and ineptness as a businessman. For decades he lives in poverty and undignified dependency. But he retains his unquenchable optimism. He is firmly convinced that if only he can be part of just one more gold rush, he will pan gold successfully and be rich again. Not only that, but he will get back everything that he has lost. In the summer of 1897, gold is found in Alaska. John Tarwater is now 70 years old and is almost certainly too old to cope with the hardships that he would have to face in Alaska. He does not have enough money to travel there, nor can he raise the even larger sum he would need to buy food supplies and equipment. In Alaska conditions have become chaotic; and, since winter is about to set in, everyone who does not have food supplies and a proper digging outfit is stopped by the authorities and sent home. Nevertheless, Tarwater leaves for Alaska and manages, without money or any equipment, to get to the interior and near the gold-fields. He spends the winter, emaciated and suffering from scurvy, in a desolate valley where he runs the household for a team of five gold diggers working there in their primitive blockhouse. Because he works hard and is entertaining (he knows countless stories from the good old days of the California gold rush, and constantly sings the old favourite of 1849, "Like Argus of the Ancient Times") they let him be. He is offered an opportunity to peg a claim on which he can perhaps, with a bit of luck, find gold valued at as much as $100 000. Tarwater refuses. To buy back what he has lost, he needs at least $300 000. He also does not want to work in the valley, but on the slopes on the opposite side of the valley, where there is an indication of an older river terrace. When spring comes and the snow melts, he drags his tired body up to the old river terrace, pulls up a few bunches of grass, and – lo, and behold – the roots are full of nuggets. A few months later he sells his claims for half a million dollars and goes home to California ...

A few words about Jack London. He was one of the greatest writing talents at the start of the 20$^{th}$ century. In his relatively short life he travelled widely, from the South Pacific to Alaska, and all over the United States. He lived in various milieus, working as a factory worker, a sailor, a gold miner, a tramp and vagabond, a student and socialist politician. He was also an excellent observer of his world, and he was able to store many details in his almost photographic memory. When he wrote, he drew on an unbelievable fund of subtle observation. So, for example, his tales about Alaska are filled with fine details regarding gold prospecting techniques. Some paragraphs from his tales could easily be included verbatim in a prospecting textbook.

Jack London was also an excellent observer of the human psyche. As a writer, he was interested in people, in their characters and destinies. In his travels he met thousands of people from every imaginable social background and of many races and he came to know their cares, their problems, their thinking and their dreams. The type of character that fascinated him most – one who appears in many of his tales in many guises – is the fighter. This is a man who fights to survive, sometimes successfully, sometimes unsuccessfully; or a man who works towards a goal he has set himself, who cannot be deterred, and who is prepared to suffer for this cause almost to the point of self-destruction.

John Tarwater is such a figure. He is careless in his business dealings, which must be a fault. But in a later stage in his life he pursues his goal to get back to the top with unequalled determination, even stubbornness. This figure, as presented to us by Jack London, was probably a composite of many observations, but it is a figure copied from life. Jack London drew on what he knew about the human soul to describe a character type that does exist and that appears in similar circumstances again and again. Thus the parallels between the character of John Tarwater and Hans Merensky, the real person, are not a mere coincidence. They confirm Jack London's extraordinary power of observation.

CHAPTER 14

# The struggle for mining rights

Merensky's predictions of a hideous rush of diamond seekers were correct, but it was not just a rush, it was an assault, and it was much worse than expected. Many people had already come to Namaqualand and had tried to secure a claim here and there and to begin digging and panning for diamonds – but now masses of people came with completely different expectations. They had heard that some "lucky fish" had found diamonds worth many thousands of pounds at Alexander Bay. Now these hordes poured into Alexander Bay and the coastal strip between the Orange River and Port Nolloth; and they were surprised and disappointed to find that there were no free claims left in the area.

But this was just one of the smaller problems. The real problem was that these people had neither the experience nor the logistic backing, the equipment or food supplies that they needed to survive in the desert. There were some who genuinely believed that they would be able to survive without these things. They did not plan to stay long. They believed that diamonds lay about loose in the sand at Alexander Bay. All they would have to do was to pick them up. They hoped to pick up enough diamonds in two weeks to be wealthy forever, and they thought they could last those two weeks. These were people of a completely different type from those who had found the first diamonds in the region. Diamond diggers like Captain Jack Carstens had spent months doing the backbreaking work of sifting sand and pebbles. They had at least had a rudimentary outfit and some economic back-up in Port Nolloth to ensure their survival. This was not the case with this flood of fortune-hunters. And the desert is harsh to those who take it lightly – a humanitarian catastrophe was on the cards.

Merensky – rightly or wrongly – felt a measure of responsibility for the events that he could foresee. After all, it was his discoveries and his name that had attracted this second wave of diamond seekers to the region. He therefore did what he thought was his duty as a human being. He drove down to Cape Town in two days, without stopping, to inform the government. Only the government could prevent this wild rush. He had to do what he could to get the authorities to intervene.

Merensky arrived in Cape Town in the early afternoon and drove directly to Parliament. Prime Minister General James Barry Hertzog was in a meeting with Frederick William Beyers, Minister of Mines and Industries, and the Minister of Finance, Nicolaas Christiaan Havenga. Hastily Merensky pencilled a brief note on a piece of paper: "May I see you please. I have something of importance to tell you." A remarkable action. Merensky had become such a well-known personality after his platinum discoveries that, when it came to any matter of geological interest or importance, he could get access to almost any politician in the country at practically any time and any place. A parliamentary secretary took the note into the meeting room.

General Hertzog soon came out into the lobby, smiling and friendly, but visibly surprised and intrigued at what could be so important. Merensky sketched the situation in Namaqualand in a few words and cautioned against the threatening catastrophe. The Prime Minister understood at once, and acted swiftly. The leader of the opposition, General Jan Christiaan Smuts, was informed and a meeting was arranged with the Minister of Mines and Industry, Beyers, and the relevant government geologist, Dr Hans Pirow. Merensky repeated his fears. He supported his argument by referring to the events in Lichtenburg and Ventersdorp. A year before, diamonds had been found there, and there had been similar rushes. But that had been in the western part of the Transvaal, in an area which was not quite as desert-like as Namaqualand. The two districts had been overrun in no time at all by almost 140 000 diamond seekers. The government had had some difficulty in maintaining law and order. Press reports about these events had appeared around the world. Even in Germany, so far away, the *Frankfurter Zeitung* had published an article on the matter. Such was the number of fortune-seekers that would have to be dealt with in Namaqualand.

Merensky's warning was soon to prove justified. By the middle of February the powerful mining companies got involved in Namaqualand on a large scale. Within a few days, numerous farms between the Orange River and Port Nolloth changed hands. Land was bought up not only there, but also inland and 120 kilometres to the south of Port Nolloth. These massive purchases alerted even the most hesitant – for them, it was now clear that there were treasures to be had in Namaqualand.

For over a week, the government discussed what it should do. Then the State took action. On 22 February, a temporary announcement stated that prospecting for diamonds was prohibited until further notice. The directive became of force in three days. Diamond diggers were given a period of grace of eight days in which they were allowed to sift and pan the piles of sand and pebbles that they had already dug out of their trenches. After that, all work definitely had to stop. The prohibition affected everyone, including the big syndicates.

This caused an uproar in Namaqualand. Everyone was indignant. There were small-time diamond diggers who had only one claim. Many of them had given everything they had to get there and to buy that option. The big mining firms had spent vast sums to acquire their diggings options and to buy land. All of them had paid money upfront and were now prevented from earning the profits they had hoped for.

Of course, the diggers and the syndicates worked until the last possible moment. Because in the last eight days they were only permitted to sift and pan, but were not allowed to continue digging, everyone secretly dug up more gravel and sand out of the trenches at night. In the daylight, they tried to sift and pan this material. H.M. Association also worked until the last minute, but they knew, down to the last half metre, exactly which material from which spot still needed to be sifted and panned. When Merensky's team stopped work at the end of February 1927, they had found, since the first find, no fewer than 6890 diamonds with a total weight of 12 549 carats and a value of £153 000.

It soon became clear that the government had lost the race against time. The measures that were to prevent a rush to Namaqualand were to prove ineffective. After the Prime Minister had been informed about the situation, the government and various politicians had intensive discussions, not only about the prevention of a humanitarian catastrophe, but also about the future of diamond mining in Namaqualand. Opinions were sharply divided and that costed time. Altogether, it took more than three weeks before the directive became of force and the grace period of eight days had passed. This time was enough for Namaqualand to be overrun by thousands of newcomers, many of whom were already very poor. For this exodus, they had sold every last bit they had. None of them wanted to go back. Many could not go back, because they had nothing to pay for the journey. They all wanted to stay in Namaqualand and insisted on an opportunity to dig for diamonds, irrespective of what the authorities in Cape Town had decided.

Then the government announced that it would table a countrywide law on prospecting, mining rights and the exploitation of diamonds and precious stones within two months. In fact, until that time, each province had had its own mining laws (the provinces were derived from the older divisions of the country into the Cape Colony, Natal, and the two formerly independent states of the Transvaal and Orange Free State). These different laws regulated certain matters differently, which led to difficulties and occasionally to mild chaos. The government was determined to end such legislative uncertainties forever.

The drafting of the law was influenced by a number of factors. The diamond rush in Namaqualand, however mad it was, was no longer the main problem. The government was far more worried about the excessive production of high carat diamonds around Alexander Bay. The diamonds found by the Merensky syndicate had meanwhile been brought to Cape Town, where they could be viewed in the offices of the H.M. Association. This exhibition created a sensation. Never before had anyone seen such a large collection of such big and perfect stones. Their colours ranged from purest white or blue white to lovely green, yellow or rose tints. The stones were not worn into rounded shapes by being transported along rivers or ocean currents. On the contrary, many of these diamonds still had their natural crystalline form with such perfection that they looked as if they had just come from the workshop of the most gifted of diamond cutters.

Some of those who came to see this exhibition were the Prime Minister, members of the Cabinet and Parliament, the Governor General and his family, foreign diplomats with their ladies and representatives from many South African mining companies. The stones made an enormous impression on all who saw them. But that was only their first reaction. Those who understood anything about the business side of the diamond industry were deeply concerned. This compact collection of high quality stones had been collected in a frighteningly short time. If that were to continue, it would result in a catastrophe for the world diamond market. Admittedly, in the preceding years, now and again a large stone with a weight of 20 carats or more had been found. But there had not been more than 10 or 20 stones of that quality per year, spread over various deposits. Here, in the space of five or six weeks, several hundred large top quality diamonds had been found. It was impossible to sell such a flood of high quality stones in the world market in a short time. To be more explicit, if Alexander Bay continued to produce such masses of high carat diamonds, that would mean the collapse of the world's diamond market.

The first to spell out the problem was Sir David Harris, the chairman of diamond monopoly De Beers and a Member of Parliament, where he was widely acknowledged to be the spokesman for the diamond industry and its workers. His understanding of the mechanisms of the diamond market was unequalled. It was obvious that the government could not ignore the concerns expressed by such a competent man. After all, the taxes paid by the diamond industry played a large role in the financing of the national budget.

The decisive pointer of what direction the diamond industry should take came from Sir Ernest Oppenheimer, the founder of the prominent gold mining firm Anglo American. Oppenheimer belonged to the younger generation: he had only entered the diamond business at the start of the 1920s and he had firmly decided that any drop in prices in the diamond market had to be resisted at any cost. Any drop in price would irreparably tarnish diamonds' reputation as a safe investment. His motto was therefore to buy up any stones that came into the market. He saw immediately that any diamonds from Alexander Bay had to be stockpiled, perhaps for a long time. Only much later, when the situation had calmed down, could one try to slip the stones into the market, very cautiously.

There were also some labour politicians who insisted that the profits from the finds in Namaqualand should be used exclusively to serve the country. They argued that the wealth of the country should not be left in the hands of mere fortune-hunters. There was also no reason to give those who had actually worked hard there, immense wealth and digging rights in perpetuity.

By contrast, the government – like its predecessors – believed that prospecting and mining should in principle be in the hands of the private sector. Government preferred to use wise legislation to encourage investment by the private sector. At the same time, licence fees and taxes should be structured in such a way that private investors would still be able to enjoy a fair and sufficiently attractive share of the profits to act as an incentive. Only this kind of policy would ensure the welfare of the country in the long term.

The legislation had to respond adequately to this complex mixture of economic and political arguments. Thus, when the draft of the Precious Stone Act was finally tabled in Parliament in April 1927, everyone was very surprised to find that in essence the draft stated simply that gemstones in secondary deposits could only be dug by individuals. All digging rights held by syndicates or large mining companies were declared invalid. All the digging that had been done was classified as illegal, and the legislation was to be retrospective, going back to July 1926, that is, the first find made by Captain Jack Carstens.

In Parliament the draft unleashed a storm of indignation. "Expropriation" and "an attack on the right to private property" were some of the milder terms used to describe the intentions of the draft. More dramatic comments included "on the way to socialism", or simply, "Bolshevism". Other comments from the opposition questioned the health of the Mining Minister's state of mind. Outside Parliament too, people were concerned. Serious business papers in South Africa and London pointed out, not unjustly, that to some extent the draft represented a repudiation of South Africa's previous mining policy. Despite the uproar and the harsh attacks on the draft, particularly by the leader of the opposition, General Smuts, the Precious Stone Act was passed after three days' debate. The government only agreed to some minor changes. The prohibition of digging by syndicates remained the focus of the Act – which was immediately passed on to the Senate.

F.W. Beyers was a strong Minister of Mines and Industry, with great visions of the future of the country. One of his greatest achievements was a law promoting the development of the iron and steel industry, the Iron and Steel Industry Bill, Act 11 of 1927, which led to the founding of the South African Iron and Steel Industrial Corporation (ISCOR) and which became the foundation for South Africa's industrial development in the 1930s. But here, in the Senate discussion of the legislation concerning gemstones, he nearly failed. Heated debate continued to the last day of the Session, and no breakthrough was made. Senate adjourned without reaching any conclusion.

The next year was sheer torture for everyone concerned. The claims that had been pegged in Namaqualand were not being worked. Nobody could dig for diamonds, nobody earned any money. The farms, which had never been particularly fruitful in this arid land, were abandoned. Most had been sold and were not being worked. Former farmers and unemployed diamond diggers crowded into Port Nolloth looking for jobs in a poor region in which there were no jobs.

Merensky used the time in his own way. He had always operated on the principle of broadening his capital base after a significant mineral find and of finding new backers to drive the marketing of the deposit once the total potential of the deposit had been estimated. He did so again now, only this time, the capital had to come from a group of financiers who also had political influence. In July 1927,

Sir Ernest Oppenheimer joined the H.M. Association. Initially he purchased a share block for £500 000, and later he purchased the majority shareholding. For Oppenheimer, this was a breakthrough on his way to becoming the dominant figure in the South African diamond industry. Two years later he followed in the footsteps of Sir David Harris, when the latter stepped down, and became the chairman of De Beers. By the start of the 1930s he was able to introduce the reorganisation of the entire diamond business in South Africa, including a sales organisation that was internationally active.

The new Act, the Precious Stone Act, Act 44 of 1927, was again discussed in the Senate at the start of the next session and finally came into law in November 1927. The Minister of Mines and Industry, F.W. Beyers, then announced inter alia a decision on the discoverers' rights regarding diamond findings. Like other diggers who claimed finders' rights, Merensky had submitted a petition in this regard. Decisions about these requests were a difficult task. After all, the Ministry was deciding the weal or woe of individual diamond diggers. Here too, there was an unexpected outcome. The ministerial decision was that only finds that had been made in an indisputably identifiable geological location would be recognised as genuine first discoveries. This meant that the find had to be made in a geological horizon that was indisputably distinct from other layers in terms of its particular character and/or its age. In terms of the law, spots where only isolated diamonds had been found (i.e. diamonds not related to a particular layer) were not recognised as finding spots. In all, only six locations were rated as first discovery spots. They were, first, Merensky's Oyster Line, second, the diamond occurrences in the terrace with the river gravels that Caplan had given him as an afterthought or "Christmas present", thirdly, a spot where Kennedy had found some diamonds, fourth, Rabinowitz's finds at Buchuberg, fifth, an occurrence at Opperculum that belonged to the Gelgorcap Syndicate, and, sixth, a place which was an extension of the Oyster Line. Three groups claimed this sixth spot, each insisting that it had made the first discovery. They were Merensky, the Gelgorcap Syndicate and the K. & K. Syndicate. It was a tricky situation. Merensky eventually resolved the matter in his favour by buying out the two competitors. He could do so because his syndicate was liquid after Oppenheimer had joined it. Each counterclaimant received £20 000 and a 30% share of the net profits. This transaction gave Merensky all the claims in Alexander Bay. He then negotiated with the remaining three owners of finders' rights and acquired these rights too. He paid Kennedy £12 000 plus 50% of the net profits. The Gelcorcap Syndicate received £15 000 plus 20% of the profits. He kept a 75% share of Rabinowitz's claim and the remaining 25% went to the Namaqualand Diamond Company. That meant that Merensky controlled all spots of interest, even outside of Alexander Bay.

When these agreements became public, there was a new storm of protest in Parliament. The opposition under General Smuts was indignant that the new Act had led to all claims being united in one entity's hand. Minister of Mines and Industry Beyers vehemently defended the allocation of finders' rights undertaken by his ministry. These rights had been allocated to individuals after all the information had been sifted carefully. After that, these individuals were allowed to do with their claims what was most advantageous to them. They could sell their shares and Merensky had the right to purchase them. The Minister made it completely clear that the government had no intention (and no legal handle) to dispute the mining rights that Merensky had acquired in any way.

If Merensky believed that he was now safe, he was to be disappointed. The new law also provided the possibility for governmental production constraints. This clause had not been generally noted before. Now the government made use of this authorization. Merensky applied for a monthly production quota for diamonds to the value of £50 000 for the Oyster Line. The government refused and would only agree to a quota of £6000. Merensky protested with a memorandum of undertaking that he submitted at the start of March 1928, together with his partners – Gustav Adolph Becker, Sir Ernest Oppenheimer and Sir Abe Bailey. He argued that the enterprise could only operate viably with a higher production quota. It would also mean more jobs created in the otherwise poor Namaqualand. In the end, the government agreed to unlimited production, but with the proviso that all the stones that were found had to be delivered to the government. Oppenheimer's political clout is almost certain to have played a role in this decision.

On 1 May 1928 everything was in place. The H.M. Association could continue its work. This time the Association had good equipment and employed 60 diggers and additional indigenous labour. After 14 frustrating months, Merensky had reached his goal and could begin to reap his well-earned reward.

Almost at the same time, he was to have another indirect success. On the north banks of the Orange River on the other side of the border, in South-West Africa (today Namibia), a continuation of the Oyster Line was found. It was also rich in diamonds of exceptional quality, just like the occurrences in Alexander Bay. Merensky was not involved in prospecting in that area, but everyone knew that this discovery was only made because of his discoveries south of the border. Since the diamond finds on the north banks of the Orange River were eventually to become the most important factor in the economy of South-West Africa, one would be justified in saying that without Merensky's work, Namibia would be a considerably poorer country today.

The prospecting work in South-West Africa brought to light something else too: years before, in 1909, Dr Ernst Reuning had undertaken a camel expedition all along the 280 kilometre-long coastal strip between Lüderitz and the Orange River. He wanted to check whether there were diamond deposits similar to those at Kolmanskop. The results had been negative. Now the old prospecting pits he had dug in many places were found again. Two of them were only 60 metres away from the Oyster Line and were barren. This requires some comment. Simply saying "tough luck" would be inappropriate. Reuning's expedition was an exploratory expedition into an extremely inhospitable desert region; and it would have been a fairy-tale coincidence if they had immediately found a diamond deposit buried metres deep under the sand. We should always remember that almost every deposit known to us today, irrespective its nature, was passed by hundreds or even thousands of people before it was found – and they did not see it. The comment must therefore focus on the contrast between the barren prospecting pits Reuning had dug and the rapid discovery of the Oyster Line by Merensky. This contrast is a textbook example of the difference between a preliminary exploration (a "looking for the needle in the haystack" approach) and a focused search for a deposit about the structure and genesis of which the prospecting geologist has already developed a clear concept.

At the same time as the H.M. Association resumed its search for diamonds, the Government also began to dig on state-owned land in the vicinity of Alexander Bay and almost immediately found considerable diamond occurrences. It was the first time that a South African government made use of the right stipulated in principle in the new mining law to mine on its own behalf. This was a shift from the old principle of leaving mining in the hands of the private sector. This deviation from former policy probably did not agree with Prime Minister Hertzog's convictions, but was a concession to the socialist policies of the Labour Party, which was the ruling party's coalition partner. This decision can be assessed in various ways. It did prevent the treasures of the land from falling into the hands of individual fortune-hunters, as various representatives had asked. It also prevented the conditions that had arisen two years earlier in the diamond fields at Lichtenburg and Ventersdorp. There, the pegging of claims on state-owned land had been run via organised races in which up to 25 000 citizens had participated. Since the starting point was always several kilometres away, the best claims were snatched by professional runners who worked for third parties. It was certainly also beneficial for Namaqualand that the government's search for diamonds created jobs, even if it was a very limited number. On the other hand, it was problematic that, despite the existing overproduction of diamonds, an additional powerful producer entered the market. This extended the bear market and contributed to keep diamond prices under pressure, and thus also the State's revenue from the taxes paid by the diamond producers.

For Merensky, the economic use of the diamond finds worked out very well, but the general developments in Namaqualand were less happy. Thousands of diggers had been impoverished and remained poor – a situation which, at the start of 1929, almost led to an uprising by the angry diamond diggers, who wanted to force the government to make available state-owned land for diggings. General Manie Maritz, who had accompanied Dr Reuning at the end of 1926 and start of 1927, played a large role in calming the heated emotions of the diggers. In the Anglo-Boer War he had been known as a hothead, and later he was regarded as a non-conformist who gave the government a headache on more than one occasion. But here it was his level-headedness that prevented a bloodbath.

A second problem was that from 1927 to 1929, the extent of illegal digging and theft from claims where mining did take place and the resulting black market trading in diamonds became absolutely excessive. The authorities were unable to control the situation in Namaqualand. Diamonds were traded in every bar in Port Nolloth. It was admittedly difficult to get the stones that had been illegally acquired out of Namaqualand. The few big roads that went to the Cape or to Johannesburg were closely watched. Since the possession of raw diamonds was prohibited in South Africa, they could not be sold in the country. That meant that they had to be smuggled to Europe. This was not easy, since passengers boarding ships in Cape Town and Durban were checked quite thoroughly. The smugglers were therefore forced to take the long road across South Africa, over the Drakensberg to Mozambique, to the port at Lourenço Marques. This took a lot of effort, but was worth it, since, because of these difficulties, the raw diamonds were sold at fair prices in Port Nolloth. Stories about this privateering are legion. Some do not lack a comical side, for example, how the diamond price was determined in the bars at Port Nolloth. There were only two categories of stones, "little" ones and "big" ones. If a stone could pass through the neck of an (empty) whisky bottle, then it was a "little" diamond and cost £1 per carat. If it did not go through, it was a "big" diamond and cost £2 per carat. There were no other categories.

But these general conditions were not the only ones that depressed Merensky. He had to face various emotional pressures. The endless wait for the acknowledgement of his claims was over, but then he had to face unpleasant animosities between him and people who begrudged him his success.

It was particularly annoying that, in the first week of December 1928, Dr Reuning published an essay in the reputable *Mining and Industrial Magazine* in which he asserted that it was he, Reuning, who had discovered the Oyster Line, and not Merensky. In a lengthy, in places rather long-winded description, he presented his version of the history of the search for diamonds on the Atlantic coast, starting with his own work in South-West Africa before the First World War, touching on the prospecting done by the legendary Fred C. Cornell, the diamond finds of Captain Jack Carstens, R. Kennedy, S. Rabinowitz at Buchuberg and the Caplan brothers in Alexander

Bay. Finally, he described how, at his own initiative, he had gone up to the high terraces and stated that it had been he who had pegged out where the prospecting trenches were to be dug that led to the discovery of the Oyster Line.

This article must have spoiled the Christmas month for Merensky in 1928. It forced him to respond quickly. His rebuttal in the *Magazine* already appeared in the first week in January 1929. It was concise and stylistically polished. Merensky referred to Reuning's earlier publications, which in no way revealed that Reuning regarded the presence of oyster shells as a possible indication of the existence of a diamond deposit. Then Merensky pointed out that only a few days before the Oyster Line was uncovered, Reuning had repeatedly tried to convince Merensky to dig much lower down, right at the waterline. Finally, Merensky quoted from Reuning's letter of 15 January 1927, in which Reuning reported on the discovery of the Oyster Line and which clearly showed that the relevant prospecting trench had been dug exactly where Merensky had asked for it to be dug. As his final salvo, Merensky included details of the employment contract Reuning had signed. It stated, almost brutally clearly, that Reuning was not permitted to prospect at his own discretion, but in every case, had to stick to the instructions he had been given unconditionally. All of this was very clearly and convincingly set out. On the other hand, Merensky was very fair and fully acknowledged that Reuning had done an excellent job in executing the prospecting strategy. Such scientific disputes, in which the issues are neither money nor patents, but "only" fame, are usually not judged and cannot, in the end, be resolved. The scientific community must weigh both sides' arguments and then reach its own conclusions. In this case, the facts were strongly in Merensky's favour. His reputation as the discoverer of the Oyster Line was untarnished; if anything, it was better than ever.

There were other enmities. The Coetzee brothers instituted a lengthy lawsuit against Merensky, demanding, in addition to their wages, which they had received promptly, a further premium of £6000 that they claimed he had promised them. Merensky did eventually win the case, but he had to go through various institutions to do so, and the case dragged on until 1931. The case upset him deeply. Nevertheless, he remained obdurate in this case, because he refused to set a precedent for other attempts to blackmail him.

Generally speaking, he had become much more careful, even "hard", in the way in which he now managed the money he had won. The suffering of the unemployed people who had come to Namaqualand moved him deeply, and he helped many of them, but he now did so very cautiously. He became accustomed to checking carefully on people's complaints and stories to ascertain that those he helped, deserved it.

But sometimes his old spontaneity and generosity did show itself. One example was a visit from the wife of a pastor of a Dutch Reformed Church. She had come from Springbok, a small town about 100 kilometres to the south-east of Port Nolloth. That morning, Merensky was sitting writing on the veranda of his hotel when the minister's wife approached him hesitantly and asked him, shyly: "I am not sure whether I can bother you, but I wanted to ask whether you could perhaps make a small donation towards the renovation of our church." Merensky, himself the son of a missionary, took it for granted that he would make a donation. He knew only too well what a blessing a small sum could be in the hands of a hard-working missionary or minister and he knew, even better, what a big role the church, as a central meeting place, played in the functioning of a community. And so he asked: "What sum did you have in mind?" The minister's wife answered softly: "We are trying to get together £500 from collections at each service and donations." Then the shy woman scraped together all her courage and asked: "I wondered whether it would be possible for you to donate £50?" Merensky leaned back and shook his head slightly, saying: "I could not do that …" He saw the poor woman shrink as if she wished the ground would swallow her up. Her face showed not disappointment, but shame. She felt that she had been quite rude to ask for such an exorbitant sum. Merensky had not intended to embarrass her and now it was his turn to be rather embarrassed. He had intended to tell her something quite different, but her reaction had cut him short. And so he said: "I beg your pardon – I have expressed myself badly. What I wanted to say was that £50 is too little! Would you permit me to give you the whole £500?" This gesture reflected his naturally generous character. In this case, it also made good economic sense to him. He did not see himself as contributing to charity. For him, such a donation was a sensible social investment, because he was certain that the fruits of this investment would benefit the general welfare of the local populace.

The physical effort required from Merensky at this time was no less strenuous. Innumerable times he had to dash from Alexander Bay to Cape Town, Johannesburg or Pretoria, to go to meetings. And then he would have to race back to manage the work on the terrain. There were various sources of irritation. The diamond yield was excellent, but there were constant problems with the workers. They were not prepared to follow his advice on a diet suited to the climate. They tended to alcoholic excesses, and did not maintain the minimum standards of hygiene required. Then there was theft and illicit digging at night. It was usually not clear whether this was an inside job, or whether Merensky's people had colluded by giving third parties a chance to do this. All of this put him under stress. Despite these unpleasant issues, he spent his few free hours writing scientific articles. They were important to him and required his full concentration. The Oyster Line was, after all, not only sensational because it was so rich in diamonds, but because it was a completely new type of deposit. Merensky did not hesitate to make his theory and expertise available to the scientific community via published papers and lectures presented to the Geological Society of South Africa. He had done the same with his platinum discoveries, even while the prospecting was still being done. All in all, in these months he worked to his very fullest capacity, pushing himself to the limit all the time.

Thus he was happy to be able, finally, to sell his shares in the H.M. Association to Sir Ernest Oppenheimer in November 1928. He did so without any regrets, because he had never intended to be a mine owner in the long term or to run the mining operations, irrespective of the type, or, even worse, to have to take responsibility for the marketing of the raw material concerned. The sale was also no problem for the other partners. All of them – Gustav Becker, Sir Julius Jeppe and Sir Abe Bailey – regarded their participation in this diamond enterprise purely as a financial engagement that had to be brought to a satisfactory close, the sooner the better. For his part, it was in Sir Ernest Oppenheimer's interest to take over the entire H.M. Association as soon as possible. Only once he had done so, could he begin to put into practice the reorganisation of the diamond market that he had in mind. This was urgent, and the government supported his initiative. The direction in which things were to move was clear. The only thing that remained was the financial details, and these were subject to hard negotiations.

First, Oppenheimer took over the shares owned by Sir Abe Bailey, who was a successful mining magnate, a much-decorated officer in the First World War and a parliamentary representative. He had made his fortune many years before and, at the age of 64, was very happy to have been involved in such a significant diamond find thanks to his intuition and with relatively little input. He had nothing more to prove, and he sold his shares very quietly. The sale of Sir Julius Jeppe's shares was equally simple. He was now 69 years old. He had made his fortune by developing land, particularly in the Johannesburg area (Jeppestown). Later he had become Sir Abe Bailey's partner, and like his friend and partner, he saw this diamond enterprise as a lovely end to a long and distinguished business career.

The negotiations with Gustav Becker were somewhat different. He came in with a very high price. At that time, he owned 24 475 shares in the H.M. Association, that is, 39,16% of the total number. He wanted £750 000 for his shares, plus a seat on the Board of De Beers. That was in the spring of 1928. Oppenheimer refused this demand. It was not very clear what bothered him more, the seat on the Board or the high price asked. The negotiations stopped, but resumed four months later, since both Becker and Oppenheimer felt that the transaction should not drag on indefinitely. In the end, Becker sold his shares for £500 000. This means that Becker got an average price of £20 per share, and he had paid £1 per share when he bought them.

The negotiations with Merensky were even more difficult. He held 20 750 shares, that is, 33,2% of the company. One cannot even really speak of any negotiation, because Merensky refused any discussion. He simply named his price and was not prepared to talk about the matter again. This was a carefully planned tactic. He knew that haggling was not one of his strengths and he also knew that he would be told that the diamonds found at Alexander Bay could not be sold at this time and that he would have to accept a discount. He was not prepared to listen to this argument at all. Instead he presented his one and only (good) argument with some force. The gist of what he said was this: "This is the best deposit of diamonds of gemstone quality that has ever been found. It is unlikely that anything like this will ever be found again. I want one million pounds for my share."

The usually very shrewd lawyers of the opposing party were annoyed by this negotiation tactic, and Oppenheimer too is said to have been visibly irritated by this. But, as he was extremely pragmatic and saw that the £1 million had become a fixed idea with Merensky, after some time he had the lawyers indicate that De Beers might agree. Merensky read the signal and was immediately prepared to accept all kinds of clauses in the agreement that he saw had only been included to save face before the Board and the shareholders. The agreement was signed on 9 November 1928. For his shares, Merensky received £1 006 000 and an additional £100 000 over and beyond the agreement for diamonds that had already been delivered. The million was paid over in four payments, £256 000 when the agreement was signed and £250 000 respectively on 1 July 1929, 1 January 1930 and 1 July 1930. A face-saving clause stated that up to £66 500 would be subtracted from the fourth payment if by that date a total of at least 65 000 carats worth of diamonds had not been found in the licence area. As in the few months since the start of mining operations, the yield was no less than 315 000 carats already, and as Merensky knew that the deposit was by no means exhausted, he had no problem in signing this agreement.

The Oyster Line had given him enormous success. In only 20 months, the value of his shares had risen from £1 to £50 each. All in all, he had made a profit of £1,15 million from the sale of this exceptional deposit.

---

**Textbox 9 – The diamond cartel**

In 1929, Sir Ernest Oppenheimer became chairman of De Beers. Those years were probably the most difficult ones in the history of that business. Nobody knew for how long the company would be able to continue to buy up diamonds and to keep prices stable in that way. The concern about what would happen to the South African diamond industry if prices dropped, affected everyone.

As so often happens, this precarious situation offered an opportunity. It lay in the insight that standing together would enable everyone to benefit. Oppenheimer recognised this opportunity. He used all his negotiation skills and persuasiveness to muster the interests of all the players in the South African diamond industry in a way that no one had ever believed possible, and also to get the producers in other African regions (Angola, the Congo, East Africa) to agree to coordinate their supply and prices with the strategy designed by De Beers. This resulted in a syndicate which was in reality a rigidly controlled cartel. The heart of his consistently sustained business policy was maintaining the value of any purchased diamonds. In this, the cartel served the interests of the producers, as well as those of the diamond cutting industry and of the traders. At the same time, the end consumers benefited from this value retention. The Central Selling Organisation (CSO), which Oppenheimer created to regulate the sale of diamonds, played a central role in carrying out his business policy.

By 1926, the accumulated worldwide diamond holdings were already estimated to be 140 million carats. There was a corresponding effort to find ever more consumer groups to absorb the supply, initially in the USA, long the most important market for diamonds, but then also in other countries. "Diamonds are forever" said an advertising slogan at the end of the 1930s, and 15 years later, Hollywood stars Jane Russell and Marilyn Monroe sang "Diamonds are a girl's best friend". A diamond engagement ring for every young bride-to-be was elevated to an absolute must. In Japan, where a diamond engagement ring was not traditional before the Second World War, by 1970, no fewer than 70% of all brides were given such a ring.

To sustain the value of a diamond once it had been sold, it was vital to prevent the emergence of a secondary market. The CSO had to act in two spheres: Sudden disproportionate price increases by individual producers had to be prevented, since they could trigger sales and speculative profiteering by those who already had diamonds. On the other hand, prices were not allowed to drop, because that would lead clients to feel insecure. Where there was any oversupply, stones were bought up and stockpiled. Otherwise everything possible was done to make the pricing of diamonds as non-transparent as possible. In the end, a total of no fewer than 5000 valuation categories were introduced! The criteria used are carat, colour, clarity and cut. While weight as a measure that determines the price is something a layperson can still understand and perhaps use, the almost innumerable distinctions between different shades is not an accessible criterion. The other criteria are clarity and cut, which looks at the quality of the craftsmanship that has been brought to bear on the stone. The latter criteria can only be evaluated by experts. This implies – at least from the point of view of buyers – that diamonds do not represent standardised wares, but individual pieces with unique attributes. This means that they are difficult to sell. Since the profit margins of the individual trade arena are also very high, it is almost impossible to sell privately-owned diamonds, unless the seller is prepared to accept a discount on the original purchase price, often more than 50%.

But development did not stop there. After the Second World War, huge new deposits were discovered. By 1976, Russia was already producing 16 million carats per year. In 1979, the occurrences in Argyle in Western-Australia were discovered, and the annual production there today is 35 million carats. Admittedly, most of the diamonds from there are not of gemstone quality, while the vast majority of the stones are destined for industrial use (for example, for use on drillbits). Nevertheless, these numbers exploded all imaginable dimensions: 35 million carats of diamonds represent seven tons! These gemstones had therefore not only lost their rarity value, but had become mass-produced goods.

There have been other changes. Today, South Africa is no longer the world's premier producer; and the richest diamond mine in the world today – Jwaneng – is in Botswana. At present, De Beers probably only has direct control over about 25% of the world's diamond production, or 50% of the yield of the raw diamonds of gemstone quality. But De Beers still has a much bigger influence on price formation. The CSO was dissolved in 2001 because of image problems, but the close networking between diamond producers continues to exist. Just as before, 80% (according to some sources, 60%) of all sales on the world market are concluded in terms of De Beers' conditions. None of the rumoured figures have been indisputably confirmed; that too is part of the nature of this syndicate. This is also true for the estimated value of the CSO's "buffer stockpile", in which it is said that in 1999/2000 there were diamonds valued at 5,5 billion euros or 4 to 5 billion US dollars. But it is certain that the Russian producers did initially try to market their own diamonds, and that it took a few failures to convince them to entrust the CSO with this task. With the Australian producers too, longer negotiations were needed before they conducted their sales via the CSO and according to their suggested pricing concepts.

The situation is therefore rather confusing. Diamonds are bought, not despite the fact that they are expensive, but because they are expensive and because their value is regarded as stable. They are gemstones, but more than that, they are a status symbol with a social value. In buying diamonds, there is a kind of consumerism at work that relies on people's need for recognition. In the general economic literature, this is referred to as the "Veblen effect" (called after the first person to describe this phenomenon, the Norwegian-American economist Thorstein Veblen (1857–1929)). The amount of literature written on this phenomenon, as on the diamond syndicate itself, is vast. In Germany, Helmut Braun (Regensburg) has published work on this, and he specifically commented on the "illusion of value" that underpins every diamond sale.

In conclusion then, it must be said that diamond prices are kept artificially high and that the prices are not determined by supply and demand. The syndicate controls the market by means of agreements and finely coordinated actions, resulting in a falsification or the elimination of free competition. This makes it a genuine cartel. The beneficiaries of this system are the producers, the processing industry and the traders. All of them profit from the "ordered conditions" of this market and the excessive prices. It is perhaps less clear who is harmed by this system. The end consumers do not see themselves as victims of the system. Many of them would simply not buy diamonds if they were less expensive or lost their glamour status. These buyers have paid the current prices to get exactly what they wanted.

CHAPTER 15

# The turning point in Merensky's life

The income that Merensky had received from diamond mining from May 1928 was considerable. Now the £1 million from the sale of his shares was added to that. He was now a man with a large fortune. Sir Ernest Oppenheimer, who, despite the difficult take-over negotiations, was kindly disposed toward Merensky and admired his specialist abilities, commented: "You won't often meet a man who comes in with sixpence in his pocket and leaves with a million pounds."

Merensky thought differently about all of this. He did not think that he had "unexpectedly" come into a fortune. He felt that his current success was the result of long years of hard work and had been hard-earned. But then, he was also not someone who would overestimate this wealth. When he was asked how he felt about it, he answered rather unglamorously that he did not feel like a millionaire at all. He said that he was tired and stressed and really needed a holiday. This was indeed his main feeling. After the stress of the past three years, he was exhausted. For some time he had been thinking of travelling to Europe for a few months, to go hunting there and to rest.

But first there were a number of things he still had to arrange.

When he finally returned to Johannesburg, his circle of friends greeted him by making a huge fuss over him. When that was over, his closest friends took him aside and urged him for God's sake to be a little more careful this time and not to try to manage his finances himself. They told him the unvarnished truth about his weaknesses: He could not manage his money; he simply could not keep together his money; he was too generous with it, both with real and with false friends; he could not say no and he was unwilling to check on the veracity and viability of any financial proposition that was brought to him. "Do whatever your heart desires," his friends said, "go looking for gold or for diamonds, go prospecting for what you want and where you want, but do not try to run your own financial affairs!"

The person who spoke his mind most clearly was Gustav Becker, who had been one of Merensky's first backers in both the platinum and the diamond prospecting projects. He had become very rich through Merensky, and he saw it as his duty as a friend to convince Merensky to manage his fortune sensibly this time, or even better, to have it managed for him. He was surprised to find that Merensky did not only agree, but had been thinking about this problem for some time. Merensky had learnt something after all. This insight had not come overnight. He had already shown some insight after his platinum finds, when he had deliberately avoided new speculations on the stock exchange. A few weeks after he had found the Oyster Line he had realised that this time, if he did the right things, he might make a fortune. From then on, he had worked towards this goal and had insisted on a high price when he negotiated the sale of the shares with Oppenheimer. At the same time, he developed a plan to manage his new wealth and structure his future. Now the time had come, and he started to muster his facts.

Merensky established the African German Estate and Investment Company Ltd., a company that was meant to run his affairs. This did not mean that he placed himself under any kind of guardianship. He retained full power of attorney over his money, and where he wanted to invest his money was his idea, but no more money left his hands before the planned investment had been checked in detail by lawyers and experts. From 1929 onward, he was advised on legal matters by Alexander (Alex) Douglas, a Johannesburg lawyer, and some time later William Warmback was engaged as his financial adviser, accountant and auditor. Both men were to become close confidants of Merensky and took care of his affairs beyond his death.

The holding company was to prove to be a very fortuitous decision over the next few years, in at least two senses. For one thing, the money was kept together or invested very carefully. For another, Merensky did not have to worry about the financial details of his investments. From now on he could afford to concentrate on what really interested him. This was significant, because it enabled Merensky to be extremely creative in the next few years and to put into action a lot of new ideas.

The name of the holding company, the African German Estate and Investment Company Ltd., may seem odd to many at first glance. What was the word "German" supposed to denote in this context? We know that by this time Merensky had long decided to stay in South Africa and that he felt that he was a born South African. On the other hand, he had never hidden his German background or origins. It was where his family lived and his mother tongue was German. But the name had nothing to do with a national or even political confession. Such an attitude would have been completely alien to his nature.

Nevertheless, the name of the holding company did indicate an intention: Merensky had decided to invest part of his fortune in South Africa, and part of it in Germany. The idea of spreading his investments geographically for the sake of greater security was probably not the impetus behind this decision. At any rate, Merensky is not recorded as ever stating that as his rationale. He was thinking of two other things.

Firstly, he wanted to assist in the development of the technical equipment of South African mining. On the basis of his mining studies he was, after all, technically trained. He also knew the German manufacturers of mining machinery and ore dressing plants quite well and knew where in South Africa there were possibilities for multiple uses of such machinery and plants. He wanted to bring together these two sides of mining. The idea was not a new one. He had already worked toward such cooperation before, for example, when in 1926 he had brought several tons of platinum-bearing ore to Germany so that ore dressing experiments could be done. Later he had extrapolated the idea of strengthening the technical know-how within the South African mining sector by focusing on human resources. He often encouraged specialists to come to South Africa and when he encountered a young immigrant that had special skills, he was always prepared to help him to make a start or was willing to pass him on to someone who could help him.

The second reason why Merensky had included the word "German" in the name of his company was more private. He wanted to buy a hunting estate in Germany, and this German hunting seat was to be managed from Johannesburg. Merensky – like his father before him – was an enthusiastic hunter. During his time in the military and at university, he had often hunted in Silesia. In the years between 1904 and 1928 he had not been able to indulge his passion for hunting because of the stresses of his career. Now, when things were going well financially, he wanted to pursue this passion in Europe again. He had already taken preliminary steps in 1928. At the time, the negotiations regarding the sale of his diamond concession to Oppenheimer had just begun.

But things were not that far yet. At the moment, all he wanted to do was relax. One afternoon he was sitting in the Rand Club, where he had lived before the war and where he still felt very comfortable. The Club had not changed much. It was still the preferred meeting place of all who had anything to do with mining or prospecting. As always, it was still an exchange of note, where news spread and rumours were whispered. One still encountered veterans from the heyday of gold digging in the 1880s. Then there were the representatives of the next generation, who now set the tone. Very young ore seekers and geologists who were still dreaming of their future came there, as did the speculators – lucky ones and unlucky ones – and there were sometimes tales of botched lives. So it was just logical that it was at this spot, where Merensky had made so many contacts, that a meeting was to occur that would change his life.

Merensky was sitting in the Rand Club, relaxing, when someone tapped him on the shoulder, saying, "Hallo, Merensky, how are things with you? I hear business is good …" The voice belonged to Sir Lionel Phillips, one of the old guard from the early gold digger times on the Rand. After many ups and downs in his life, he had finally gathered a considerable fortune. Now, late in life, like so many of his generation, he had decided to go into farming and spent most of the year on his farm.

Merensky liked him, because Lionel Phillips was a man of sterling qualities. He invited him for a drink, and of course, the conversation naturally first turned to the diamonds at Alexander Bay. But then Phillips asked: "And what are you planning next, Merensky? I hope you have a few diamonds left to buy a farm with?" The question was not strange, because anybody who was anybody in the Transvaal, whether he was a general or a politician, was also a farmer. If anyone made a fortune in gold mining or in diamonds, he also spent his old age on his own farm, unless he had roots in England and went back there.

So it was not surprising that Merensky nodded and said that yes, he had already considered that. Then Phillips said: "Well, think about it, Merensky, I want to sell my farm Westfalia. I think that it might be just the one for you." Merensky pricked up his ears. He knew the farm and he knew that it had belonged to Phillips for a number of years. It was in Duiwelskloof in the north-eastern Transvaal (today the Limpopo Province) and was a large estate. Back in 1904, the year when Merensky first arrived in South Africa, he had been there for the first time. Westfalia lay on the eastern slopes of the Woodbush Hill, which is part of the northernmost reaches of the Drakensberg, that mighty range of mountains running from north to south in the eastern Transvaal into the eastern Cape. The farm lay in a depression open to the east, where the moist winds from the Indian Ocean were trapped. Unlike the rest of the Transvaal, where the Drakensberg prevented rain clouds from reaching much of the rest of the province, the area received good rains. The soil on Westfalia was deep, fertile humus; ideal farmland. Back then, in 1904, it was a well-kept farm on which peanuts, tobacco, coffee and cotton were grown. Around the small farmhouse there was a lush vegetable garden and on the slopes there were all kinds of fruit trees. The owner in those days was a German called Plange, an energetic farmer who knew how to make something of what nature offered him.

The best thing about this farm was the view. The farmhouse lay on a slope and looked out over the widening plain, over fertile fields, grazing land and wooded, gently undulating ranges of hills. Merensky had liked these very much on his first visit, and he had returned there again later, but not in the past few years.

Plange had died some time ago. His widow had run the farm a few years longer, but had then sold it to Lionel Phillips in 1914. Phillips had not bought it for himself, but for his son Harold, who had recently died, and so the farm was on the market again. Lionel Phillips wanted to sell it. Merensky found this very interesting, because Westfalia was a little piece of land that would be a pleasure to work. He agreed to go there the next week to look at the farm again.

That is what happened: When Merensky crossed the Drakensberg and stood on the Magoebaskloof Pass, he once again looked out over the vast vista of the wide land to the east, a view that had captured his heart many years before. But when he got to the farm, things were very different from what he remembered. He knew what a well-kept farm looked like and he also knew how to recognise a farm that had been neglected. This farm had been very badly neglected. Even worse, the farmland was dry and barren. The lush grazing and the small streams that had run in the hills were all gone. Where water had once sparkled, there were now dried up dongas, and where there had once been green fields, there were now only empty, deeply eroded slopes.

He did not know how this could have happened in this valley in which the moist wind blew. Had there really been no rain here? No, this was not the case, or the deep erosion dongas could not have been cut into the soil by the water. It had rained, but the water had run off very quickly. Had this been caused by human neglect? There were various signs that suggested that that might have been the case, as a glance at the plantings sufficed to reveal that they had not been well tended. Harold Phillips had clearly not been a farmer with any ambition. The farm showed that the late owner had not loved the soil very much. He had clearly had no real understanding of the fact that to get something out of the soil, one had to put something into it. Merensky asked himself whether this farm could ever be rehabilitated to what it had once been. If it could ever be done – which would be a wonderful thing to do – the task would take years.

Now for the first time, Merensky's team in his African German Estate and Investment Company was to prove its worth. When he was already on his way to Europe, his advisers and experts negotiated with Lionel Phillips. Soon after he arrived in Germany, he heard that he now owned Westfalia. He had paid £40 000 for this vast estate, which he knew had once been one of the most beautiful in the Transvaal and which he hoped would be one of the most beautiful again.

CHAPTER 16

# A summer in Mecklenburg

Merensky travelled to Germany in the spring of 1929. The next few months were to be among the most peaceful and carefree that he ever experienced.

The start of the journey was not much to his liking. When he went on board in Cape Town – in those days one still travelled to Europe by ship – journalists from all the news agencies and newspapers represented in Cape Town lay in wait for him at the docks.

He was photographed and then photographed again and then he was asked question after question. How would the diamond market develop? Would there be more outstanding finds like the one in Alexander Bay? How did he see South Africa's position in the international platinum trade? What were his plans? One question after the other, and most formulated in such a way that in all good conscience he could not answer.

What could he say about the future development of the diamond or platinum market? He knew from experience that finding a deposit, no matter how promising, was only one cog in the vast world market mechanism. If a new platinum deposit were to be found in Australia or Russia tomorrow, things would look different by tomorrow evening! And his own plans? Yes, he had some, but should he really tell anyone that he was so exhausted that all he wanted was some peace and quiet and to breathe the cool evening air in the German forests? Nobody wanted to hear him say any such thing. So he gave rather monosyllabic, noncommittal answers: "Yes." "No." "That could be very interesting ..."

But these interviews paled beside what he was to face when he arrived at the Adlon in Berlin. The fuss made of him there was unbelievable, and there was much more excitement than four years earlier. Then he had still been relatively unknown, an exotic explorer from far away Africa. Nobody had known much about his personal circumstances, so the journalists had free rein to write the most fantastic things about him. Some described him as a lucky devil who had stumbled onto a fat platinum vein without having to do much for it; others painted him as an indefatigable hunter for the hidden treasures of the earth, who had followed his childhood dream of a big find for many years. But this time, the members of the press had done their homework. They knew the production figures, prices and all about the complex interface between supply and demand. The Berlin economic reporters were particularly well informed about the platinum market. As a result of the Russian dumping strategy, the platinum price had dropped from its 1928 price of £18 per ounce to £11 ¾. Questions rained down on him. Would the South African platinum companies try to stabilise the market by curbing their production? Or would they continue a price war with the Russians? Would the diamond syndicate be able to keep its prices stable? And would it continue to buy up all the stones found in South Africa? And what would happen if synthetic diamonds were to hit the market? These were more questions that he neither could nor wanted to answer. It was absurd to expect him to make any pronouncements abroad on the business policy of South African firms. As journalists shot questions at him, he was blinded by a storm of camera flashes – sheer torture.

The journalists had barely departed when visitors were announced, people whose names he had never even heard, with bizarre visiting cards. Complete strangers forced their way into his presence and tried to convince him to become involved in vast enterprises. The things they wanted to build or sell in South Africa were unbelievable – and he, Merensky, was to finance it all! Naturally they all claimed that the investments they offered were "dead certs". The businesses they represented held no risk at all, or so they claimed. Merensky did not wish to discuss such nonsense with people he did not even know. Now it was very helpful to him to point out the existence of the holding company he had established in Johannesburg. When a visitor threatened to swamp him in a wave of words, he simply asked him to put his ideas on paper and then to send the business proposal to his office in Johannesburg. Then he would politely show out his unwelcome guest and be rid of him. The people who simply wanted to borrow money were easier to endure, because one could get rid of them more easily.

The Adlon might be a comfortable hotel, but Merensky was drained by these events. Four days after his arrival, he fled the hotel and took refuge with some friends, Major Malcomess and his wife, in Lichterfelde.

It was this major who arranged one of the finest hunting experiences Merensky would ever have: hunting on the von Bülow estates in Mecklenburg. As with many estates after the hard years of the Depression, cash was welcome and they welcomed the opportunity to take in a paying guest. This made sense. The von Bülows had three estates close to one another: Rodenwalde, Goldenbow and Albertinenhof. The family lived in the manor house on Rodenwalde. The houses on Goldenbow and the Albertinenhof were not in use, but were quite habitable. The estates were in the middle of a wide, lovely forest, rich in game.

The Malcomesses had made careful arrangements. The hunt was leased, not only for this summer, but for five years, until 1934. Merensky also had an option to buy Rodenwalde. If he wanted to take it over, the von Bülows would move to Albertinenhof. Until he had made a decision, Merensky would stay at Goldenbow. The moment when he left for Goldenbow is documented: on May 1929, he wrote from Berlin to a friend of his youth, Horst Correns: "... *in der nächsten Woche will ich nach Goldenbow gehen ...*" ["... in the course of the next week I will go to Goldenbow ..."]. The house there was one of the very few manor houses built in the early Baroque style still left in Mecklenburg. The grandfather of the current owner had restored it at considerable cost from 1862 onwards. It was an imposing, manorial building, even if the interior did seem a little outdated. But Mrs Malcomess had seen to it that at least some of the more odd old-fashioned pieces were replaced by something a little more comfortable. Merensky's more mundane needs would be taken care of by the estate manager and his wife, which made sense, as the wife had once worked as a cook to a member of the nobility. The experienced head forester was ready to accompany Merensky on the hunt.

The events that followed had their comical side. When the arrangements were made, somehow there was a misunderstanding about this hunting guest. Major Malcomess had mentioned in passing that Herr Merensky was very famous in South Africa since he had made large diamond finds in the last few years. The family took in this information and let their imaginations run wild. In their nightly conversations he became a "nouveau riche millionaire". The active imaginations of the younger members of the family embroidered the picture until they had completely the wrong idea of what the guest would be like. Naturally he would arrive with his own private chef and a huge staff. The story got wilder and wilder, and after a few days, they were convinced that he would bring two mistresses with him, a white one and a coloured one. At this stage, their father intervened and strictly forbade any further speculation about their guest. Nevertheless, the brothers still argued hotly about how many elephants their guest might have shot.

Obviously, in real life, Merensky was rather different from what they had imagined. Because of his quick exit from the Adlon, Merensky arrived somewhat earlier than expected, and there was nobody to fetch him from the station. He rented a car in Schwerin and arrived in Goldenbow practically unannounced and, of course, alone. The estate manager received him and telephoned Rodenwalde immediately. Since the head of the house, Henning von Bülow, was absent at that moment, his 17-year old son, Jürgen von Bülow, saddled a horse and rode over to Goldenbow to greet their guest and to see that everything was prepared to his satisfaction.

When he arrived, he saw someone wandering from the house to the stables, clearly one of the guest's servants. Jürgen von Bülow greeted him as he rode past and hastened to the house. He was surprised to be told that the man he had just passed outside was the new guest. General amazement grew when the estate manager's wife told people the next day that, after he had eaten the opulent supper she had prepared for him, Merensky had praised her culinary skills and had thanked her, but had then, very modestly and very kindly, asked whether she could also prepare good, wholesome, ordinary meals.

He would prefer plain food, because overly fancy dishes were not really to his taste.

The next surprise was reported by the head forester, a man who spoke little, but saw much. He had accompanied many gentlemen out hunting: experienced hunters and clumsy beginners; kindly elderly gentlemen and young whippersnappers whose behaviour displeased him, although he did not show his displeasure. He had expected the guest from South Africa to be a good shot, but he was surprised by the guest's open-mindedness and his interest in life in the Mecklenburg countryside. What really floored him was his discovery that this gentleman, who came from so far away, knew all about the German hunting world, knew about hunting seasons and when not to hunt and was knowledgeable about the need for and problems surrounding the care and protection of game. How was he to know that Merensky had learnt everything, but everything, that one could learn about hunting and forestry in the home of the parents of his friend von Thaer?

By this time, the von Bülows already had an inkling that the hunting guest they had agreed to host was somewhat different from the man they had expected. They left him alone for a few days to settle in and then invited Merensky to Rodenwalde for dinner. The family was eager to meet him. As so often in Merensky's life, his charm, his quite modest behaviour and the wise way in which he responded to individual people impressed his hosts. The children were admittedly somewhat disappointed, because they would have liked to hear something about the adventures that he must have had, but as always he was reticent when it came to telling people about his life in the veld.

The invitation was repeated. Henning von Bülow was three years older than Merensky and it was not long before the two old gentlemen had become friends. It was to become a lifelong friendship, even though they came from different worlds – Henning von Bülow, a refined nobleman and former gentleman-in-waiting to the Grand Duke of Mecklenburg-Schwerin and Hans Merensky, geologist from South Africa, famous discoverer and doctor honoris causa at the Technische Hochschule in Berlin. But perhaps it was precisely for that reason that they had a lot to talk about, and it was particularly the objective, clear way in which each spoke about his world that brought them closer together. They also discovered that they had several things in common. The prices of wood and agricultural products from Mecklenburg as raw materials depended on events in the markets and market conditions. There were several similarities with the ups and downs in the metal markets that Merensky had experienced, to his own cost.

The two gentlemen were to discover a very different and unexpected point of contact: They were both knowledgeable about wine and loved to philosophise about their preferences. Both regarded the wines from the Rheingau as the crowning glory of German viticulture, but beyond that, they disagreed. Merensky preferred the Steinberg from Kloster Eberbach, which he valued because these wines in their best years were expressive and richly spicy. By contrast, Henning von Bülow believed that Schloss Johannisberg produced the noblest of cultivars. They had long discussions on the matter. When they had exhausted all arguments based on the taste and had discussed the technical aspects of winemaking (without being able to convince each other of anything), they fell back on citing the history of wine. Von Bülow argued that, after all, it had been the Benedictine monks (who were truly the best viticulturists of all) who had planted the first vines on the Johannisberg. Merensky was not impressed, because, as he pointed out, the Steinberg had first been planted by Cistercian monks and the vineyard was at least as old as the Johannisberg. The fact that the Metternichs had taken over the Johannisberg did not convince Merensky of the superiority of the vineyard either. Von Bülow, who was cultured and well read, had many other arguments in his armoury. Merensky finally gave in when von Bülow brought the big guns of great literature into the field in defence of the Johannisberg and quoted Heinrich Heine:

*Mon Dieu, wenn ich doch*
*soviel Glauben in mir hätte,*
*dass ich Berge versetzen könnte,*
*der Johannisberg wäre just derjenige Berg,*
*den ich mir überall nachkommen ließe.*

["My God, if I had so much faith that I could move mountains, the Johannisberg would be exactly the mountain that I would want to follow me."]

It was a titanic struggle which was ultimately undecided, but it gave the two gentlemen an excuse to spend many mild summer evenings tasting wine and chatting about hunting and the way of the world, both in Rodenwalde and in Goldenbow.

Merensky became friendly with the children too. They admired him. First, there was the youngest daughter, Jutta von Bülow, who was 21 years old. She had got married the year before; and she and her husband stayed at Rodenwalde. Sometimes she had some business to do in Schwerin, where Merensky also had to go from time to time. Sometimes he needed ammunition, sometimes he fetched some wine that he had ordered to taste and sometimes he went to have a signature certified by a notary. Whatever the occasion, he did not miss an opportunity, after completing his business, to fetch the young woman and take her and some of her friends out for a meal. The ladies knew exactly where they wanted to go – the best restaurant in town, *Bei Uhles*. Afterwards, there would be a boating party and sometimes they stopped off at a *Konditorei* or coffee shop. When he greeted them in the late afternoon, he thanked them most cordially for their company and gave each of them a large *bonbonniere*. No wonder that they were delighted by so much gallantry. For Merensky, such afternoons were often quite tiring, as he still had hearing problems, and it was sometimes difficult for him to discern everything the merry young women said in the cheery chatter, but he thoroughly enjoyed the company of these carefree young people. He had not been this joyous and free of anxiety in years.

He hunted a lot in these weeks, and sometimes he was accompanied not by the head forester, but by the young Jürgen von Bülow. The hunting area was so large and the game was so shy at this time of year that a stranger to the woods needed a guide if he was to shoot anything at all. Usually they sat in the raised hide from early evening, and it could take a while for the game to become active. That left them a lot of time to talk.

Once Merensky asked his young companion what he wanted to do as a career. It turned out that everything had been discussed and decided in the family. The agricultural holdings would pass into the hands of Friedrich-Carl, Jürgen's older brother by nine years, and he, the younger, was to enter the diplomatic service. Considering his social skills, this seemed like a good choice, particularly when one considered the large number of well-known personalities that the family had produced since the early Middle Ages. In the past 120 years alone there had been five: Count von Bülow-Dennewitz, who refused to let Napoleon's troops under the command of Marshall Oudinot get through to Berlin at Großbeeren in 1813 and who, some months later, beat Marshall Ney at Dennewitz, and intervened at Waterloo at a decisive moment in the battle; the State Secretary for Foreign Affairs and Bismarck's close confidant, Bernhard Ernst von Bülow; his son, Bernhard Prince von Bülow, the Imperial Chancellor under Emperor William II; Karl von Bülow, the Field Marshall in the First World War, and finally, his own grandfather, who had been the Minister of State for Mecklenburg-Schwerin. But perhaps it was precisely this illustrious set of relatives that put off the young von Bülow. In any case, Merensky sensed that he was not entirely keen to take up a career as a diplomat. Some gentle probing revealed that Jürgen von Bülow wanted to farm, just simply farm! He did not want to live in Berlin or in any of the other capitals; he did not want to be walled in; he wanted to be in nature. He told Merensky this quietly, but clearly. Merensky thought back to when he had chosen his own profession. It was 36 years ago that he and his friend Albrecht von Thaer had sat in a hide on a similarly balmy summer night. Then he had realised that he had to take up a career in which he could be "free". "Anything, as long as I am not hemmed in," had been his motto from then on. He thought about his father, the missionary, whom he had told of his choice of career and his desire to be "free" soon after. The missionary had been a little surprised, because his other sons had picked more "traditional" professions: law, the church, the military. But then he had looked at his son seriously, and he had said: "If you are really sure that this is the right thing for you, then do it." And Merensky spoke the same words to the young von Bülow, encouraging him to make his dream come true. To encourage him further, he added: "If you do not know where to farm later, I have just bought a large farm in the Transvaal. There is a lot to do in the next few years. If you want, you can come there any time you wish. You can stay for two or three years, then at least you have seen something of the world – that is never wasted time, and then you can decide what you want to do next."

That is what happened. Not long after that, Jürgen von Bülow completed his *Abitur* and registered at the Agriculture Faculty in Bonn. After a few semesters Merensky arranged for him to go to

London to learn English. In 1935 he came to Westfalia. It did not take long for him to accustom himself to the work and, after two years, it was unthinkable that he would leave. Jürgen von Bülow became Merensky's right hand and stayed with him until the end of Merensky's life. He was also to be one of the four administrators of his estate.

Merensky had spoken to Jürgen von Bülow because he wanted to help this young person, who seemed to be worthy of the effort, to make a life decision. He did not know at that time that what he said would have a decisive effect on his own life.

For Merensky, 1929 was a turning point. He attained financial independence, passed financial decisions to his holding company, bought Westfalia, took time to take a breather in Germany and to clear his mind of the weight of all he had had to think about over the past few years, and now, there was the fortuitous encounter with this young man who was to become one of his most important co-workers. All this was a unified, coherent process. Merensky left behind his former sphere of activity; and when the year came to an end, he started a new stage in his life, one which was to be characterised by immense creativity. Admittedly, he was no longer young. He was 59 years old and had led a hard life. He was not worn out, especially not mentally, but his body could no longer take so much punishment that he could realise all the ideas that he was to have in the next few years all by himself. So it was a happy chance that he had this young man from Germany with him, an energetic man who could develop the enthusiasm to turn much of what Merensky dreamt of into reality and who was able to represent him effectively with his polished manner, both in negotiations and at social functions. Jürgen von Bülow was a lucky find for Merensky.

That summer in Mecklenburg was also significant for Merensky, because toward the end of his stay he decided to take up the option to purchase Rodenwalde. Love for the forest and for hunting was in his blood, and Rodenwalde met all his expectations regarding a hunting preserve. There was more. He liked the manor house because it was large and he could invite many guests there. There was a well-kept old park with a tennis court and beautifully laid out flower borders. He loved this rural and yet cultured atmosphere and so he arranged for the offer to purchase. The sale was signed before a notary on 24 February 1930. At that stage, Rodenwalde's hunting lease was valid until 1934, but Merensky used this opportunity to extend this lease, as well as the right to use the wood and timber resources at Goldenbow, by another 15 years – in other words, until 1949.

The purchase price for the 1100 hectare estate was 750 000 Reichsmark. That was a large sum, but it was still a good buy. Because of the agrarian crisis at the time, the price per hectare in Mecklenburg dropped from 1083 Reichsmark in 1928 to a mere 557 Reichsmark in 1932. According to the agreement, Merensky paid 584 000 Reichsmark cash and took over a mortgage to the value of 166 000 Reichsmark.

In the next few years, up to and including 1938, Merensky came back to Rodenwalde regularly to hunt, but never for very long, usually only for six to eight weeks. He never came alone, but always brought business friends and hunting guests. He was always accompanied by his nephew Carl-Theodor Klugkist, who now worked as his private secretary and took care of Merensky's business correspondence (which was considerable) even when he was away from home. Klugkist was one of the sons of Merensky's youngest sister. He had graduated in agriculture, and Merensky valued him because he worked so hard.

For Merensky, Rodenwalde was not just a hunting estate. He was very aware of his obligation to save the estate's substance. That is why he already invested about 400 000 Reichsmark in the first five years. This was spent on refurbishing the manor house, remodelling the outdated farm workers' cottages, the improvement of the land and the purchase of the newest agricultural machinery and equipment. Later, a new house for the forester and a new school in the village were built. We know about this because the leader of the national socialist Reichsstelle für Landbeschaffung [Office for Land Acquisition], which was constantly officially looking for inadequately managed lands to resettle them, took a position on Rodenwalde on 5 November 1935. It said: *"Die objektiven und subjektiven Voraussetzungen für eine Inanspruchnahme liegen vor. Der Betrieb wird jedoch infolge der außergewöhnlichen Aufwendungen des Besitzers für die Umsiedlung zu teuer."* ["The objective and subjective conditions for an expropriation and resettlement are present. However, because of the exceptional expenditure of the owner, the compensation to be paid will be too expensive."]

In the 1930s, Merensky purchased two more estates. He bought Süßwinkel, an estate near Breslau, from the Crown Prince of Saxony. The estate actively delivered agricultural and forestry produce and brought in revenue from the start. But here too, Merensky mainly bought the estate because of his passion for hunting. Between the two world wars, this estate was regarded as the best hunting ground for pheasants. Not satisfied with this, Merensky also bought the Gutzmin estate in Pommerania. It lay amidst great forests, and was pure forest land rich in red deer. Here too, Merensky had to invest a great deal. Originally the estate had belonged to a Herr von der Osten, who had been the Emperor's adjutant.

All three estates were lost to Merensky in 1945 at the end of the war. Süßwinkel and Gutzmin were in the provinces that fell to Poland and were expropriated. This invalidated Merensky's testamentary stipulations regarding these two estates. Süßwinkel was to go to the von Thaer family, to whom Merensky was still close until the end of his life. Gutzmin was intended for the eldest son of his younger brother, the pastor Ernst-Adolf Merensky.

Rodenwalde fell victim to land reform in the Soviet-occupied zone, where all estates and domains that had more than 100 hectares under cultivation were seized. There was partial compensation. Since Hans Merensky never married and had no children, during his lifetime he transferred his fortune to a trust, established under South African law. The Merensky Trust could therefore claim some compensation for damage and losses during and immediately after the Second World War. This claim was recognised in terms of the South African Custodian of Enemy Property and the Trust was paid £250 000. This sum only partially covers the claim. Discussions about further arrangements started with the German government after the German reunification, but the matter has not yet been resolved.

CHAPTER 17

# The creative farmer

After Merensky's return to the Transvaal, Westfalia became the focus of his life. He put all his energy into the farm. In the next few years he dedicated himself exclusively to this task. It may be hard to believe, but for several years he did not touch his geologist's hammer or his magnifying glass.

Some geologists prefer to skip this period in Hans Merensky's life. That is understandable if the focus is purely a paper on ore geology and industrial minerals. But if one wants to tell the story of Merensky's life, then the years he devoted exclusively to his farm are an essential part of the fuller picture. After all, he was more than a geologist, and in these years he was also to become an ecologist, a protector of nature, an agronomist and a cultivator of plants. He effectively took up a second career; and here too, he was to achieve exceptional successes.

It was obvious that once he had decided to rebuild Westfalia, he planned to realise something special. It was not that he wanted to build himself a home. A home, a place where he could rest and find peace, was never a priority to him (he never married). His thinking went much further. He wanted to leave something behind, something purely physical, that could convey a specific message. This thought matured over the years. The messages that he wanted to convey to the world were faith in progress and the conviction that it is worth working for progress. In this, Merensky followed in the footsteps of his father, who had also left behind something that testifies to progress, namely his mission station, Botshabelo. The mission station has stood for 140 years as testimony to the pioneering spirit of that generation. It has since been declared a South African national cultural monument and has become a popular tourist destination.

Although in the 1930s Westfalia became the place on which Merensky's thoughts centred, he did not stay there all the time. He travelled a lot, and regularly stayed in Johannesburg for weeks on end. There he did business and maintained his many contacts. He still enjoyed going to the Rand Club to see old acquaintances and to hear the newest rumours, but instead of staying there he rented a suite in the Carlton Hotel, which was close by. This hotel was the ideal backdrop against which he could meet his social obligations. Now he met Members of Parliament and Cabinet Ministers, knew all the financiers and was sought out by the "Rand Lords" and head geologists of the big mining firms, who all valued his experience and his considered opinion regarding the viability of mineral occurrences.

He combined business with pleasure in many of his invitations to the Carlton. These events were soon legendary for Merensky's generosity. The ambience was extremely elegant, and only the best food and drink were served. This reflected his sense of cultured hospitality. He would appear in impeccable tails with a piqué waistcoat; the women wore full evening dress and were each received with a bouquet of roses. Merensky liked giving compliments and could be very gallant on such occasions. Usually, in the course of the evening, he would also present the ladies with a "lucky stone" – an understatement typical of Merensky, since the lucky stone in question was a diamond, a sapphire or a ruby. Women who often graced these occasions could eventually boast a small collier!

Merensky knew what women liked, and his parties were not the only occasions on which he gave gems to them. When, for example, the South African Ladies' Tennis Team left for an international tournament, he could not resist giving each member of the team a tourmaline "for luck" before her departure.

Of course, on such an evening at the Carlton, the women in their turn wanted to ask Merensky all they had always wanted to know from him: "Dear Mr Merensky, how does one find diamonds?" He had a few standard answers ready to trot out, very charmingly, in response to such questions, for example: "Quite simply. With a pick and shovel, some patience and lots of luck!"

It was inevitable that the women would take the opportunity to ask some more personal questions that they had long wondered about and that their husbands could not enlighten them on, because men are not that interested in such questions: "Why, dear Mr Merensky, didn't you ever get married?" Here too, he would smile and say: "Well, you know, dear lady, when I was young, I was too poor to ask any young lady to marry me – I really could not have kept her in a style that would be worthy of her. And then I was never in the city for longer than three days at a time, and then I would be out in the veld for weeks. And if I had ever attracted any lady's attention, well, by the time I came back from the veld after three months, she would have found someone else long ago. And now – well, yes, now many women might like to marry me, but I do not know whether they really want to marry *me*." Then he would smile gently and return to the agenda.

Such a picture of his financial situation in his younger years was probably somewhat exaggerated, since he had had some good years before the First World War. But otherwise it was accurate. When Merensky was still in Germany as a student and young professional, he may well have thought of getting married once he had established himself professionally; but when in his first few years as a professional geologist he was always travelling in the veld, he reached the conclusion that this vagabond's life was incompatible with starting a family. Then came the very difficult years when he was bankrupt, when he was interned and the period after the war, when it would have been impossible to think of getting married. This was followed immediately by the relentless search for platinum and diamonds, which had required extreme physical and mental effort from him and had left no room for him to think about anything else. Now, at the start of the 1930s, he was free of such anxieties and his financial circumstances were good, but he was around 60 years old and he had found a lifestyle that suited him. He enjoyed pursuing his passion – hunting – with great intensity, and had become a confirmed bachelor.

However sociable Merensky was by nature and however sophisticated his social life in Johannesburg might have been, the luxury in which he lived there was not something he needed in his private life. There, he tended to be quite undemanding. He enjoyed the simple life as he knew it from his youth and as was customary on the farms.

That does not mean that on his farm he lived like a hermit. His life there was quite sociable. There were small get-togethers between the Europeans living and working on the farm; they met for sundowners; and there was, of course, the tennis court. Merensky liked playing tennis, but was not a crack player. Since he did not like losing (even great men have their weaknesses), he preferred to play against women. Since he was so charming about it, they were happy to oblige. All his friends' hints that he might learn more about the game if he took on better partners, were quite fruitless.

The tennis court was the only place where one ever saw Merensky without a tie. He even came to breakfast on the farm correctly dressed in a jacket, waistcoat and tie. On the many photographs from the time when he was prospecting for platinum and diamonds, even when panning, he is always correctly dressed and wears a tie.

The clearest example of Merensky's love of a simple life is the farmhouse on Westfalia, which was known as Top House because of its location. On the one hand, it was beautifully situated, looking out over a breathtaking vista of the widening valley and over the Lowveld. On the other hand, it was a simple farmhouse with a corrugated iron roof, and its only luxury was a wide veranda. This was typical of the simple architectural style of the time when the house was built in 1903. It had not been modernised, except that a telephone had been installed. Until his death, Merensky refused to change anything about the house. It was quite enough for him and met his modest needs – he was not demanding when it came to himself.

Merensky often had guests. Among them there were some important personages – the Governor and his wife, mining magnates and active or retired politicians such as General Smuts, who was one of his friends. These guests were housed in one of the houses built for one of the estate managers. These were noticeably larger and more modern than Top House. Merensky thought that that was only right, as the managers had families. By and by, the number of employees grew because other agricultural land was also managed from Westfalia. Several new houses were therefore built, and they were naturally equipped with all the modern conveniences of the 1930s. But none had a view like Top House.

The hospitality for which Westfalia was known has been preserved to this day. One of the managers' houses has been converted into a very pleasant guest house. In this guest house, there is a valuable old Chinese vase which came to Westfalia 30 years after Merensky's death, which reminds us of an episode from his life. We know that Merensky never hesitated to assist young people who seemed to be worth helping to get a start in their professional lives. Around 1929, his Silesian friend, Horst Correns (who was someone he knew from his youth and with whom he had often hunted), who worked as a district forest officer in Pommerania, wrote to him, asking Merensky whether he could do anything for his son. The son was then between 20 and 22 years old and was working in Hamburg as salesman in a position with very few prospects. Merensky took it for granted that he would try to help. Because of the economic depression he found no suitable position in South Africa and various references and recommendations sent to friends who traded in Bremen, Hamburg, London and East Africa did not have the desired results. There was much correspondence between Merensky, his friend Horst Correns and later also the son. Merensky continued to exhort the young man not to stop trying. As soon as the depression ended he would find something that met his expectations. Finally, in 1934, the young Correns started an import-export business in China. But soon there were new problems because the bank insisted on a sizeable start-up deposit to open an account for him. Since the young Correns could not raise such a sum, Merensky came to the rescue and lent him the money. It may have been £1000 or even £2000. Two years later, the young man was doing so well in his business that he could start to pay back the money. On this occasion he wrote to Merensky and thanked him again for his assistance. Merensky replied very cordially, and wrote, among other things: "*Sie brauchen mir nicht zu danken. Machen sie ihren Weg in der Welt, sie machen mir damit eine große Freude.*" ["You do not have to thank me. Make your way in the world, and you will give me much pleasure."]

Many of the handwritten letters that Merensky wrote in this exchange of letters survived. Thirty years after Merensky's death, Correns Jr., by then already quite a bit over 70, visited Westfalia and brought three gifts with him. The first was the antique Chinese vase; the second was Merensky's letters, which both father and son had kept carefully all those years; and the third was a set of photographs of Merensky. Among them there was one that shows him around 1893 as a practical mining trainee in Upper Silesia. He had sent this photograph to his friend Horst Correns. In his own archive, he did not have a print of this photograph, and until Correns Jr. donated it, no one else knew it existed. Without the letters that Correns Jr. brought with him, the entire episode would never have been known to us. That would have been a great pity, because it is so characteristic of the kind of person Merensky was. He helped many but did not speak of it, and did not like anyone to make a fuss of what he did.

Although Westfalia was known for its hospitality, the meals served on the farm were simple. No expensive delicacies were brought to the farm from elsewhere, because the farm was self-sufficient. There was a huge vegetable garden, which was very well kept, and thanks to Merensky's hard-working gardener, Zimmermann, there was almost every kind of vegetable. Merensky knew Zimmermann from the years 1914–1919, which they had spent together in the internment camp. When Merensky worked in the Alexander Bay area during 1927–28, he frequently had to go to Cape Town, Pretoria or Johannesburg for meetings. He employed Zimmermann as a driver because he needed a reliable chauffeur in those days. Trips to these meetings involved frequent drives during the night. Journeys would be organised in such a way that Merensky could join the meetings immediately after arrival at the destination. When Westfalia had been purchased, Zimmermann accompanied Merensky to the farm, attending (in the beginning probably also to other things) to the supervision, the care and the extension of the domestic garden. Being an enthusiastic gardener, this work soon became Zimmerman's main occupation – something that, from time to time, caused Merensky some small problems: Zimmermann could on occasion be quite stubborn and also showed it. This became especially evident when he was of the opinion that there was interference with his gardening work, or when, on occasion, his few helpers in the garden were commandeered for a short time from his keeping for urgent work at another place. On these occasions Zimmermann grumbled so vehemently that Merensky felt uncomfortable. Sometimes he even yielded and reversed his decision. This did not happen out of conviction but "for the sake of peace and quiet". There existed an interesting relationship between the two. They knew each other for more than 35 years and had worked closely together for over 20 years, and although they certainly were no friends, they respected each other. Merensky knew that he had a reliable chauffeur and an excellent gardener and Zimmermann was in turn conscious of the fact that he had a no-nonsense, clear-headed employer who, with regard to his employees, was always fair and consistent. Zimmerman was probably a few years younger than Merensky. He left the farm about one and a half years before Merensky's death for a well-deserved retirement.

Mrs Zimmermann was the housekeeper. The dishes that were served were simple ones, served on Boer farms for generations. They were what Merensky remembered from his childhood. They were also served when there were guests. Merensky sometimes joked about the simplicity of the life he led on the farm. He might comment, while receiving his guests: "You are now on a farm and your host is an old Bushman. Everything here is quite primitive, sorry." Or he might say, during the main course, looking about mischievously: "I can't wait to see what the pudding is tonight …" and then he would pause, and when the guests looked at him in anticipation, he would say, as if in passing, " … my cook can make two kinds of pudding."

He might joke about the food, but he took the intensive work needed to get the farm up to date and back to its former glory seriously.

The first task that Merensky undertook on Westfalia was to start the battle against aridity and continued bad soil erosion. Merensky had his own way of solving such issues. On the one hand, he favoured a scientific approach, and on the other hand, he realised full well that in agriculture there are no quick fixes. He knew that he would need to have patience and that time worked for the farmer, if he knew how to guide the process.

His approach meant first taking stock, then gathering additional facts, including observations and advice from elsewhere, and then thinking carefully about the whole thing. Where the matter was very complex, he consulted experts and, if necessary, instituted additional scientific studies. At last he reached a decision about what he wanted to do. Then he would run a small experiment. If the experiment was technically possible and promised to produce good results, the method would be implemented much more broadly and considerable amounts of money were poured in. From the start, the goal was to make the enterprise a profitable investment.

He acted accordingly. Stock-taking of Westfalia showed that the springs had dried up, and that many slopes had lost all grass and were rent by dongas caused by water erosion. The plantations had suffered badly. Many of the fruit trees were almost dead.

Then came a surprising discovery. These phenomena did not affect only Westfalia, but had also been noted on neighbouring farms. In some cases, the damage was so bad that some of the owners were about to sell up and leave.

From the outset, Merensky did not accept the widespread claim that it had been a bad year with less rain than usual. He was also not convinced that there had been a change in the climate. However, he wanted to check whether his suspicions were correct, and therefore he visited the mission stations in the surrounding areas. Generally, these stations measured precipitation and kept records that went back decades. The missionaries confirmed his suspicions. There had been good and bad years, but there was no indication that the rainfall had dropped considerably compared to that 30 or 40 years earlier.

Then he went to see the village elders in the area. This visit was not only to talk about the weather, but was also a formal call. Every time there was much lengthy talk. But it was worth it, because the people living in the villages were excellent observers of nature and they had a good memory for detail. In these conversations, there was general agreement that the streams had dried up about 15 years earlier. This had not happened suddenly, but came to pass gradually, and the stream beds had now been dry for about eight or ten years.

Merensky knew he could exclude geological factors. There were no earthquakes in this area. There had been no landslides and there was no mine in the vicinity that could have affected the groundwater levels.

The next stop would be to ascertain what human interventions there had been that might have had an effect. Merensky consulted experts. He discussed the problem with foresters and experts he went to see at the agricultural colleges. What had changed radically in the past ten to twenty years? They soon discovered the change: eucalyptus trees! Large tracts of land on Westfalia and the neighbouring farms had been planted with these trees in the past twenty years, because the sale of eucalyptus as a wood used in the mines was so profitable. The disadvantage was that eucalyptus trees need a very large amount of water to grow as quickly as they do. If the plantations are situated in the catchment areas of streams, the trees extract the water from the soil before the water reaches the springs and the streams and the areas down the slope from the plantations then dry up. That was what had happened on Westfalia and some of the neighbouring farms. Of course, Merensky acknowledged that the catchment areas could not be bare. The tropical cloudbursts that drenched Westfalia from time to time came down with such force that it was essential to protect the soil from the drops battering the earth by providing leaf cover. This implied a very delicate balance between planted areas and deforestation; and this balance had to be restored and then carefully maintained.

Once he had clarified all this, Merensky decided to thin out the eucalyptus plantations considerably in many places. Since such extensive forestry activity had already been started, he decided in addition to have the monotonous pine plantations (which had also been planted to supply timber) cut down, and had them replaced with indigenous trees. The rehabilitation of the plantations also affected two smallish neighbouring farms, which he bought up for this purpose. Due to these purchases and other acquisitions, Westfalia eventually grew to a very large farm of around 5000 hectares.

Merensky thought that these measures would take a long time to have an effect and he was surprised to find that there was a relatively rapid change. Already in the second year after the eucalyptus and pine trees had been cut back, the soil in the original catchment areas of the dried-up streams was more moist, and soon the streams began to flow again. At that time, Merensky was always accompanied in his inspections of the farm by his gardener and factotum, Zimmermann. He would carry a large bowl with him, in which, directed by Merensky, he was to try to catch the water produced by each spring. Merensky would stand next to him with a stopwatch and tried to measure and calculate how much water was produced per minute. This was a difficult procedure, and it never quite satisfied Merensky's need for exactitude. Nevertheless, the measurements they took eventually showed that the water levels were rising slowly but surely. A few years later, the water flow was regular enough to make it sensible to build a dam in the valley, along the road to Tzaneen, and to dam the water flow. This work was completed in 1936. Merensky paid the considerable sum of £40 000 for it. This was the same amount as he paid for Westfalia in 1930! But the investment was worth it, because it meant that the farm now had a permanent water reserve. Later, in dry years, the dam even supplied water to neighbouring farms. The dam, which is called the Hans Merensky Dam, is still operational today.

Admittedly, the dam brought its own set of problems. It silted up quickly. This phenomenon is common in dry areas everywhere. Because the soil is not trapped by much vegetation, when it does rain, a lot of soil is washed down any slope. Mudslides wash into the dams and fill them up quickly. This also happened here. The next urgent and essential step was to stop erosion on the slopes.

Some of the slopes endangered by erosion belonged to neighbouring farms. In order to have a free hand, Merensky leased these properties. There were other eroded places on his own farms, but these were in the environs of African villages. As with all large farms, the villagers concerned had been given certain surface areas to use as they saw fit. In return, they provided labour for farm work at fixed times. In almost all cases, these villages were situated on slopes or on the hilltops. The villagers had a very specific way of tending their land. Before they began to work the fields, they burnt weeds or bushes. This was not labour-intensive and was quick to do. But at the same time, it was a recipe for desertification. The first biggish shower of rain swept away the mineral-bearing ash and large amounts of topsoil. The problem was aggravated by the fact that the villagers owned large numbers of livestock, so that the land became overgrazed – which further destroyed the plant cover.

These circumstances forced Merensky to look at the agricultural techniques used by the indigenous population. Since he was primarily concerned with the rapid and lasting rehabilitation of the zones threatened by erosion, he offered the villagers an opportunity to resettle in the meadows down in the valley. These were more fertile and easier to tend. Once this process had been completed, he began to stabilise the slopes by planting grasses there, and this was successful. The sedimentation of the dam was drastically reduced, even though it could not be prevented completely.

In the course of this resettlement, the contractual labour conditions for the indigenous labourers were renegotiated – something that necessitated some intervention in the traditional lifestyle followed so far. This implied long discussions with the village elders before the changes could be implemented. Until that time, the villagers had to work on the farm for 90 days per year in return for having the right to live on the farm. Now Merensky took on the labourers, gave them fixed jobs and gave each of them a small piece of land that they could use for themselves. This land was easier to work than that previously allocated to them. Ultimately, that improved their standard of living. They learnt how to fertilise their fields and that meant that there was no further necessity to burn the fields, a tedious task. Both the resettlement and the employment of permanent labour were extremely significant for the development of the farm, because the new system meant that the labourers eventually developed a genuine sense of belonging to the farm.

Merensky did not think much of continuing to follow time-honoured but now slightly outdated pathways. "We are living in modern times," he said. "Today we have an opportunity to experiment with crops and plants that we did not know before or could not get here – and since that is possible and will promote progress, we should do it." The word "progress" had become one of his mantras.

From the mid-1930s, Merensky often had visitors on the farm who wanted to learn more about how he had counteracted soil erosion or about his cultivating, breeding and forestation programmes. When they were experts, he was happy to have them and he enjoyed discussing things with them. But if they were merely visitors who were curious to see the farm and all they could say after seeing it was how lovely the whole estate was, he withdrew into understatement, his favourite refuge. One of the comments he frequently resorted to was: "I am an old 'veld-man', I am a prospector, I am a farmer, but I am a dunce as far as money matters are concerned."

One of the many series of experiments that Merensky did was the planting and testing of grasses from the most varied sources. He experimented with all the kinds of grass that he could get hold of in South Africa and even ordered grass seeds from the Kalahari, from Rhodesia and East Africa. He realised that grasses had all kinds of functions. They helped to anchor the topsoil and protected the soil from being washed away, from drying out and from being eroded by wind. When they died and decayed, they added new minerals to the soil. Merensky saw the focused use of grasses as an absolute must. Even when he was a child, his father had taught him that every kind of grass found in the veld said something about the nature of the place where it grew. The inverse then also had to be true: for every place and every type of soil on Merensky's farm there had to be an optimal type of grass. He spared no effort to identify that type for each area. This eventually made Westfalia one of the best-known grass farms in South Africa. In the end, it supplied all the farms in the then north-eastern Transvaal with grass seeds. Merensky's first biographer, Olga Lehmann, recorded an event that occurred in his later years that shows how important the issue of grasses and their function was to him.

One of the visitors that often came to stay with him and that had become a close friend was General Jan Smuts. Their paths had often crossed, in good and in bad circumstances. Now the two elderly gentlemen sat on the veranda at Top House and their conversation was animated. What did they talk about? The one, a former Boer general, had been the South African Prime Minister for years; a close ally and friend of Churchill; a British General Field Marshall from 1942; one of the founding members of the United Nations and the initiator of the Preamble of the Charter of Human Rights of the United Nations, in short, an international statesman of note. The other had been awarded many academic honours, and was the most successful discoverer of mineral deposits and deposits of precious ore and gemstones that had ever lived. They spoke – the reader can probably guess – neither about politics nor about diamonds: they debated the characteristics of different grass species, the merits and disadvantages of this or that species, and with an intensity that would have been suited to any scientific colloquium.

Another area that concerned Merensky was his citrus plantation. Some slopes had already been planted with navel oranges in 1892, right at the outset of farming activities on this piece of land. Unfortunately, the trees did not bear much fruit, and the oranges were small and did not look very appetising. The manager responsible for the plantation was of the opinion that these trees should be replaced by new ones. Merensky did not agree, because he thought of things in the long term. He argued that if a tree could survive with poor care for so long and continued to bear fruit (albeit a poor crop), then that tree had enough vitality and was valuable. It had a root system that had developed for over 40 years. A young tree would need more than ten years to develop such a root system. No, these trees should not be replaced, but needed better nutrients.

The first thing he did was to terrace the eroded slopes on which the citrus trees stood. Then he added manure and phosphates to the soil, loosened the soil and sowed grass and peas between the trees to prevent the soil from drying out. The trees responded. They became stronger, the fruit was better and, over time, these rows of orange trees became a magnificent orange plantation.

In the course of this rehabilitation, Merensky was soon confronted with another problem. To supply the plantations with the necessary nutritive elements, he needed large amounts of compost and manure. This implied that he had to get some cattle. Over time, he bought three more farms, of which two were some distance from Westfalia: One of these farms, Vlakpoort, near Northam, was used only to breed cattle; the other, Kalkfontein, near Warmbaths (now Bela-Bela), was used to plant grass on a large scale as cattle feed.

One of Merensky's comments shows how important he believed fertilising the soil to be. When he was asked about his plans (his interlocutor expected him to say something about his next prospecting project), he answered with a straight face: "If I have any ambition, it is to produce 2000 tons of compost per year." He enjoyed giving such unexpected answers and leaving the person he was talking to quite speechless. But, in the end, he was merely telling the truth.

Merensky did not only want to plant things on Westfalia that had been planted there before, but also wanted to try something new. He had plenty of ideas. He was given new ideas through his numerous contacts with various universities, both in South Africa and in

Germany, and by his trips to Europe. Sometimes his co-workers just groaned when he came up with yet another new thing to try. Often they later had to admit that his notions could be realised. Once it was growing grenadillas; once he tried growing tremas trees, which provide a semi-soft wood eminently suitable for making boxes and simple planks. Today the Merensky Trust is the second largest supplier of timber in South Africa and besides wood used for props in South African mines, it supplies every kind of building timber, as well as high-quality wood for furniture, panelling, joinery, laminating and construction.

One of his ideas that initially seemed rather outlandish was the attempt to grow avocados on Westfalia. Avocados had been grown in South Africa before, but they were scarce. They were also quite expensive, if they appeared on the market at all. Merensky started some research on the matter. He discovered that most avocados were grown locally in Natal and in the eastern Transvaal and that there were about ten different varieties. He got hold of samples of each, and ordered root stocks from Mexico, Guatemala and the West Indies. He experimented with all these types and tried growing them in various places. Here too, he was successful. His plantations flourished. He was the first to cultivate avocados higher up on slopes – before that, they had only been planted in valleys. Today, 70 years later, Westfalia is the biggest avocado producer in Africa. A large percentage of the crop is exported.

Merensky was similarly successful in his endeavour to plant pecan nuts, which had not been planted in the region before. Twelve years later, the farm boasted 600 pecan trees, each of which produced 20 to 30 kilograms of pecans.

Of course, not all his ideas worked. There were a number of enterprises that he stopped after a while, as they did not go as he wanted. That included a brief involvement in the sugar industry. Through various transactions he had become a partner in a sugar cane plantation in Natal which was already showing some profit. Merensky dreamt of combining planting sugar cane with breeding cattle. He therefore imported Friesland breeding stock and conducted feeding experiments with the waste products of sugar cane processing. Since the experiment would have a significant impact on the entire region, he even attracted support from the Ministry of Agriculture. However, the other partners did not agree. They did not want to waste time on lengthy experiments but wanted to invest their profits in a chocolate factory. The capital investment could easily be calculated, and there would be a guaranteed buyer for the sugar that was produced. Merensky did not think in such short terms. He was not interested in being part-owner of a chocolate factory which was only run on commercial grounds, and so he sold his shares.

On the other hand, since he had attained his fortune, he did ensure that the enterprises he was engaged in were profitable, but always on the premise that they served progress in some way. He did not see profitability only in financial terms. There were cases where he saw the greatest profit to be an increase in the general welfare of the people and the evironment. An example of this is his involvement in bee-keeping. The impetus for this enterprise was the influx of wild bees to the farm in the dry years, so much so that they posed a threat to humans and livestock alike. Sometimes they frightened or stung teams of horses or mules so that they bolted, or swarms invaded the packing halls where oranges were being packed. The only way to protect the staff and animals from being attacked was to smoke out the bees' hives – a risky business, considering the fire hazard. On this occasion, Merensky noted that the local people absolutely adored wild honey.

When he noticed this, he saw it as an excellent opportunity to do something that would benefit the general state of health of the villagers. But before he acted, he wanted to check how much they really liked honey. So he put two pounds of sugar and a bottle with a pound of honey on a table. Then he asked first the black people working in his house, then farm workers and finally also a village elder that happened to visit him what he could give them as a gift – the sugar or the honey. They all wanted the honey and stuck to their choice even when he offered to increase the sugar on offer to three pounds. At four pounds of sugar, some hesitated, but only when the quantity of sugar offered was increased to five pounds did everybody decide to take the sugar rather than the honey. Despite the limited number of people he had asked, this was a conclusive result.

On the basis of these small-scale statiscics, Merensky could now put into action his plan to improve the villagers' nutrition in good faith. He did this in a way that was typical of the way he liked to work. First, he ordered books on bee-keeping and studied them thoroughly. These books are still on the shelves of his study in the Merensky Archive today. Then he sent three assistants to Pretoria to do an apiary course. When they returned, a number of hives were bought, apiaries were constructed and honey production was tried out on a small scale. When it worked as planned, 300 hives were set up on the farm, and soon he could market honey. About half was sold to cover the costs of producing the honey. He had the other half of the honey production distributed regularly to the villages. Financially speaking, keeping bees was not a profitable business, but for him the profit lay in broadening the local diet. Since he was also able to persuade the villagers to cultivate their own vegetable patches, after a few years the nutrition and health of the villagers living on his farm were noticeably better than those of people on the neighbouring farms.

Hans Merensky was generally and genuinely concerned with bringing about an improvement of the socio-economic conditions under which his farm labourers lived. He spent a lot of time teaching them more effective agricultural methods, for example by teaching them to plough and to erect windbreaks. In time, he was to expand this local endeavour, and established a training farm in the valley at Tzaneen which was designed to introduce improved farming techniques in the district as a whole.

Thanks to Merensky's impressive multi-sidedness and flexibility, his interests constantly continued to expand. That eventually inspired him to finance two purely scientific projects that were important for all of South Africa. The first study focused on whether the well-known uplift (or superswell) of the South African subcontinent, which had been proven beyond doubt by elevated old beaches and the elevation of the Oyster Line, resulted in continuous desiccation of the region or climate changes. He succeeded in involving the leading German geographer, Professor Erich Obst (1886–1981) from the Technical University of Hannover, and his then assistant, Professor Karl Kayser from the University of Munich, in this study. The first results were promising. Sadly, the project suffered a major setback. In 1939, the Second World War broke out. Unfortunately, all the scientific material that had been gathered was lost in a bomb attack on Hannover, including a manuscript for a twelve-volume textbook. However, the term *"Große Randstufe"* [Great Escarpment], coined by Professor Obst, was retained in scientific literature. The term refers to the elevation of the interior of the subcontinent all along the north-south line demarcated by the Drakensberg.

The second project was no less interesting. It focused on the strong sunlight in South Africa. Did it have an effect on people's health? This research was later expanded to include the health of animals and plants. The project was led by Professor Grober from the Institut für Klinische Medizin [Institute for Clinical Medicine] in Jena and the assistant in the Institut für Humanmedizin [Institute for Human Medicine], Frau Dr G. Riemerschmid, who set up six measuring stations in South Africa. Here too there were surprising and promising initial results, which showed that large parts of South Africa have a solar constant comparable to or better than that in the best European health resorts. Unfortunately this programme also fell through because of the war.

One of Hans Merensky's greatest achievements was his support of South African universities, with which he had constant scientific contact. He donated the University of Pretoria's library, which has been extended several times since. At the University of Stellenbosch, he made it possible to establish a Chair for Forestry and donated the money to erect the Hans Merensky Physics Block – which extended the study and research possibilities in the Natural Sciences at that university. As always, Merensky's eagerness to promote progress inspired his patronage of the sciences.

---

**Textbox 10 – Eucalyptus as timber**

Eucalyptus are indigenous to Australia and Polynesia. There are about 160 known types of eucalyptus; some trees, others shrubs. The trees grow very quickly. In timber plantations they can be cut down after only six to seven years. In terms of returns, this is an unusually short period. Because of this and a few other interesting properties, eucalyptus was exported and then planted in many other countries around the middle of the 19$^{th}$ century.

In Africa, eucalyptus wood was used to fire the first trains, notably where there were no local coal deposits. So, for example, the Belgians laid out eucalyptus plantations at regular intervals all along the Katanga line, which they had built to transport copper right across the Congo Basin to the Atlantic port of Matadi. In South Africa, the huge need for timber in the mines forced the cultivation of eucalyptus.

An interesting characteristic of eucalyptus is the exceptional hardness of the heartwood. If the trees are allowed to grow for longer, the wood can also be used as building timber or for railway sleepers. Some species boast a hard, reddish to pinkish grained wood. This is known in South Africa as "saligna" and is used for high quality furniture and panels. In addition, eucalyptus oil, which is extracted from eucalyptus leaves, has several medicinal and therapeutic uses.

Because they grow so quickly, eucalyptus trees need extremely large quantities of water. Depending on where they are planted, this can be an advantage or a disadvantage. In areas where water supplies are limited and must be shared with other plants, it is not unusual for too many eucalyptus trees per area to stunt the growth of other plants. On the other hand, in damp, feverishly hot depressions, eucalyptus stands can contribute to the reduction of excess damp. In some areas eucalyptus trees are therefore called "fever cure trees". On level valley floors, provided that the trees are not planted too close together, the trees can provide shade for other cultivars. The trees also drop lots of leaves and therefore protect the soil from drying out, creating a rich humus layer.

CHAPTER 18

# Gold in the Orange Free State

It took six or seven years to rehabilitate the soil and plantings on Westfalia to such an extent that Merensky could afford to take a breather. Of course, in the years that followed, he still had many more ideas to improve the structure of the farm and put these into action. But 1936 marked a little pause. The most important things had been done. Now the plantations had to be left to grow in peace and only supportive action had to be taken.

For Merensky, who was now 65 years old, this meant that he had time to think about other things again. It was natural that he should return to prospecting activities. For the people living on the farm – plantation managers, foresters and business employees – this came as a surprise. They all had only joined Merensky after he had acquired Westfalia. Among these people were Jürgen von Bülow, who had arrived in South Africa in 1935, and Carl-Theodor Klugkist, the son of Merensky's youngest sister Margarethe, who had joined Merensky in 1936. He was then 28 years old; and he had graduated as an agriculturist. Merensky employed him as his personal secretary, which made Klugkist one of Merensky's closest confidants.

These employees only knew Merensky as a passionate farmer. They knew that he had once discovered rich platinum and diamond deposits, but they had no real idea of how and where one found platinum or diamonds. The desert-like Namaqualand, which was far from the Transvaal, might as well have been on another planet. They were all convinced that his prospecting phase was long over and that Merensky had closed that chapter of his life.

From Merensky's perspective, things looked quite different. He might not have had any time in the past few years to work as a geologist himself, but he was fully informed at all times about any recent developments in the raw materials world. When he went to Johannesburg, he never failed to visit the Rand Club. He did so not purely for business reasons, but because he was by nature sociable and it was part of his personality to maintain his friendships and contacts. Thus he saw everybody who was anybody in the raw materials industry, as well as the chief engineers of the big firms, the geologists and the financiers quite regularly. Nor did he ever think himself above having a drink with a simple prospector who had just returned from the veld and who might look a bit ragged, and listening to his tales. This he did until the end of his life. He therefore always knew what was going on where, both on a large and a small scale.

That it was gold prospecting that led to his re-entry into the South African mining scene was caused by the fact that South African gold mining was experiencing an acute problem at that time. The mines in the central Witwatersrand were experiencing some declining results and there was an urgent need to find new high-quality mining possibilities.

Merensky had always been interested in prospecting for gold. First, there had been the matter of the Madagascar gold which had had such a significant effect on his life. Later he had prospected for gold in every part of the subcontinent, in South-West Africa (today Namibia), in Southern Rhodesia (in the gold fields that Carl Mauch had discovered) and, of course, in the Transvaal. In one of his first publications, which appeared in the *Transactions of the Geological Society of South Africa* in 1908, he had written about the gold occurrences of the Murchison Range in the north-eastern Transvaal.

At the start of the 1930s, it was precisely his lack of time to do geological work himself which made him do something that was to give an exceptional impetus to the South African gold mining industry. In 1930, a young German geophysicist and geologist, Dr Rudolf

Krahmann, came to see him. This young man had just immigrated to South Africa and brought with him an Ascania-Magnetometer, which had recently been developed in Germany. This instrument enabled him to follow the course of the magnetite-bearing slate of the Far West Rand (magnetite is a magnetic iron-bearing mineral), not only on the surface, but also where the layer dipped down deep under the surface and was covered by other rocks that had no magnetic properties. That was very interesting indeed, because the gold-bearing layers of the Witwatersrand usually lie at a certain distance under this magnetite-bearing layer. By determining how deep under the surface this layer was, one could also indirectly identify how deep down the gold-bearing layers were.

Merensky was a cautious geologist who was not quick to jump to enthusiastic conclusions. This was also true in this case, because at that stage this was just a new method which, it was hoped, would enable geologists to grope their way towards the gold-bearing reefs deep under the surface. On the other hand, he realised that this scientific approach was very promising and should really be pursued. So he did not hesitate to refer the young Dr Krahmann to two of the most able and energetic gold mining experts at that time, geologist Dr Leopold Reinicke and mining engineer G. Carlton Jones. Both worked for the Gold Fields Group. They took up the matter, and soon there was a new surge in geophysical depth exploration in the Transvaal. The result was the development of the (now famous) West Wits Line, about 90 kilometres to the west of Johannesburg, near Randfontein. Between 1934 and 1968, eight large gold mines became operational along this line. Their cumulative gold production has since reached a value of many billions of Rand.

Later in the 1930s prospecting continued and reached Klerksdorp, just 160 kilometres to the south-west of Johannesburg, close to the border between the Transvaal and the Orange Free State, where some gold had already been found in 1900.

At this time, a number of the trend-setting geologists wondered whether the gold-bearing reefs that dipped south and disappeared near Johannesburg might not come closer to the surface somewhere further south, in the Orange Free State. The idea was that the sequence of the Witwatersrand System might be shaped like a tilted "saucer", the northern edge of which cropped out near Johannesburg. Then the southern edge would be somewhere in the Orange Free State and – hopefully – would curve up to a depth that could be reached by mining. This problem could only be resolved by drilling. At this time, sinking a well in the extremely hard rock series in South Africa was still very difficult and very expensive. After all, no one could tell whether it would be possible to find the rocks of the Witwatersrand System deep below the surface at all. The risks of such a depth exploration were therefore considerable. If they drilled in the wrong place, all the capital invested in the process would be wasted.

It took some time before any company was willing to take such a risk. The company that did so was Wit Extensions, which acquired some options in 1934. These options were situated about 100 kilometres to the south of Klerksdorp, at Odendaalsrus. The company went into partnership with the Anglo French Exploration Company, and a year later the two firms started deep drilling on the farm Aandenk. The whole gold mining industry watched this undertaking with great interest, since it was concerned with nothing less than an attempt to find new mining possibilities for gold mining. There was therefore great disappointment when the Anglo French Exploration Company withdrew in 1936. This action caused Wit Extensions to become financially unstable. It eventually wanted to abandon the drilling operation altogether.

This was the situation when Merensky became involved. He also believed that the attempt to ascertain the whereabouts and layering of the gold-bearing strata by depth drilling would determine the future of gold mining in South Africa. Since he happened to be in Johannesburg, he decided at short notice to drive down to Odendaalsrus to have a look for himself. When he arrived in the area where the drilling was taking place, he found that it was not only financial restraints that were creating problems, but that the interpretation of the geological results had become guesswork. No one knew exactly at which part of the geological succession the drill had stopped. Consequently, no one had any idea of how much further they still had to go to perhaps reach the gold-bearing layers of the Witwatersrand System.

This was a critical situation. It was pointless to carry on drilling if one was not able to establish without doubt where one was within the geological system. The borehole should then be abandoned. But Merensky did not want things to get that far.

He therefore decided to stay on at Aandenk for a while longer and to take a very careful look at the drilling samples available. The samples – small and even tiny rock chips laid out in small heaps, aligned in rows next to the drilling rig – had been taken at one or two metre intervals while the drilling progressed. Examining them was a Sisyphean task. However, Merensky tackled this job with the same meticulous attention as many years earlier during his investigation of the dunes at Kolmanskop and later at Alexander Bay, when he looked at hundreds of sand samples under his magnifying glass. From the surface exposures further north he knew the sequence of layers of the Witwatersrand System quite well, like that of the Ventersdorp System which covered the Witwatersrand System, and so he succeeded in finding his way among the multitude of samples. At 830 metres, the drill had passed through the lava rocks of the Ventersdorp System and into the upper layer of the Upper Witwatersrand System below. Since then, drilling had continued another 400 metres and the drill was still in this formation. The gold-bearing layers, the so-called reefs, which – if they were there at all – would be in the deeper layers of the Witwatersrand System, had not yet been reached. Merensky was convinced that they should without a doubt continue to drill deeper.

He presented his findings to the managers of Wit Extensions, but the decision to abandon the borehole had already been made and was irreversible. Merensky believed the decision to be wrong. Since he wanted to prevent the abandonment of the operation at all costs, after a brief negotiation, he took over the terrain held by Wit Extensions and the entire drilling operation with a three-year option.

He had barely signed the option agreement when his decision became headlines in the Johannesburg press. The tenor was exaggerated: "Dr Merensky, the discoverer of platinum in the Bushveld and the diamonds at Alexander Bay, is about to discover significant gold occurrences in the Orange Free State." This kind of journalism made Merensky very angry. Once again there was a risk that people who knew nothing of geology would be driven to speculations in which they could only lose, and all because the press had mentioned his name in connection with the exploration. He denied the rumours.

Then he tried to explain that the drilling on Aandenk was purely exploratory, and was only intended to clarify what the sequence of layers in the Orange Free State was. It was completely unclear whether the drilling would uncover gold-bearing layers. The press could not ignore this corrective statement, but knew exactly how to rob his denial of any effect by adding comments. After all, Merensky had been lucky so often. Why should he, the well-known expert, risk many thousands of pounds if he did not have some concrete reason to hope that he would find a gold reef? And why had he added two further drilling operations to the one he had taken over? There had to be a reason! In short, he was not believed.

At precisely this time, the mining legislation in the Orange Free State changed. So far, the legislation had been rather anti-investment. Now it was adapted to match the stipulations that applied in the Transvaal. This did admittedly allow in some speculators, but the big gold mining companies were now showing an interest too. That was good news for Merensky, because it meant that he now had people to talk to about the progress of the exploratory drilling – people who took the matter seriously. In the course of such conversations he came into contact with the Anglo American Corporation of South Africa. They had just developed clearly improved drilling equipment and were using new, very effective drilling bits, ones which were not set with the large Brazilian diamonds, but with smaller South African diamonds, which were now in plentiful supply. For a start, the Anglo American Corporation cooperated financially with regard to the drilling technique. When this mining company indicated that it was interested in participating in the venture, at the start of 1937, Merensky took the opportunity to sell his option to Anglo American.

The rest of the story is quickly told. The big breakthrough came in 1939. On the farm St Helena, 28 kilometres further south, Western Holdings found the Basal Reef, which displayed good gold concentrations at that spot. During the Second World War, the exploratory work was almost completely stopped, but by then it was already known that the boreholes that Merensky had ordered to be sunk at Aandenk traversed a virtually identical geological succession. At the end of 1945, with only a small push deeper, the Basal Reef was reached on Aandenk. One year later, the first shaft in the

Odendaalsrus district was sunk. From then on the area has rapidly developed into one of the most important centres of South African gold mining.

Merensky made no (or in the best case, only a modest) gain from the sudden sale of his options. Nevertheless, experts agree that Merensky made an important contribution to the development of gold mining in the Orange Free State. His recognition that the drill hole was still above the reefs that were being sought was critical for all the work done after that. Even more important was the fact that at the decisive moment he prevented the exploratory drilling on the farm Aandenk from being abandoned. Without his intervention, the opening up of the Orange Free State gold field would have been delayed for many more years. Although all the mining companies were interested in the progress of the drilling, none of them could have acted as quickly and decisively as Merensy, in his capacity as individual entrepreneur, was able to do.

People have often wondered why Merensky sold his option so quickly. After all, as the later events were to prove, he had been absolutely correct with the additional drilling he started. There were three reasons why he sold at that stage.

First, Merensky had reached his original objective. He wanted to prevent the all-too-soon abandonment of the drilling started by Wit Extensions. He believed that this exploratory drilling was vital for the future of the South African gold mining industry. When Anglo American declared that it was prepared to take over his option and all the drilling, and when other mining companies began to be active in the Orange Free State, his presence was no longer essential. One must remember that throughout his life, Merensky never wanted to be actively involved in large scale mining. He refused such involvement after he had discovered the diamonds, just as he had done before when he had found platinum. For him that would have been a completely different line of business as the one to which he as a geologist was trained for and wanted to pursue. The fact that he was now wealthy did not change that. He was also glad to give up the option because depth prospecting that includes any drilling requires a very high financial investment. Most of his capital was invested in Westfalia and other projects. The means available to him were not unlimited.

The second reason was his deep-seated unease with any kind of media storm. One should not underestimate this motive at all. The many months that Merensky had spent in Alexander Bay, surrounded by disappointed, impoverished and despairing people, had made a strong impression on him. The miserable situation of these people then had been caused by the fact that they had responded to the exaggerated accounts in the press in which his discoveries and name had been mentioned. The fact that he had not been responsible for these reports did not matter to him. Now, once again, the press was publishing exaggerated headlines about him. He did not want to experience another situation such as that in Alexander Bay.

But there was a third reason, which was perhaps the most important. Merensky had in mind a completely different prospecting project. This was a project that he believed to be promising and that – however surprising this may sound – he regarded as more sensible than prospecting for gold. It was the search for chrome ores.

---

**Textbox 11 – Chrome ore deposits**

Chrome, a steel-grey, shiny heavy metal, has a specific mass of 7,19 and a melting point of about 1857°C. Its industrial significance is based on the fact that – together with nickel, cobalt, manganese, molybdenum, niobium, tantalium, vanadium and tungsten – it belongs to the group of metals used in the manufacture of stainless steel. The presence of chrome increases the compressive and tensile strength of steel and increases its resistance to metal wear and tear. Special types of steel with a higher chrome content can also resist rust, acidity and heat. Another important use of chrome is the chroming of metal and plastic surfaces.

Between 65% and 70% of the global utilisation of chrome ores is in the steel and metal processing industry. Here chrome cannot really be substituted with any other metal in the qualities that it gives special steel alloys. Another 15% to 20% of all the chrome mined is used in the chemical industry. Chrome oxide and chromates are primary materials used in the manufacture of pigments for paints and lacquers and in the tinting of glass. Chrome salts are used in tanning and in the manufacture of fungicides and substances to protect wood. The remaining 10% to 15% are used in the manufacture of fireproof materials. Because of the high melting point of chrome, and given its low chemical reactivity, chrome ores are used in the manufacture of fire-resistant stones and fire bricks and compressed fire-proof materials for smelting furnaces.

The element chrome occurs quite widely in the crust of the earth. Among the many chrome minerals that occur in nature, there is only one, chromite, which occurs in sufficiently compact amounts to allow the ore to be mined. Chrome ore deposits have been found in about 25 countries. Therefore it is unlikely that the ore will run out. Mineralogically speaking, chromite belongs to the spinel group. Chemically, it is a mixed crystal and its formula is $Cr_2O_3 \cdot FeO$. The chrome oxide ($Cr_2O_3$) can be replaced by varying amounts of aluminium oxide ($Al_2O_3$) or iron oxide ($Fe_2O_3$), and instead of FeO, magnesium oxide (MgO) may be present. The result of that is that there is practically no chrome ore that is like another and that the theoretically possible highest $Cr_2O_3$-content of 67,9% is almost never found in chromite in nature.

Chromite deposits are orthomagmatic. They are connected to basic and particularly ultrabasic rocks. We can distinguish between two broad main groups of chrome ore deposits. The first comprises lentil-shaped occurrences found in orogenetic zones. That means that they originated when mountain chains were formed. The most important deposits of this kind are found in Kazakhstan; and there are some in Albania, Russia, Turkey, Iran and in the Philippines. Often these deposits consist of a largish number of small ore bodies that lie more or less closely together, some containing only a few hundred, others several tens of thousands of tons of chromite ore. However, the metal concentrations are often very high. Until the development of the chrome ore deposits in the Bushveld, this kind of deposit was the exclusive supplier of chrome ores to the world market.

The second main group of chrome ore deposits are layered deposits. They are found in the Bushveld (an area stretching across Limpopo, the North West Province and Mpumalanga) and in Zimbabwe. The individual chromite seams are often only a few decimetres to a metre thick, seldom more. Often several seams lie on top of each other, and in many cases that means that they can be mined together. The metal concentrations of these ores are noticeably lower than those in the first type of deposits, which is found in orogenetic zones. However, the seams can be followed for kilometre after kilometre, so that the reserves in a deposit are vast. Worldwide, this type of deposit contains more than 90% of the available chrome ore resources. It was Merensky who was the first to examine and prospect this type of deposit, which had hitherto been regarded as uneconomic. This shift was to affect not only South Africa, but also the rest of the world.

CHAPTER 19

# New successes: chrome ores and vermiculite

Merensky arranged the handing over of his drilling on the farm Aandenk to the Anglo American Corporation. Then he went to the northern Transvaal without any delay. He wanted to look for chrome ore in that region. He had some big plans, and these were to become a prospecting campaign on a grand scale.

His interest in chrome ores was not sudden, but had grown over the years. The catalyst for this interest had been the conversations he had had with the South African politicians and industrial leaders since his return from Alexander Bay. They also discussed the necessity of industrialising the country and particularly of developing a steel industry. Merensky welcomed these notions. It was not that he had anything against mining platinum, gold or diamonds. He understood these branches of the economy to be very interesting in that they were very lucrative for the country and created employment. However, diamonds and precious metals were largely exported and were not processed in the country. The ability to process materials and manufacture things from them was exactly what the country needed. Only with the help of manufacturing industries could the wealth of the country be brought to the larger population. The first step was to develop a steel industry.

Now, in 1937, Merensky wanted to make a personal contribution to this industrial development. He wanted to identify chrome ore deposits and prepare them to be mined.

It has long been known that South Africa has chrome ores in the Bushveld. However, the first tentative attempts to mine the ore was only made in 1917, and the first real production – a modest 4570 tons – was only recorded in the official statistics in 1924.

Merensky was well equipped to prospect for chrome ores in the Bushveld in several ways. He knew the area well from the days when he had prospected for platinum there, perhaps better than anyone else. Then he had observed a number of chromite seams in the Lydenburg district, and he also knew that these seams lay below the Merensky Reef in the Bushveld's stratigraphical sequence. What he had to do now was to locate the areas in which the chromite seams were thickest and try to trace them over a longer distance.

By coincidence, his former prospector Busschau had brought to Merensky's notice the fact that the farm Jagdlust was for sale. This farm was situated on the eastern edge of the Bushveld, between Pietersburg (today Polokwane) and Lydenburg. There were known to be chrome ore occurrences in the area and to Merensky the farm seemed to be the ideal starting point for a prospecting campaign. He therefore decided to buy the farm – something he could do quite happily, since the farm met some of his agricultural needs as well. If he found no chrome ore, he could still use Jagdlust as a cattle farm.

The farm Jagdlust was, however, not the only starting point for his search for chrome ores. Merensky already owned another farm, Vlakpoort, on the western edge of the Bushveld, in the Rustenburg district. He was currently using Vlakpoort for cattle, but knew that there was a small chrome ore occurrence on the farm. To round off his interests in that area, he acquired digging rights on two neighbouring farms, Haakdoorndrift and Varkvlei. This enabled him to prospect for chrome ores on both sides of the Bushveld.

Promising results soon came from Jagdlust. With careful instructions as to what Merensky wanted done, his old confidant Busschau oversaw the field work. It did not take long to identify a group of chromite seams that lay close together. The largest had a thickness of just a metre; others were only 30, 20 or even just 10 centimetres thick. All in all, the seams added up to 2,40 metres. These chromite-bearing layers could be traced right across the farm to its boundaries. Merensky sensed that this could be a "large" deposit, and did not hesitate to buy up the neighbouring farm, Winterveld, too. Here too the chrome ore layers were well developed. The seams just did not appear to end! Eventually, they traced the ore-bearing layers on the surface for a stretch of 11,2 kilometres. From this line of outcrops, the chrome ore seams were dipping at angles between 10° and 20° to the west. A rough calculation showed that this was the biggest coherent chrome ore deposit found in the world thus far. Merensky was highly satisfied.

Now systematic testing analysis of the ores began. Merensky already guessed that the chromite concentrations would not be very high – and his suspicions were confirmed. The average concentration of the samples was around 46% $Cr_2O_3$; only an average ore quality. The good chrome ore deposits in the world had concentrations of 50% $Cr_2O_3$ and sometimes substantially more. It was such high-quality deposits that the big steel firms needed. When Busschau saw the analysis values, he was disappointed and wanted to stop prospecting. He did not believe that they would find a buyer for a chromite deposit with such low metal content.

Merensky saw things differently and remained confident. There were certainly a number of serious disadvantages to this deposit: The chromite content was not very high, the ore contained a lot of iron, the road infrastructure to the deposit was poor and the closest international port, Lourenço Marques (today Maputo), was 550 kilometres away. On the other hand, the ore mass available was huge. Merensky was sure that the industry would not ignore a deposit of this magnitude. Whoever invested here could count on many years of productive mining. In addition, the chromite seams were practically unfractured. There would therefore be no unpleasant surprises during the mining. With regard to the undesirably high iron content of the ore, Merensky relied on the ingenuity of the engineers. He was sure that metallurgists would soon develop processes that would be specifically designed for the Bushveld chromite. In short, it was only a question of time before these deposits would be mined and become one of the big suppliers to the world markets. Until then, he could use both farms for grazing. Thus they were not wasted money. He was in no rush to sell the chrome ore deposit.

Once again, Merensky was right. The exploitation of the occurrence was delayed by the outbreak of the Second World War. After the war there was no immediate demand for chrome. But in 1952, things began to change. One of the biggest United States steel companies, Union Carbide Corporation, purchased the deposit for £500 000.

The development continued. Today, chrome ore is mined not only in the areas that Merensky prospected, but also in many other places in the Bushveld. After Kazakhstan, South Africa is the richest country in the world when it comes to chrome ore and with regard to easily mined chrome ores with $Cr_2O_3$ concentrations between 44% and 46%, it is the world leader.

After successfully completing his prospecting, Merensky hurried back to his farm, where mountains of work awaited him. The big projects on Westfalia had been initiated, but there were innumerable details that had to be taken care of. There were new decisions to be made every day, and Merensky's people were glad that he was back to take the helm. From the perspective of the purely agriculturally-oriented team on Westfalia, the whole excursion to the "gold-drilling holes" in the Orange Free State was nothing more than an elderly gentleman's little hobby. They did not see any evidence of concrete results. As for the chrome ore expeditions – well, the "Doctor" (as they called Merensky) might see them as successful, but in the end all his efforts brought him nothing, other than a post-dated bill of exchange. The main effect of these excursions was, from their vantage point, that now they actually had two more farms to look after, Winterveld and Jagdlust. Of course, nobody at Westfalia would have dreamt of criticising Merensky's spontaneous prospecting excursions, but everyone took it for granted that his passion for prospecting had now been satisfied for ever. What else was he to look for, anyway? He had prospected successfully for every imaginable kind of metal, and all the big deposits in South Africa had been discovered already – or so they believed. In any case, in the spring of 1937 Merensky would have completed his 66th year. At that age, most other men would be enjoying their well-earned retirement.

But Merensky had no intention of retiring. For his age he was quite fit, and had no physical problems other than increasing deafness. He had also perfected the art of delegating time-consuming detail work so that he could conserve his energies and focus on the essentials. This was a technique he had always used, and it was part of his winning recipe.

Among the matters that he was particularly concerned about at the time was to find additional grazing closer to Westfalia than his farms in the Bushveld. In the spring of 1937, he therefore travelled about in the Lowveld east of Westfalia to see whether he could find a useful piece of land to buy for grazing. He was accompanied by an old acquaintance, Max Ruh, who knew the area well. They visited various farms, but found nothing that met Merensky's requirements.

When they were about to give up their quest, Merensky happened to ask Ruh in passing: "And is there nothing else here in this region that is interesting?"

Max Ruh shook his head, but then something jogged his memory, and he said: "I do not know whether it will interest you – do you remember old Cleveland? He is digging at Loolekop and he is looking for mica."

"And? Has he found anything?" Merensky asked. "So far, nothing," replied Max Ruh. "All he has found so far is that 'rotten mica'. That is probably like that new American stuff – you know what I mean, Doctor?"

Merensky pricked up his ears. He knew Loolekop. It was a small, conical hill, rising out of the dense bush in the Lowveld, and around it a variety of minerals had been found. However, so far, nobody had been able to prove that there was a specific deposit there. Merensky had also prospected there some time before the First World War, but all his digging had revealed was small quantities of copper ore. He remembered Cleveland. He was an individualistic prospector who worked alone and followed up on his own ideas, but he was hardworking and capable. If Cleveland had been digging there for some time, there had to be a real reason. As to the "rotten mica", the "new American stuff" as Max Ruh called it, Merensky knew immediately what he meant: vermiculite. This was a material that was only seldom seen in the field and usually only in small quantities. Many geologists had only seen it in geological sample collections. It had never been regarded as a useful mineral, but recently, in Montana in the United States, a large deposit of this mineral had been discovered for the first time, and suddenly everybody in expert circles was talking about the rare physical properties of vermiculite. If the material is heated suddenly, it expands to between ten and thirty times its original volume. Its unique properties make it suitable for numerous industrial applications.

Obviously, Merensky, who had never seen a largish vermiculite occurrence in the field, was immediately intrigued. They packed up and left, and reached Loolekop in the late afternoon. They hacked their way through the thick bush toward the hill, and found Cleveland in one of his prospecting trenches. He was pleased to have such a competent visitor.

"What do you think, Doctor?" the old prospector asked. Merensky climbed down into the trench, scraped some samples from the side wall and looked at them under his magnifying glass. Yes, this was indeed vermiculite and clearly in relatively good concentrations, in other words, with little admixture of clay or sand. "It looks good," he told Cleveland. But Cleveland shook his head. He was not satisfied with the results of his diggings. It was vermiculite, he knew that, but he was not looking for vermiculite. In any case, there was no market for it yet, at least not in South Africa. On the other hand, he reasoned, vermiculite was a form of mica, even if it was "rotten mica". That meant that somewhere lower down there had to be some mica that had not "rotted", and that was what he was after. There were enough buyers for mica. Merensky cautioned Cleveland gently. The vermiculite could go down 20 or even 50 metres and then there was no way to reach the rock below by means of a trench. Old Cleveland nodded: "You are probably right, Doctor. I have a feeling that I am not digging in the right place here."

Merensky returned to Westfalia deep in thought. The next morning, his managers asked whether he had found usable grazing. He shook his head, looking tired. Then something happened that alarmed his people at once. After breakfast he stayed out on the terrace and stared out over the valley, as if he was dreaming. By lunchtime he was still there. They knew the signs. This was the calm before the storm, or, to be more precise, the Doctor was hatching a new plan. They had some experience of this. Once it had been the plan for the avocados, then it had been the tremas trees and the time before that, the dam. This was the thinking phase, in which he thought through all the details and implications of a new project. This phase could last two or three days, then the plan was ready to be put into action, and then came a number of detailed instructions about what exactly had to be done. But was that possible? They had heard from Merensky's chauffeur that Merensky had been to Loolekop. Was he really thinking about another prospecting project?

Of course, that is what it was. Merensky had a lot to think about. Vermiculite was undoubtedly a very interesting mineral. But should he get involved? Since in South Africa there was no mining firm that was mining vermiculite yet, he would not only have to undertake the prospecting, but also the subsequent mining of the deposit. He had always managed to avoid such involvement. He could deal with the magnitude of the project – but what individual steps would he have to undertake? First, he would have to reach an agreement with Cleveland. That would probably not be difficult, because Cleveland was not interested in vermiculite and was almost ready to give up. Then he would have to investigate the immediate environment of the trenches. This was probably not a deposit that would stretch over ten or more kilometres, but it would have to be a few hundred metres in length to be classed as a proper deposit. Then he would have to go to Johannesburg and would have to secure a concession. Cleveland had told him that all the digging rights for the area were held by a syndicate that had secured the area in case of a large copper find. Cleveland only had temporary permission to look for mica, but nothing more. Thus Merensky would have to acquire the concession. That could probably be arranged. Next, he would have to look at the occurrence in detail. That should not be too expensive: with 20 to 25 workers, it would be possible to get a good overview of the deposit in about three months – if it was a deposit. They would have to test how deep the deposit went by drilling, or even better, by means of shafts. The real problems would probably only surface later. Cleveland was quite right – there was no market for vermiculite in South Africa yet. What made the whole thing so interesting, though, was the fact that one could use vermiculite for soil melioration, because it loosened the soil. Where better to demonstrate the usefulness of this mineral than at Westfalia? If he looked at things that way, there were several points in favour of the project. Of course, a demonstration of how to use vermiculite on Westfalia would not be enough. He would not only have to organise the exploitation of the mineral, but would also have to establish a marketing company that could sell the product. The company would have to market the product actively, convincing farmers and industry to make use of the numerous applications of vermiculite. Without such marketing, the whole enterprise would fail.

Three days later, Merensky was back at Loolekop. He quickly reached an agreement with Cleveland. Then Merensky examined the surrounding area. Starting from the existing trenches, he could trace the vermiculite for over a kilometre in one direction and following a perpendicular line for some hundred metres. It seemed that the surface of the occurrence formed a large oval. In every place in which he dug a little way down, he found small fragments or crumbs of vermiculite. That was enough for now.

Then he drove to Johannesburg and purchased the concession. Soon after that he began to investigate the terrain. The work was led by his assistant, Dr Hans Gelletich, one of those hard-working and capable young immigrants that Merensky helped at the start of their careers. His reasons for doing so were quite simple, but logical. In Merensky's words: "Capable and hard-working people deserve to be helped and the country will benefit if the expertise that they bring with them is used in the right way." Gelletich was born in Budapest in 1908, had studied geology in Austria and had come to South Africa in 1934. He had initially worked with Dr Rudolf Krahmann (one of the most renowned geophysicists in South African history) and had prospected for gold, but had then (probably on Merensky's advice) returned to Europe for a year, to graduate from Merensky's *alma mater*, Berlin-Charlottenburg. From 1937 to 1941 he worked for Merensky, at first prospecting for gold in the Orange Free State and then prospecting for chrome ore in the Bushveld. Now he worked very hard on consolidating the discovery of this vermiculite occurrence. He was to become more famous later, though, because he soon realised that Loolekop was not only geologically very interesting, but was archaeologically rich in prehistoric stone tools. He was very active in locating and archiving such tools, and when Dr Gelletich died a few years later (much too young) he left behind a significant collection of these tools.

The investigation of the vermiculite occurrence soon showed that the occurrence covered an area of more than a square kilometre. That was clearly much bigger than Merensky had expected. So it became another big prospecting campaign. All in all, his team dug

3000 exploratory pits. At 15 metres, the vermiculite was still present everywhere. It went down 24 metres in places, and even deeper in others.

This meant that it was an occurrence that in terms of its tonnage was comparable to the only other known deposit, at Libby in Montana. There was one essential difference: in Montana the vermiculite always occurred with some asbestos. At Loolekop, that was not the case. At the time, nobody paid much attention to this difference, but forty years later, when the health risks posed by asbestos became better known and asbestos was shunned, the asbestos content in the deposit at Libby led to this mine's premature closure. The real surprise regarding the Loolekop occurrence came from the laboratory tests. The value of such an occurrence depends particularly on the expansion factor of the vermiculite. The more the material expands when it is suddenly heated, the greater the number of applications. The American vermiculites had an expansion factor of 12 to 18, which was enormous. The vermiculite from Loolekop expanded its volume 26 times when it was shock-heated! The quality of this vermiculite far surpassed that of the American vermiculite. In the Lowveld, Merensky had discovered vermiculite of the best quality ever found at that time, in a deposit comparable to that in Montana.

---

**Textbox 12 – Vermiculite**

Vermiculite refers to a group of layered ferrous magnesium aluminium silicates that have absorbed water and incorporated it in their crystalline structure. Since the percentages of the main components of vermiculite – namely silicium oxide, aluminium oxide, iron oxide, magnesium oxide and water – vary in a considerable bandwidth, there is no uniform chemical formula that would apply to all types of vermiculites.

In the field, vermiculites look like scaly, flaky, loose soil-like aggregates, whitish yellow, often golden yellow, brown or grey, not very hard (1,5 Mohs) and with a density between 2 and 3. Laypeople who see it for the first time often describe it as "rotted mica".

Vermiculites are not primary components of rock, but are always converted materials that came about because water was later absorbed. The original minerals into which the water had been absorbed could have been biotite (an iron magnesium mica), phlogopite (a magnesium mica) or other basic silicates, such as amphibole, pyroxene, olivine or serpentine. The absorption of the water could have occurred as a result of weathering close to the surface and/or hydrothermal processes. (Watery hydrothermal solutions originate in magmatogenic processes, but tend to circulate further to much further from the originating magma chamber at temperatures of 150 to 450 °C. They play a deciding role as the medium of transport in the formation of certain ore deposits.) When the vermiculites absorb water, certain mineral transformations occur, including in particular the removal of potassium.

When vermiculite is suddenly shock heated, the intra-crystalline water evaporates. Since it cannot escape, this process results in an accordion-like expansion of the material, which puffs up perpendicular to the layered structure of the minerals. This very typical expansion upwards led to the name "vermiculite" (*vermiculus*, Latin = little worm), which was coined by T.H. Webb (1824). How much the vermiculite swells up essentially depends on the quantity of water absorbed. It can expand to between ten and thirty times its original volume. Then the specific mass of the materials drops from 2 or 3 to 0,016 or 0,064.

The expanded vermiculite is technically versatile. It is a material which conducts heat poorly and it has a fairly high sintering point of around 1050°C. This opens up multiple possibilities for use in thermal insulation and fire protection, often in places where asbestos was formerly used. Vermiculite is used in compressed fire-proof materials as insulation in industrial ovens and kilns and in chimneys. When it is mixed with cement, it functions well as fireproof plaster. In metallurgy it is used to coat pouring ladles and melting pots and to guide the cooling speed of large mouldings. It is particularly important in agriculture and horticulture, where it is used for melioration (a kind of soil improvement). Its high absorptive qualities make it possible for vermiculite to store large quantities of water without losing its loose consistency. It can therefore assist in the management of the hydrological balance and can be used as a carrier of fertilisers, herbicides and insecticides. When it is used as a packaging material, it provides thermal insulation and protects against shocks. If there is an accident, it can absorb dangerous liquids immediately. This quality is important in laboratory accidents and it is used, rather more mundanely, in cat litter in many households.

The world vermiculite production is now about 520 000 tons per year. Of this, about 36% comes from South Africa, almost exclusively from Phalaborwa (what was once called Loolekop), today the most important vermiculite deposit in the world. The USA produces 29% of the global supply. Most comes from South Carolina. The exploitation of the deposit at Libby in Montana, which was the largest vermiculite deposit in the period after the war, was stopped in 1990 because the vermiculite ore was contaminated by asbestos. At that time, the deposit could still have been mined for a further 35 years. There are smaller occurrences in Russia, China, Brazil and Zimbabwe.

CHAPTER 20

# The last coup

Time passed. On Westfalia there was unbelievably much to be done, because the various sidelines that had been added over the years had expanded the area under cultivation considerably. Then, suddenly, came September 1939 – war had again broken out in Europe. Like many others, Merensky was not prepared for this event at all, and he had no idea of the extent of what would happen.

He was even more surprised by the blow that was to strike him personally when war broke out. At the start of 1940, the authorities informed him that he should prepare himself to be transferred to an internment camp. Merensky was horrified. More than that – he was indignant, and deeply shocked. This could not be happening in a civilised state! The idea of putting him behind barbed wire a second time; he who had been born in South Africa and had devoted his entire career to this country; he who regarded himself as a South African as few others did; he who had done so much for this country. Throughout his life, Merensky was never arrogant or vain, but he knew exactly how valuable his discoveries had been, not just as personal successes, but as building blocks for South Africa's economic development. His friends and acquaintances were just as shocked.

All of them, even the younger ones, knew Merensky's life story, and the older ones remembered very well in what a terrible condition he had returned from the internment camp in 1919. It was unlikely that he would survive being interned a second time.

The scientific community responded very clearly to any hostility shown towards Merensky. The University of Pretoria awarded him a doctorate honoris causa on 9 December 1939, three months after the start of the war. The procedures to honour him in this way had been started months before, and the members of faculty saw no reason to abandon or postpone their plans to award him this honour merely because war had broken out.

The indirect honour conferred upon Hans Merensky by the Geological Society of South Africa was perhaps more subtle. Its president, R.T. Bridges, entitled his 1942 presidential address "The Geologist: His work in South Africa". In his speech he did not mention any names, but three quarters of his address focused on the superb discoveries of platinum in the Bushveld and diamonds in Alexander Bay. Every person in the audience knew who was meant and why the address was held.

In the end, Merensky was not interned. Instead, he was placed under house arrest. That meant that he was not allowed to leave Westfalia for the duration of the war. It is more or less certain that this decision was made because of the intervention of General Smuts, who was Minister of Justice on the day when war was declared and who became Prime Minister a few days later. For General Smuts it was not just a personal favour that he granted to Hans Merensky as his friend, but also a political decision. Smuts, who had been Prime Minister before, and who had been at the hub of political power for decades, was one of the people who could clearly recognise the significance of Merensky's discoveries for the future of South Africa. Perhaps he sensed that, although Merensky was already 68, he had not yet reached the end of the road as a geologist and discoverer and would still do even more for the country.

Jürgen von Bülow was not so fortunate. He had become one of Merensky's most important co-workers doing a number of successful experiments regarding the planting of eucalyptus, with the long-term aim of establishing large eucalyptus plantations. A year earlier, he had married the daughter of the geographer Professor Erich Obst (who came to South Africa in 1934/35 due to his involvement in the research project on the uplift of the South African subcontinent mentioned in Chapter 17). Now he had just become a father, and a short time afterwards, he was interned.

The same happened to Carl-Theodor Klugkist, whose internment was to end tragically. He died in 1943, during a stay in hospital. This was an enormous blow to Merensky, who had had great plans for Klugkist. For him, Klugkist was the only member of his family that he believed to be capable of taking his place in leading some of his enterprises. Even a few years later, Merensky was to write in a letter to a business acquaintance *"Klugkist fehlt mir doch sehr"* ["I do still miss Klugkist"].

For Merensky himself, house arrest on Westfalia was probably not the worst that could happen. He had everything he personally needed and he was surrounded by people who supported him unconditionally. The fact that many nationalities were represented among his staff played no role. At the start of the war Merensky had made it clear that everyone could have his or her own political opinion, but that he would not approve of any attempts to change anyone else's mind. That had been enough.

For the rest, Merensky was able to continue his agricultural and forestry development on Westfalia and the neighbouring farms without any constraints. Indeed, his projects developed very successfully during the war. Nevertheless, Merensky remained deeply angry and even bitter about the attempt to intern him again.

As it turned out, things are never as bad as they seem. Twice during the war the Government asked Merensky to give an expert appraisal of certain phosphate occurrences. What had happened?

During the early 1940s, with the Second World War continuing in Europe, South Africa had to make a number of significant decisions. From 1942 onward, the country began to suffer a shortage of superphosphate, a key fertiliser. South Africa had hardly any phosphate occurrences of its own, and until the autumn of 1939 it had met the local demand by importing phosphates from Morocco. These imported raw phosphates were then locally processed into superphosphate. When the war began, there were still large stockpiles of untreated raw phosphate. The regular delivery of further supplies stopped eventually, but it took some time before the stock of raw phosphate ran out. From the third year of the war, there was an acute shortage of fertilisers and this obviously resulted in great problems for agriculture in the country.

The phosphate ores that had been imported from Morocco until the start of the war came from very young geological formations, the Tertiary. There are practically no such phosphate ores in South Africa. However, in South Africa the crystalline basement contains occurrences of phosphate minerals, such as apatite, a calcium-fluorphosphate. It is possible to produce fertiliser from this mineral, even though it is more expensive and difficult to extract the phosphate from apatite than from phosphate ore derived from geologically young formations. The Soviet Union, which also has no young phosphate deposits, had used this procedure successfully and had managed to free itself from the need to import phosphates.

In South Africa, this idea had already been mooted in the early 1930s. In 1931, the South African Phosphate Company had prospected in the valley below Loolekop and had been able to prove the presence of phosphate-bearing rock. Two years of test mining had shown that it would not be profitable to extract these phosphates. The poor quality of the phosphate ores and the inadequate transport infrastructure made it impossible to establish an economically viable phosphate mining industry in what was then still a very isolated region.

It was this occurrence that the government sent Merensky to look at during the war when they realised that there would be a fertiliser shortage. He was to check whether it would be possible to mine the apatite now. Unfortunately, the reasons that had led to the closure of the pilot project ten years earlier still applied and the war-related shortages still carried weight. The appraisal was therefore negative. This was the right thing to do professionally, but the matter bothered Merensky, and it niggled at him. Since he was a farmer himself, he shared the suffering of his fellow farmers.

The war ended. Unfortunately, the general situation did not improve as quickly as people had hoped. The news that came from family and friends in Europe was worse. Like many people of German origins in South Africa, the United States and South America, Merensky took it for granted that he should send care parcels to Europe to relieve the acute food shortages. He did not send only one or two parcels every month, but 120 to 150. The list of people he supplied was long. In addition to his only surviving sister, his nephews and nieces and his Silesian friends, there were the Duke of Mecklenburg, with whom he had hunted, and the now elderly General von Lettow-Vorbeck, to whom he felt some obligation because his late brother Albert had been one of his confidants as a major in East Africa during the First World War.

Then came 1946. Merensky was turning 75. His employees regarded it as a matter of course that his career as an actively prospecting geologist was over, especially as there was so much to do at Westfalia. But once again, they were wrong. For Merensky, it was an absolutely absurd situation that South Africa, which was otherwise richly blessed in minerals and other raw materials, should be exposed to the risks of being dependent on imports for its phosphates. This situation gave him no rest and he had been brooding on it for years.

One morning he again stayed on the veranda after breakfast and stared down into the valley. Normally, at that time, he would go down into the citrus plantation or some other plantation or field to check on things. When he was still sitting there by noon, his people knew that it was not the view he so loved that was keeping him in his chair, but that a new planning phase had begun. What could it be this time? Nobody thought of prospecting, not even for a moment. Everybody was sure that he wanted to initiate a new agricultural project. This assumption was quite logical, because now, when peace had come, there were many new opportunities to order young plants from anywhere in the world, to import new machinery or to experiment with new methods for testing improved processes.

For a while, no one dared to interrupt Merensky's thoughts, but then von Bülow, who had rejoined Merensky, enquired what problem he was wrestling with. Merensky looked up and said, very quietly: "I *must* still find a large phosphate deposit …" Then, after a long pause, he added: "That will be my farewell gift." It was noticeable that Merensky, who was always extremely polite to people, and who had never told anyone that he must do anything, but always said, very amiably: "Would you do this or that …" had suddenly said: "I must." This was unusual for him, and so was the fact that he was determined to find a large deposit from the start. He put himself under enormous pressure, which he had never done before. Later he explained what he had been thinking about for so long: the crisis that had come about because of the shortage of fertilisers during the war, and which had caused a lot of damage, should never be repeated. He felt that this shortage had been like one of the biblical plagues of Egypt. It seemed almost grotesque to him that this could have happened in a country which was perhaps the richest in raw materials in the world. All that he and the many geologists working in South Africa had found in the past few decades, all the platinum, all the gold and all the diamonds, was meaningless if they could not find what they needed to enable the farmers to preserve their plantations, fields and grazing from desertification.

He knew exactly what he was looking for and where to look. He turned to von Bülow and said: "You know Loolekop, where we tested for vermiculite?" When von Bülow nodded, he said: "You can do me a huge favour by driving there and bringing me a particular rock. Climb up the hill from the back; there is a path that has been cut through the bush and that goes to the hilltop. You do not need to climb all the way to the top, but should stay at a level about 80 metres below the hilltop. Then you turn to the west and walk around the hill. After a couple of hundred metres, you will find a very conspicuous tree, quite windswept. It should still be there. When you reach the tree, you are almost there. You continue at the same level. About 200 metres along the slope, you will find a large rock with an irregular surface. When you look at it, you will see small greenish apatite crystals. That is the rock we are looking for. Will you bring me that rock?"

It would not have occurred to von Bülow to refuse to do anything Merensky wanted, but this time he was rather worried. He was not a geologist and, other than an introductory course in soil science he had done 15 years ago, he had had little contact with the subject. It was a daunting task to find a single, specific rock in the dense Lowveld bush, on a hill overgrown with thorn trees and shrubs. Therefore he asked, cautiously: "When did you see this rock?" Merensky thought back for a moment and then said: "I think it was 1908, but the tree should still be there and I don't think the rock could have moved."

Von Bülow left. As the crow flies, Loolekop is only about 100 kilometres away from Westfalia, but he knew that the road he was to take was much longer. When he arrived, Loolekop lay, as it had done for centuries, arid, under the blazing sun. The paths that had been cut through the thorn bush years before had become overgrown again and were no longer usable. Von Bülow fought his way to the hill. When he thought he had reached the right elevation, he tried to walk around the hill to the west – and, lo and behold, after a few hundred metres, he found a conspicuous, windswept old tree, standing out above the other vegetation. Another 200 metres on he reached a part of the slope without much vegetation where there were numerous small pieces of rock. Near the middle he saw a somewhat larger chunk of rock with a noticeably uneven, bumpy surface structure, but there was no sign of greenish apatite crystals such as Merensky had described. However, if any rock there was the one he meant, this had to be the one. It weighed almost 20 kilograms. Von Bülow dug out the rock, dragged it down the hill and loaded it into his car.

When von Bülow arrived back on Westfalia, Merensky had already gone to lie down for his afternoon nap. Von Bülow laid the rock on the veranda table, and then he sat down on one of the wicker chairs and waited to see what would happen next. Soon after half past three, Merensky reappeared. He had clearly slept well and was very cheerful. When he saw the rock on the table, he greeted it like an old friend whom he had not seen for 40 years: "Ah, that is our apatite rock, isn't it?" He turned to von Bülow, saying: "I hope it was not too difficult."

Von Bülow shook his head: "No, no, not difficult, but I did not see any green crystals!"

"Yes," Merensky said, "the rock is badly weathered. It has to be cleaved." He took his geological hammer and with two quick sharp blows, he split the rock. "There you can see the apatite," he said and pointed out some green speckles. Then he took his magnifying glass and looked at the freshly cleaved surface centimetre for centimetre. After a while he pushed the rock aside and said softly: "It is the best apatite ore we have – I think we should investigate it thoroughly."

From then on, things went quickly. Merensky already had a work plan in mind. He asked Von Bülow to leave for Loolekop the next week with 12 labourers and to clear the whole hilltop. He would join them in two weeks and would peg out the lines for the prospection trenches. At the same time, they decided not to make public the aim of the prospecting they would do, but to allow the labourers and outsiders to believe that they were digging for vermiculite again.

Merensky soon came to Loolekop. He spent a lot of time walking across the length and breadth of the terrain, taking soil samples and looking at them with his magnifying glass. After a few hours, he called von Bülow over and said: "A surface inspection makes me think that the apatite-bearing rock covers most of the hilltop. That is more than I thought. I think it will be worth checking this very carefully. That can take a year. We will put aside £30 000 for that; I think it will do."

Von Bülow was amazed. £30 000 was a vast sum. But then, had Merensky not spoken of a "big" deposit? Only – even a Merensky could not know whether a deposit was going to be big or small before testing began.

Irrespective of such speculations, Merensky immediately began to peg out the lines for the exploratory trenches, and by the end of the day, the hill was spiked with pegs. The work began and soon the marked terrain was criss-crossed by trenches. As soon as a trench reached a depth at which the rock was no longer mixed with loam and sand, samples were taken and prepared for analysis.

After a year, the hill looked like a battlefield with trenches and pockmarked by shells. There were trenches here, there and everywhere, piles of soil and multitudes of pegs, designated with numbers and tape in different colours. The workers no longer had any overview of where there was "good" or "less good" apatite ore. But Merensky knew exactly where anything was, and he worked with dozens of hand-drawn plans in which the trenches were marked and the results of the analyses were noted.

When the year was over, Merensky said: "This is not enough! I think we need to step up the work and use more labour. I think we should put in another £30 000." That was what happened next. Now there were 200 labourers working on the site. But that was not all – these labourers had to be supplied with food, drink and all the necessities. Loolekop lay deep in the bush; and it required an entire supply chain to keep the labourers supplied with everything they needed.

In the beginning, Merensky stayed in Westfalia and only drove out to Loolekop once a week to inspect the work and to pick areas where samples were to be taken. As the work progressed, he came back more often, and in the end he had a small wooden shack built for him on the hilltop, in which he then stayed overnight. He sat on an old crate covered with empty sacks. He lived there in conditions as spartan as those he had lived under in earlier days. Despite the blazing heat, he marched up and down between the individual trenches, looked at rock fragments under his magnifying glass and picked spots where samples were to be taken.

The reason for the fact that the investigation ran for more than the planned year was that the occurrence was markedly bigger than Merensky had initially thought. This meant that many more samples had to be sent for analysis than had originally been planned. In the course of the work, Merensky realised that he should not look at the terrain he was investigating in isolation. It was clearly part of a bigger structure that included Loolekop as a whole. The vermiculite deposit was part of the complex, as were the apatite occurences of the test mine from 1930 to 1932 in the valley below. Merensky commented: "The people from the South African Phosphate Company were not far out, there is a large phosphate occurrence here! They just began to prospect in the wrong place and then made the mistake of starting the test mining too early. They should have widened the radius of their field investigations." He did so himself and repeatedly found traces of copper minerals and finally also traces of radioactive minerals. This made the whole structure even more complex. It would be very interesting to resolve the relation between these finds, Merensky thought. He realised, however, that this would be a lengthy process. He had neither the time nor the means to do that. Therefore he concentrated on the apatite occurrences. He was convinced that the investigation of the other mineralisations would happen by itself when the mining of the phosphate ores began. He was proven right.

At the end of the second year the investigation was still not quite complete. The extent of the occurrence in terms of the surface it covered was now known, but the depth to which the deposit went still had to be tested. Merensky made available another £10 000 for this. For this investigation a drill was used, but this choice proved to be disadvantageous, because it took ages to get the drill to the site, which delayed the completion of the project. It might have been faster to dig test shafts. There were a number of other problems as well. Once, in the rainy season in summer, the Olifants and the Letaba rivers, both of which one had to cross to get to Loolekop, were in flood, which meant that the supplies could not get through. The foodstuffs had to be dropped from a plane. Another time, a whole set of analyses were faulty. Like any experienced field geologist, Merensky always sent some samples for a second analysis under another designation and so he had discovered that a whole series of results were now flawed. That could be resolved, but it cost time.

At last, after two and a half years, the prospecting work was completed. Merensky appeared to be very satisfied. His co-workers in the project, who had long since lost any real overview, asked him: "So, what have we found?" Merensky smiled and said: "You remember how much phosphate fertiliser South Africa needs per year ..." Of course, they did not know exactly how many tons that would be, but everyone knew that it would be vast quantities. "Well," said Merensky, "the apatite ores we have here at Loolekop will be enough to meet South Africa's phosphate needs for the next 100 years!" He said that quite calmly, without showing too much emotion.

Von Bülow and the others were all the more speechless. So this was the "big" phosphate deposit Merensky had spoken about two and a half years earlier. It was an unbelievable success. Before his people could break into jubilation, Merensky damped their enthusiasm with a pragmatic remark: yes, it was a big deposit, but that created a number of problems, precisely because of its dimensions. To mine the phosphates on their own would not help the country much. The phosphate ores had to be dressed and converted into superphosphate immediately. Then it would have to be transported and distributed to the rest of the country. There were many thousands of tons that had to be moved. Conversely, huge quantities of materials had to be brought to the area to start the mining process. In short, it was essential to build a railway system in the Lowveld to enable access to and transport from the area. It had to be planned in such a way that mass-produced goods could flow in both directions without any problems. An agrochemical industry also had to be established around Loolekop.

Merensky, who was always fully aware of the technical requirements and economic consequences whenever he was prospecting, could also name many relevant figures off the cuff. An investment of £12 to 20 million would be needed to develop the entire complex, that is the mining operations and the processing plant, the establishment of the agrochemical plants, including warehouses and the development of the infrastructure that was needed. In order for the various parts of the sub-projects to converge seamlessly, it was probably advisable for the backing to come from one source. Of course, from the very beginning, there had to be a comprehensive master plan. That was the only way to prevent costly misinvestments.

Merensky believed that a project of this magnitude had to be instituted by the state, because, although all his life he had worked in mining in the private sector, he felt that the decision as to whether an industrial centre should really arise around Loolekop was a matter of national interest. The development had to be desired and supported by the government. He explained all this in an impromptu speech to his co-workers and closed with the words: "Now we will have to see what we can do in Cape Town."

Unfortunately, his friend General Smuts had just stepped down from his position. Merensky therefore requested his long-time financial adviser, William Warmback, to contact the government on his behalf. Merensky did not want to make any profit from his phosphate prospecting. He was prepared to hand over the completely explored deposit to the government in return for the £80 000 he had spent. Warmback flew to Cape Town. When the politicians and ministers began to grasp how large the deposit was, they were both surprised and delighted. South Africa really needed a guaranteed source of phosphates, and that was what it had lacked during the war. But then, when the Minister of Finance, Nicolaas Christiaan Havenga, and William Warmback discussed the overall costs of the project, as projected by Merensky, the Minister of Finance got cold feet and decided that the State could not afford to participate in this huge undertaking. He gave Merensky permission to use the concession himself or to sell it, as he saw fit.

Merensky was disappointed when he was confronted with Havenga's decision. He was now 77 years old and physically weaker. He wanted to see the project get off the ground before he died. So he did not hesitate and made a public announcement that the deposit was for sale. The announcement created a sensation. A deposit with a supply guaranteed for 100 years, certified by the famous Merensky, was worthy of such notice. However, Merensky imposed some conditions: the potential buyer had to be able to supply the necessary capital to start the work, and had to be prepared to submit a project plan and a financial plan that covered the entire project.

The first person to approach him was Dr Hendrik Johannes van der Bijl, who ran the African Metal Corporation. The initial meetings were very promising, but then Dr Van der Bijl suddenly passed away, and Merensky had to look for someone else. Some smaller mining companies that expressed an interest were quickly excluded, because it did not seem likely that they would be able to raise the necessary capital. Merensky was determined to prevent the deposit from being passed from one company with low capital resources to another. That would have ruined the project's renown.

Then the Otavi Mining Company submitted an offer. Otavi was a noted mining company from the former German South-West Africa which had long ceased to be in German hands and which was now under the control of the South African Custodian of Enemy Property. The company would have been an interesting partner, both because of its financial background and because of its renown in mining circles. However, the Custodian was not prepared to allow Otavi Mining such a large investment, and in South Africa there were some reservations about allowing a former German company to operate on its soil, even if this was not said openly.

When this contact also failed him, Merensky instructed Jürgen von Bülow to approach Sir Ernest Oppenheimer, who immediately grasped the significance that such a large phosphate mine would have for South Africa. Preliminary discussions with Anglo American began, followed by a memorandum of understanding and then the establishment of a joint committee. With regard to the available know-how and the financial strength of the company, there could be no better partner. There was no other firm in South Africa that was quite as suited to undertake the planning and implementation of such a megaproject.

Soon after this, a number of influential voices were raised in the Ministry of Trade and in the Industrial Development Corporation against the decision that the Minister of Finance had made. Later, third parties claimed that these reservations were actually aimed at excluding Anglo American, or Oppenheimer himself. There was a rumour going round that there was some opposition to allowing Anglo American to take the lead in the South African fertiliser industry, in addition to its prominent position in the diamond and gold mining industry. In reality there is no evidence to support such claims. It is a fact, however, that there were grave differences between the Ministry of Finance and its opponents inside the government. The domestic finance experts did not want to face the costs and risks associated with the project and clung to the principle that mining is the prerogative of the private sector. From their point of view, the state should create the necessary framework, but should not get involved in mining projects.

There were a host of opposing arguments that were in favour of state involvement. The Ministry of Trade stated that it would save foreign exchange to the tune of £2,7 million if South Africa could stop importing raw phosphates. The state could then also control the price of the end products and could protect the farmers from excessive fertiliser costs. The Industrial Development Corporation also did not want to pass up a chance to develop the hitherto neglected north-eastern parts of the country.

To get its foot in the door, the Industrial Development Corporation started by buying the Phalaborwa Phosphate & Vermiculite Company's rights to mine phosphate. For these rights, it paid £350 000. This company was one of the two small mining companies that were mining vermiculite at Loolekop, aside from the much larger operation that belonged to Merensky.

When Merensky heard about this sale, he was visibly annoyed. He was particularly irritated by the fact that the government could be so uncoordinated internally. But after thinking it over for a while, he said: "Well, I suppose then that we will eventually get to where we want to be." With that he meant his notion that a project of such national significance needed to be planned at a national level and be supported by the state. He decided that if the government wanted the phosphate project after all, it should have it. Von Bülow, who was often Merensky's diplomatic representative, was given the thankless task of informing Sir Ernest Oppenheimer of Merensky's decision. Oppenheimer was not at all pleased with the withdrawal of Merensky's offer, but he was enough of a pragmatist to accept the situation.

Now Merensky's advisers began to negotiate with the government. The original offer to give the government the phosphate rights at a price which would just cover Merensky's original outlay of £80 000 was not upheld. Merensky now wanted £370 000. He argued that the Phalaborwa Phosphate & Vermiculite Company was smaller than his enterprise and had far smaller phosphate reserves, and the State had paid £350 000 for the rights held by that company. He did not drive the prices – the price had been suggested by the government's own choices. Because the government wanted to get the whole business over and done with without too much fuss and media attention, Merensky's suggested price was accepted.

The newly founded state-owned Phosphate Development Corporation took over the phosphate rights. However, Merensky's Transvaal Ore Company kept the central triangle at Loolekop in which the vermiculite pit was and for which Merensky owned all other digging rights. This was to be significant, because some time later this area proved to be the centre of the copper mineralization and became very valuable indeed.

An agreement of such financial dimensions naturally had to be ratified by the Cabinet. Because the Minister of Finance couldn't be reached, the Minister of Economic Affairs, Hon. E. Louw, had to explain the dossier to the Cabinet. Later he admitted that he had had a rather hollow feeling, considering the vast sum involved that had to be debated. A year later, however, it was clear that by adding this point to the agenda he had set in motion a very profitable deal for the government. The agreement had barely been signed before the government began to work on a master plan to develop the project and the region as a whole. Renowned experts and engineering bureaux were involved. Such a master plan obviously also included a rechecking of the ore reserves. The result was sensational. The value of the deposit was estimated to be £300 million. That was more than 400 times the price that the government had paid both companies for their phosphate rights. The next day the press reported on it, and not long after that the news reached Westfalia over the telephone. When the call came through, Merensky was out doing his morning rounds in the plantations. When he came in, his co-workers told him the news, visibly worked up at the vast sum. Merensky nodded amiably and said that he had expected that. He added: "It was supposed to be a gift after all – a farewell gift …"

CHAPTER 21

# The last years

When the sales agreement for the phosphate concession was signed, it lifted a huge weight from Merensky's shoulders. There had been moments during the work on Loolekop when he had doubted whether he would be able to complete this project. From the start of the project he had known that the deposit was a good one, but he had wondered whether at the end of the prospecting phase it would be possible to develop the deposit speedily enough for him to still see the start of phosphate production.

This anxiety was not unjustified, because throughout the entire prospecting period on Loolekop he had been pushing himself to the limits of his physical endurance. His family doctor, who came to see him regularly and had been doing so for a while, had taken a strong line against any major exertion. He had expressed this warning more or less at the time as when Merensky decided to undertake the prospecting. The occasion for this warning had been a light case of bronchitis which the patient had been suffering from for some time and which did not seem to want to clear up. This worried the doctor. But Merensky vehemently rejected any hint that he should restrict any of his activities. After all, he was "only 75". More than that – he invited the doctor to join him for a cup of tea and then very cordially explained what he planned to do for the next few months and how important this undertaking was. Since the entire prospecting plan was already mature by the time he first mentioned it, he was able to present his plans with enormous enthusiasm and conviction. When he described the objectives of a prospecting project, he was always eloquent, but the doctor was not impressed, because he and his patient were operating in completely different worlds when it came to this matter. So Merensky was surprised to find that after their conversation over the teacups the doctor was not as enthusiastic as Merensky about his plans. Instead, the doctor said dryly: "Nevertheless, I think you should go down to the coast. You need a holiday and you need a change of air. At your age you must make the time for that."

The punishment for being so foolishly recalcitrant – because that is what Merensky was – soon followed. A few days later the bronchitis had worsened to include a severe ear infection on both sides, accompanied by a dreadful headache, and eventually both eardrums burst. It took some time for Merensky to recover a bit, and that delayed the start of the digging. Then he drove out to Loolekop every few days, but that was tiring, since he only left in the evening and was then on the road for much of the night. When he had the hut built on Loolekop for himself, things were not much better: in the summer months, in daytime, it was unbearably hot in the simple wooden structure. There were some days on which he was so exhausted that he did not even manage to walk between the individual trenches (this was not easy in any case, as there were huge piles of excavated soil that he had to walk around or climb over). Hence, he had someone carry him from one trench to the next and sometimes to a tree, to rest a little in the shade.

Merensky wanted to reach his goal of developing Loolekop into a phosphate deposit at any cost, come what may. For a long time he refused to admit that he would probably not be able to complete his plans in his current state of health. His family doctor warned him repeatedly, but Merensky was resistant to any advice. Fortunately, a total collapse could be averted. At some point the doctor finally succeeded in sending a very weakened Merensky south for six weeks, to the Cape, where he could recuperate in a healthier climate. This "dedication to his work" was only too reminiscent of his behaviour after the accident with the mule cart while he was prospecting for platinum and in which he had broken some ribs. The difference was that then he was 23 years younger and had far greater physical reserves.

The prospecting continued in his enforced absence. Of course, Merensky wanted to know exactly what was going on, almost hour by hour and blow by blow. Thus, almost every day the newest analysis results and the sketches of the places where the samples had been taken, were sent to him. In turn, he bombarded von Bülow with telegrams. Twice in these six weeks, von Bülow had to drive down to the Cape to take Merensky rock samples and plans to appraise. Each of the two round trips took von Bülow more than 4000 kilometres.

It is therefore understandable that Merensky was relieved about the signing of the agreement with the government. Now he finally returned to Westfalia. There, lovingly taken care of by his people, his health improved. He knew that he did not have much time left, but he was not anxious – he knew that his life's work was done.

Then he had another success after all: he was able to sell his chrome deposits on his farms Jagdlust and Winterveld. The sale was initiated by von Bülow, who often had to complete difficult missions on Merensky's behalf. In December 1951 the American geologist Eugene N. Cameron (1910–1999), Professor of Economic Geology at the University of Wisconsin, passed through Johannesburg. He stayed with von Bülow. Cameron was on the way to Southern Rhodesia to look for chrome ore deposits in his capacity of consultant for the Union Carbide Corporation. The Americans had thus far sourced their chrome ores mainly from the Philippines and Turkey, but they did not regard either of these two sources as entirely secure; and they were looking for an additional source in a Third World country. Von Bülow drew Cameron's attention to the considerable advantages of looking at the chrome ores of the Bushveld, and then things snowballed. The American inspected both farms. Then he visited Merensky in Westfalia. He returned there at the start of 1952. Negotiations began, and soon they had agreed to a price of £500 000. The sales agreement was signed four weeks before Merensky's death.

As always when a deal was concluded successfully, Merensky rewarded those who had helped to create this success. These rewards usually took the form of a cash payout, but could also be remission of a loan he had made to a co-worker to buy a house in Johannesburg or something like that.

Merensky did not plan any new undertakings after his return from Loolekop. From now on, he was concerned mainly with putting his affairs in order and finalising his plans about how to leave everything after his death. He had begun to put things in order some years before and his last will and testament contained detailed and carefully thought-through testamentary stipulations and was fixed by the establishment of a trust (later turned into a foundation). What remained to be done was to discuss the last details and to fix who was authorised to deal with what during the transitional period. Thus 1951 became crucial to the arrangements for Merensky's succession. Von Bülow acted as the General Manager for the Transvaal Ore Company and was responsible for the forestry business, Max Ruh was in charge of the vermiculite mining on site and the newly appointed Dr J.C. Fick (previously appointed by the Ministry of Agriculture in Pretoria) became Westfalia's manager-in-chief.

Merensky wanted to ensure that the farm would continue to be developed along the lines he wanted even after his death. In the last months of his life he therefore had many individual conversations with his farm employees. In these discussions, he impressed upon them the importance of caring particularly for this or that part of the plantations after his death or to pay particular attention to something. Occasionally, he also urged them to continue the experiments with the planting of various types of grass. Or he reminded them that the citrus plantations required particularly intensive care. Or he pointed out that some time in the next few years, dams should be built in two places that had already been identified; or that the planting of trees in the newly established eucalyptus forests should be consistently continued. Above all, the marketing of the trees was to be done very selectively. Basically, the plantations should be thinned out after seven or eight years, but some trees should be left for about twenty years so that they could be sold for high quality building timber. He was particularly concerned about the care for the indigenous African domesticated cattle and the Namaqualand ponies. Both breeds were resistant to many diseases, and Merensky had noted with concern that these animal breeds, kept by the indigenous local people, were endangered. There was good reason to believe that, unless something was done to preserve them, both breeds would soon become extinct. Kalkfontein, one of his grazing farms, was to be a refuge for these endangered breeds. Later, when there was greater understanding and tolerance for such matters, they could be used in experiments to cross these breeds with European ones to create a new, disease-resistant cross-breed. Merensky's interest in these cross-breed trials went back to a family tradition. His father had also looked into the matter very closely and 60 years earlier had published a scientific article on the "*Akklimatisation des Pferdes in Südafrika*" ["Acclimatisation of the horse in South Africa"].

Merensky repeatedly discussed all these ideas that he had for Westfalia with his divisional managers, von Bülow and the other leading figures in his employment. None of these conversations left the people he was speaking to with a sense of his giving orders for the years after his death. He much preferred to persuade his people that what he was suggesting was what was best for the development of the farm.

Many such conversations have been retold, but many more reports and short anecdotes from the last ten years of Merensky's life have been preserved that highlight his human traits. We have to thank Merensky's first biographer, Olga Lehmann, for noting down all these anecdotes. Her book appeared three years after his death and she was able to interview many of his contemporaries and people who knew him when she was researching her book.

Some of these reports confirm Merensky's always discreetly caring attitude to his co-workers, irrespective of whether they were of European or African origin. Once, for example, the wife of one of his employees needed an expensive operation. Merensky encouraged the husband to make all the necessary arrangements at once – after all, he said, the cost was not a problem, as the husband was owed a bonus anyway. The man knew nothing about any bonus, but at the end of the month the extra payment appeared on his salary slip. The bonus covered the cost of the operation and the hospital bill almost exactly – probably no coincidence.

On another occasion, Merensky heard that one of the children of one of his employees had an exceptionally bad attack of malaria. As his family doctor was just coming to see him, he did not even let the doctor get out of his car but got in and immediately took him to the house where the child was. Apologising profusely for his unannounced visit and for intruding and for bringing someone with him as well, he had the doctor check on the child. The diagnosis revealed that the child was not suffering from malaria, but from advanced blood poisoning. Merensky was now able to organise that the child be taken to hospital immediately, saving the child's life.

Another trait that emerges from these stories is the empathetic sense of humour with which he responded to small mishaps. For many years, he had urged the African women in the nearby kraals to plant vegetable patches. He hoped that this would improve the nutrition of the local Africans. At the same time he wanted to give the women a chance to sell some of their vegetables to earn some money of their own. To encourage them, he had promised to buy their surplus vegetable supplies at any time. One day, a boy brought him a bowl of healthy-looking beans. He was paid. Three days later he brought some more, and a few days later another supply. Merensky showed his pleasure, but then he was told that the boy had secretly picked the beans in Merenky's own kitchen garden. Now Merensky was in a double bind. On the one hand, stealing a few apples and pears (and in this case beans) was a pardonable sin, especially in a ten-year-old. On the other hand, he had to act, not least because his gardener, Zimmermann, was very angry and had said so; his garden meant everything to him. He and Merensky had known each other for a very long time and had become close over all these years. Mrs Zimmermann was in charge of Merensky's bachelor household. He did not want to upset either of them, so he looked stern and stressed that something like this should not be allowed to happen again. When Zimmermann had left, he told his estate manager in a much milder tone: "Very shrewd, this boy. But I suppose his business sense is good ... And picking beans is quite a lot of work, so he is not lazy – and that is the main thing."

Sometimes his sense of humour was quite mischievous. One day a truck driver came to see him, and told him in great detail that his vehicle had been stolen. He claimed that he had often driven on farm business. Now, he said, he had lost his source of income. Could Merensky help him? Merensky could not remember ever having seen the driver. He asked what the registration number was, and while

Merensky chatted to the driver, his secretary made a telephone call or two and discovered that the registration number they had been given did not exist and that the police concerned, in Duiwelskloof, knew nothing about any such car theft. The secretary passed her employer a note telling him this. When Merensky had skimmed the note, he spread his arms expressively, and smilingly told the driver: "You are a lucky man! The police have let me know that your vehicle has been found and that they have it at the station. All you have to do is pick it up – but first, have a cup of tea with me!"

However, Merensky did not always react quite as humorously, especially when he was importuned very rudely. Robbie Maddison – a young man who had started to work on the farm just after the Second World War – told of such an occasion. One Sunday, he sat in the farm's gatehouse when two unannounced visitors arrived and insisted on seeing Merensky. They had something important to show him, they said. Robbie telephoned the Top House, but Merensky declined to see these people he did not know. However, they kept on insisting and forced Robbie to call the main house a second and even a third time. When Merensky realised that Robbie Maddison could not get rid of these unwelcome guests, he instructed Robbie to bring them up to the house. He received the two on the veranda, standing, with an unmoved face. As soon as they stepped onto the veranda, the houseboy appeared and asked what he could bring them. It was customary in hot countries to offer guests or even strangers that came to one's house something to drink. Unsmilingly, Merensky said: "Water for the gentlemen, tea for Robbie and me." Then he turned to the visitors: "What brings you to see me?"

One of them took a small packet from his jacket pocket and clumsily unwrapped several layers of newspaper to reveal an ore sample that shimmered golden yellow. He held it out to Merensky, who stood unmoved and only said: "And?" What followed was, as Merensky had expected, a lengthy explanation. They had worked in the Lowveld (they mentioned a very isolated area). They said that they had found copper ores. Merensky took the sample, picked up a magnifying glass from a side table and looked carefully at the sample. Then he gave it back and said: "Yes, it is a nice piece of copper ore." Then he waited to see what they would do next. They hemmed and hawed, but eventually said that they wanted to investigate the area more fully and wanted to dig trenches. They wanted to know whether Merensky did not want to become involved – after all, he knew what was what. Merensky took the sample again and looked at it from all sides, without his magnifying glass. His face showed no emotion. Then he gave back the sample and said curtly: "This sample comes from the pit at Messina, which has already been investigated. There is nothing more to develop. Robbie, would you please escort these gentlemen to the farm gate." Then he turned and went into the house without any further greeting.

The pair was struck dumb, and Robbie Maddison was speechless. He had never seen his employer like this. When they got into their car, he heard the one hiss at the other: "How the hell did he know that?" Robbie did not know either. A few days later he asked Merensky whether one could really tell from which mine an ore sample came. Merensky smiled and said: "In principle, yes, but sometimes it is difficult. But that was not necessary in this case. These were two conmen who could never have worked in the bush for any length of time. And the sample! Wrapped up as if it was made of glass and so perfect that it was just too good to be true. Ore samples found in the bush are weathered and quite unobtrusive."

Merensky had a strong sense of the beauties of nature, and not just grand landscapes or glorious sunsets. He also loved smaller things he found literally at the roadside. One day, for example, while he was out walking, at the edge of the bush, he observed some guineafowl scratching about for food. There was a ditch between them and the road. The ditch ran parallel to the edge of the bush and after a shower of rain there was often water in it. When he had seen the birds there a number of times in the afternoons, he began to carry grain in his jacket pocket to feed the guineafowl. The birds soon got used to this and would fly over the ditch to meet him when he threw some grain on the road. He began to take along a little boy to carry a small bucket with grain for him. One day the guineafowl appeared with a number of chicks. The adult birds flew over the ditch as always, but the chicks stood at the edge and cheeped helplessly. That evening, Merensky called one of his craftsmen and asked him to build a small bridge at this point. The man was happy to do so, but suggested that the bridge should be moved down the road a little, because then the Doctor could get into the woods better. Merensky insisted that the bridge be built at precisely that one spot – it was not for him, but for the chicks. The good man was speechless, but, as always when their revered Doctor expressed any particular wish, he got what he asked for. Two days later there was a little bridge with guard rails made of upright planks on either side so none of the chicks could fall into the ditch.

One of the biggest problems Merensky experienced in the last few years of his life was his increasing deafness. He could follow a dialogue without too much difficulty, especially if it was about a topic he was familiar with. It was much more difficult when he had to follow a conversation in a big group switching from one person to another, or when a stranger (usually someone who wanted to borrow money) approached the aim of his visit in a roundabout way. Merensky was very unhappy when he lost the thread of the conversation, so his close associates tried to protect him from such visitors whenever they could. Sometimes, however, he himself undermined their efforts because he was so amiable, and just could not help it. One day, for example, he received some men from the South African Soil Conservation Board and took them around on the farm. This was not surprising, as by then Westfalia was already regarded as South Africa's model of the successful prevention of soil erosion. The conversation between the small circle of experts flowed easily, as they spoke the same language, and the visit was a great success. Soon thereafter, though, there was a conference about measures for soil conservation, and, on the basis of this good experience, a whole group was sent on an excursion to Westfalia. Merensky did not feel up to dealing with such a large group, and his manager-in-chief, Dr Fick, guided the visitors over the farm. Afterwards, he invited the participants to have some afternoon tea at his house. The guests were disappointed not to see the famous Dr Merensky either during their tour of the farm or at the function afterwards. Meanwhile, Merensky had taken his usual afternoon stroll. When he came back, not far from the house, he saw two chauffeurs sitting under a tree, waiting for the group. They greeted him politely. Merensky started to chat to them, and eventually invited them to have some tea with him on his veranda, as he thought they should have some refreshment before they started the long drive back. This came to him quite naturally: He was never so lofty that he did not enjoy talking to so-called "ordinary people". "One can learn a lot from every person" was one of Merensky's mottos. The participants in the excursion, including some highly ranked professors and top ministerial officials, were much less impressed when they heard of the cosy teaparty at Merensky's house!

Merensky was always fond of being sociable. In good times and bad times alike, he valued having friends around him and loved having a meal with them. This was also true of him in the last few years and months of his life. He no longer gave great receptions like the ones he had once given in Johannesburg, but liked small dinner parties, with this or that couple, and usually over a bottle or two of good wine. He also loved playing cards, especially Bridge, and even more Skat (a German card game), because that was not quite as serious as Bridge – and reminded him of his youth. Because the last German Kaiser had been an enthusiastic Skat player, the game was popular among officers and students alike, and 60 years later, Merensky still enjoyed the game. One can say that until his very last day Merensky lived and enjoyed his life to the full. Nevertheless, he was prepared for the end. A few days before his death, he said to Dr Fick: "When my end comes, then I will die without fear or regret, because I know that I have lived a good and successful life."

On the last day of his life, 21 October 1952, his family doctor tried to persuade him to stay in bed for a few days and to look after himself – he had been a little weak for days due to light bronchitis. He protested strongly, because he wanted to play Skat that evening. In the afternoon, as usual, he had tea with his manager-in-chief, Dr Fick. When they rose from the tea table, the telephone rang. It was von Bülow, calling from Johannesburg, where he was negotiating an agreement. He told Merensky that he would arrive on Westfalia the next day. "*Wunderbar,*" said Merensky, "*dann können wir das ganze auf deutsch besprechen, das ist einfacher.*" ["Great. Then we can discuss the whole thing in German. That's much easier."] These were his last words. He went to lie down to rest a little. Half an hour later, Dr Fick, who was worried, sent young Robbie Maddison to the Top House to see whether Merensky was all right. Robbie peeped through a crack in the door and reported that Merensky was sleeping and was snoring lightly. An hour later, his co-workers realised that he was sleeping forever.

As he had wished, his ashes were dispersed in the forests on the Rosendal farm that belonged to Westfalia and that he had loved particularly. He did not want to be buried and particularly did not want a grandiose tombstone. However, a year after his death, a memorial was erected above the Top House, one that was appropriate to his personality and his life. A small park was laid out at a point from which there is a good view of the valley. There is an unpolished rock, inscribed with the words

HANS MERENSKY
1871–1952

In a large circle around the memorial there are 81 trees, one for every year of his life. All along the paths leading from the park, many kinds of shrubs and trees have been planted that are indigenous to the north-eastern Transvaal, in this country that Merensky loved so much and that he had chosen as his second home country.

CHAPTER 22

# A lasting legacy

Before one can assess Hans Merensky's life, one needs to look briefly at his personal development, which caused his life goals to change successively.

One can identify several distinct chapters in his professional life. The first chapter ran from 1904, the year when he immigrated to South Africa, to 1911, the year of the stock exchange collapse. These were the years in which, as a young geologist, he did well financially, thanks to his excellent training, his easy-going personality and his ability to adapt to the conditions in the country. His enthusiasm for his profession and his hard work constituted the other basis of his success.

The second chapter ran from 1911 to the middle of 1924. This was a time of great worry and stress for Merensky; a time of poverty and sometimes despair. His misfortunes began slowly. 1911 and 1912 brought along the gradual decline of his fortune, mainly due to losses on the stock exchange – a downward spiral that reached an ultimate low with Merensky being declared bankrupt in 1913. It was only at that moment that he finally realised that his finances had slipped beyond his control. Then came his internment – the most difficult time in his life. In the last year of his internment, he reached his physical and emotional nadir. After his release in 1919, his financial problems continued, but gradually his natural optimism got the upper hand again. Despite all his difficulties he finally began to believe that he would again have success as a geologist once the economic crisis had passed.

The third chapter, from 1924 to 1930, was that of his two first big finds. Around the middle of 1924, he discovered vast platinum deposits in South Africa, which made him world famous and enabled him to repay his debts. In 1927 he discovered diamonds at Alexander Bay. Barely two years later, he became a very rich man when he sold his concessions. That enabled him to change his life from then on completely.

The fourth chapter, which began in 1930 and lasted until about 1949, was characterised by an almost breathtaking burst of creativity. The fact that by the start of this phase of his life, Merensky was already 59 years old, makes it all the more remarkable. He bubbled with new ideas and, because he was financially independent, he was able to pursue those ideas and realise his plans. The biggest event of this period (and a turning point in his life) was the fact that he purchased Westfalia. From then on, rehabilitating the farm and developing it into a model farm became the focus of his energies. Nevertheless, he continued to work as a geologist, although his motivation was now quite different. Before, he had prospected to earn a living, and because of the pure enjoyment of discovering new deposits. After 1930 he only prospected sporadically, and then in a very focused way, for ores or minerals that he believed or knew would be important to the future economic development of South Africa. These prospecting campaigns brought him more financial success, but making money was no longer a reason for him to do something. He regarded the economic use to which the country could put his finds as far more important. From an accounting perspective, it might even be said that he sold his last great discovery, the phosphate deposit at Loolekop, to the State almost as a gift.

The last chapter of Merensky's life began in 1949, when he signed his testament. It was the winding down of a long life, filled with hard work; and in many ways it was a fitting crown to his accomplishments. He succeeded in consolidating the many achievements of his life. He had developed a detailed foundation concept and put in place a convincing succession plan. He had been preparing both in his mind for years.

But before one comes to a final conclusion on Hans Merensky's life, there are still a number of questions that need to be explored. To begin with: What was the secret of his big successes? Or to put it differently: How was it possible for someone suddenly to discover significant deposits, the existence of which had clearly eluded his predecessors in places in which hundreds of experienced geologists had already worked?

A second significant question would be to ask what became of his large fortune? What became of his scientific manuscripts, maps, geological notes and correspondences?

Thirdly, one should ask how lasting the effect of his discoveries and his enterprises were – and question whether the deposits he found delivered what they promised. How did his agricultural and forestry enterprises develop after his death?

Lastly, it would be interesting to see what Hans Merensky's reputation is today – and to take stock of the way in which today's scientific community and South Africans in general view Merensky's achievements.

To answer the first question, with regard to Merensky's discoveries: Some of his contemporaries would have liked to relativise the significance of his discovery of platinum in the Bushveld. They argued that, back then, platinum had been "in the air", so to speak. The time was simply ripe. It is true that in 1923 and 1924 there were other prospecting teams looking for platinum. But it was Merensky who found it and who found it in more than one place. This was pointed out on several occasions by Percy Wagner, one of the most significant South African geologists of that time. Not only did Merensky and his team find the first platinum in the Lydenburg district, but he then followed up on his idea of tracing the platinum-bearing reef all around the edge of the Bushveld. He did so at a time when everyone else was still trying to get options only near the first finds. That way he consequently discovered the platinum reef in the Potgietersrus area and after that, when everybody else had almost given up, the platinum-bearing layers near Rustenburg, hidden under thick peat layers.

It is of course undeniable that, as many envious people have said, Hans Merensky was fortunate to have received an initial impulse from someone else for all his big discoveries – the platinum, the diamonds, the gold in the Orange Free State, the chrome ores, the vermiculite and the phosphates. The first indicators of the existence of platinum in the Lydenburg district came from a farmer, Lombaard. The diamonds found at Alexander Bay were discovered while Merensky was away in Johannesburg, looking for backers, even though they were found in the places he had pegged out. The gold in the Orange Free State was finally reached through drilling after Merensky had already sold his concession and had left the Free State. His old prospector, Busschau, had drawn his attention to the chrome ore occurrences on the farm Jagdlust. The vermiculite occurrence on Loolekop was already being investigated by the old prospector Cleveland, and a third party had prospected for phosphates in the area 16 years earlier, even if they did so in the wrong place. On the other hand, it is clear that without Merensky's intervention, none of those deposits would have been identified as promising at that stage. They might well have been ignored for many years, if not decades. Without Merensky, Andries Lombaard and his brothers-in-law would have lost the desire to continue prospecting. Dr Reuning and all the others that were searching for diamonds at Alexander Bay would never have thought of going up to the higher terraces. The exploratory drilling in the Orange Free State would have been stopped before the gold-bearing layer had been reached or the geological sequence had been clarified to lay the foundation for the gold finds there. Nobody else thought of following the admittedly known, but apparently insignificant chromite seams in the Bushveld across longer distances. Even when the unusual extension of the chrome ore deposit had eventually been recognised, for a very long time Merensky still remained the only person to recognise the international rank of the find. By the time Merensky visited old Cleveland at Loolekop, Cleveland was on the point of abandoning his diggings because vermiculite did not interest him. If Merensky had not happened to drive out to see what Cleveland had found, it is likely that Cleveland would have stopped his work at that spot. It is not certain whether anyone else would have been prepared to prospect at Loolekop again soon. Similarly, the identification of the nearby phosphate deposit might have been delayed by years without Merensky's actions.

It was probably no coincidence that Merensky's intervention was repeatedly needed to grasp the significance of the traces of ore that had been found and to kick-start the development of such occurrences as deposits. Clearly, for each of these occurrences he was "the right man at the right time", the one to give the deciding push.

Probably Merensky's successes can best be explained by the fact that he was divinely gifted with multiple talents. Where there was nothing, even he could not find anything, but if there was a deposit somewhere, even if the visible signs of its presence were very slight or unclear, he possessed an entire palette of personal traits that enabled him to uncover the deposit and to assess its development potential accurately.

Merensky was a superb geologist and had an exceptional ability to observe detail. But that alone would not have been enough. There were many good geologists in South Africa at that time, but in addition to his geological training, Merensky also had what was possibly the best mining training available at the start of the $20^{th}$ century. This combination was certainly something special. He always benefited from it. Not only did it enable him to recognise that an ore occurrence extended in this or that direction, but it also enabled him to include the technical conditions that could promote or hamper the eventual exploitation of the occurrence in his calculations and to assess the economic viability of a project. Whatever he did, he was always able to keep in mind a comprehensive overview of the project as a whole.

Moreover, he was a visionary and could look into the possibilities that would open up in the future. His personal ideas about the development of a future industrial complex at Loolekop is an example of this. By the time he concluded his prospecting for the phosphates, he already had a clear mental picture of how things would develop at that site. Twenty years later, all that he envisaged had been erected and was in full operation. His thinking about the chromite ores in the Bushveld was similarly farsighted. Until he investigated the occurrences, people did not believe that they would be usable in the steel industry, but Merensky trusted the ingenuity of the metallurgists, and he was right.

Merensky's most important trait was probably his ability to think creatively. Based on the indications that he observed in the field, he was able to imagine the existence of new types of deposits, the structural plans of which had hitherto never been observed and which had consequently never been described before. This applies to the platinum-bearing reef in the Bushveld and to the diamond deposits of the Oyster Line. In the latter case, it took 18 years for anyone to believe that what he suggested could even be possible.

His professional qualifications and abilities were complemented by his personal attributes, which determined his style of working and the way in which he communicated with people. He could work almost to the point of complete exhaustion. He had an extremely strong will that drove him in his work. Moreover, his will was often equalled by his eloquence and his ability to encourage his companions to continue when he sensed that they were losing hope or that their courage was waning. This was vital when he was prospecting for platinum. On the other hand, he was able to assert his authority in a way that enabled him to put his ideas into action even when he had to deal with people who did not share his opinions. This can be seen in his prospecting for diamonds at Alexander Bay. On yet other occasions, he was able to employ a softer tone to persuade his co-workers to do what he wanted and to urge them on. He was able to infuse a healthy team spirit and he was masterly in his leadership of men. His creativity and his gift for motivating his co-workers were also the basis for his successes in the development of agricultural and forestry aspects on Westfalia.

With regard to the second question – Merensky's legacy – the following can be said: Because Merensky was unmarried and had no immediate relatives who could inherit his estate, he began to think about his legacy early on. He wanted his farm to continue, and hoped that the multitude of different projects that he had started would be completed. He wanted this development work to benefit South Africa as much as possible. This dream could only be realised with the input of a team of experts – and he wanted the best. Given these dreams, it was clear that he could not leave his fortune to an individual or a group of people, or to members of his family. This does not mean that he had turned against his nephews and nieces – on the contrary, even while he was alive they already received large sums from him and in his will he left them generous legacies. However, in the interest of the farm, he wanted to prevent family arguments or an individual's financial difficulties from affecting the efficient running of the enterprise. He thought about this for a long time and asked for advice from his lawyers. In the end, he drafted a testament that Alex Douglas cast into the necessary legal form. He handed over 90% of his fortune to the Hans Merensky Trust while he was still alive, and designated the trust as the heir of the remaining 10%. His four closest confidants were appointed as the trustees, namely his long-time lawyer Alex Douglas, his financial adviser William Warmback, Jürgen von Bülow and Carl Rolfes.

The transfer of the investments to the Trust was subject to two essential stipulations:

Firstly, the appointment of the Trust as the proprietor of Merensky's enterprises was only a temporary arrangement. After at least ten years, and after no more than 25 years, the Trust should be transformed into a foundation. Merensky chose this time interval because he believed that the farm would only have developed into its final structure at that time. He wanted the Trust to be changed into a foundation because nobody could predict the economic, political and social conditions under which the Trust would have to operate in a few years' time. He did not think that it made much sense to prescribe the business strategy that the Trust should follow beyond his death. He argued that a foundation with foundation managers who were independently responsible for their decisions, and who were largely free to make decisions within a set framework, would essentially be a more flexible instrument.

Secondly, he stipulated that after his death all the projects he had initiated had to be continued for at least another ten years. This reflected Merensky's personal conviction and experience that in agricultural enterprises one had to think about a longer term and should not give up too early. In the years leading up to the transformation of the Trust into the Hans Merensky Foundation, the Trust was also to expand the capital surplus so that there would be enough resources available to the Foundation.

The mandate of the Foundation was broken up into core activities, the purposes of which were defined very carefully, and an extended set of activities which would allow the Foundation managers more freedom of action. The core activities included research on the prevention of soil erosion and the improvement of South African soils, particularly by introducing natural mineral materials such as vermiculite; research on the cultivation of citrus at various elevations; and experiments in breeding and cross-breeding European cattle with African breeds, to combine the higher meat and milk production of the first with the exceptional resistant to various diseases of the latter.

The extended activities allowed the trustees or the later Board of Directors of the Foundation more freedom to decide on what it wanted to do. Thus the Foundation could decide to support foreign research on matters relating to agriculture, forestry, animal husbandry, medicine, ore geology, mining techniques and chemistry, in so far as they serve the interests of "general progress" (a term Merensky liked to use). Moreover, two funds were to be financed and overseen. One was to support the training of students and practitioners of all races; the other the erection and maintenance of the appropriate schools, training and welfare institutions to do this.

Before the estate was wound up, after his death, various legacies were to be paid out. There was again a high sum to be paid out to his relatives. About £74 000 went to personal friends. The first of these was Major General (retd) Albrecht von Thaer, who had been living in the Emsland since the end of the war and who survived Merensky by seven years. Then there were his other Silesian friends from his youth. Another £41 000 went to charity: the Berlin Mission, the Hermannsburg Mission, the universities of Stellenbosch, Pretoria, the Witwatersrand and Potchefstroom and diverse schools and libraries, not only in South Africa, but also in Windhoek. The employees leading his enterprises received £50 000. This was a bonus for loyal service, but also a bonus for the future, because it was important to Merensky to attach his experienced staff to the Trust after his death. His house staff also received a sizeable sum. The total of these legacies came to a round £237 000. Withdrawing such a large sum from his enterprises all at once was obviously impossible, so the testament allowed the legacies to be paid out in instalments over a period of ten years. All in all, the foundation concept was very cleverly devised to function well.

Merensky and his designated trustees signed his testament and the transfer documents late one evening in May 1949, on his farm Kalkfontein. As the farmhouse on this farm was much more simply furnished and had fewer amenities than the one on Westfalia, this remarkable transaction, in which Merensky parted from a fortune worth millions, was concluded by candlelight.

One can begin to answer the third set of questions (namely that surrounding the further development of Merensky's various enterprises) by starting from the fact that the deposits Merensky discovered have all, without exception, been mined with great economic success. In some cases, where there was initially no market for the mineral concerned, as Merensky had predicted, it took some time for the value of the deposit to be realised, but once it was, the economic success was all the greater.

In the past decade, South African platinum production has overtaken that of Russia, which used to be the premier producer. Whereas, for a while after the Second World War, each of these two nations produced 45% of the world's platinum metals, by 2004, South Africa produced 75% and Russia only 17% of the world's production. South Africa produced mainly platinum; Russian production focused mainly on the industrially equally important palladium. Johnson Matthey, the leading platinum dealer, estimated South Africa's 2005 share of the world production of platinum to be as high as 77,7%.

From an economic point of view, platinum mining is of immense importance to South Africa. In 2002, as many as 17 platinum mines were in production and they produced 25,1% of the total profits from South African mining.

The diamonds from the Oyster Line at Alexander Bay have long been mined. The focus has now shifted to the north side of the Orange River, to Namibia. Since the Oyster Line and other high terraces continue there, Namibia is rich in particularly lovely gem quality diamonds. More than 50% of Namibia's Gross Domestic Product (at times it was more than 80%) comes from the profits of diamond production.

Merensky's work on the gold occurrences in the Orange Free State later proved to be highly significant. Admittedly he had not continued his work until the gold occurrences had been finally verified, but had passed his results to industry once he had worked out the problem of the geological sequence of layers. His predictions about the promise of gold in this area were to come true in every way. The area around Odendaalsrus has since become an important new source of gold.

The vast chrome ore deposit found in the northern Transvaal in 1937 was sold for half a million pounds to an American steel company, the Union Carbide Corporation, in 1952. That was many times the sum that Merensky had spent on the prospecting work and concession rights 16 years earlier.

Even more remarkable is the accuracy with which Merensky predicted the development of the world market for chrome ores. When it was first discovered in 1937, the chrome ore deposit on Jagdlust could not be sold. At that time, low percentage chrome ores were not regarded as interesting, but Merensky was convinced that, considering the vast extent of the deposit, industry would immediately want to acquire the deposit once the necessary metallurgical processes had been developed. Today, this type of ore dominates the chrome world market. In the Bushveld, chrome is mined in about 20 chrome ore mines. According to statistics published by the U.S. Geological Survey, in 2004, South Africa produced about 47% of the world's chrome ore. This places the country in the leading position in terms of both the mining production and world reserves (72,4%).

The development around Loolekop has been almost fantastic. There Merensky had first discovered vermiculite and then phosphates, but also traces of copper and radioactive minerals. In the mid-1950s, a drilling programme designed to investigate phosphates showed that the radioactive mineralisations were not economically interesting, but that the copper traces belonged to one of the largest copper deposits in the world. The mineralisation goes down to a depth of more than 1000 metres. Since then, vermiculite, phosphate ores (apatite) and copper ores have been mined in the area in separate opencast mines.

The Phalaborwa Mining Company (PMC) was established to mine the copper ore. Today the company belongs to a consortium in which Rio Tinto is represented by 46,6% and Anglo American by 29%. Loolekop as an individual hill has disappeared completely. Where the hill once stood, there is now a funnel-shaped opencast mine, several hundred metres deep. At its top edge the mine has a diameter of 2000 metres. It is the largest opencast mine in Africa. Between 1964 and 2002, four million tons of copper were smelted from the ores from this mine. From 2002 onward, the mining process has been changed from opencast mining to underground mining. This will produce another 1,4 million tons of copper (metal) by 2022.

The vermiculite deposit now also belongs to the Phalaborwa Mining Company. With an annual production of about 200 000 tons, it is now the world's largest vermiculite producer. About 90% of the vermiculite produced here is exported. South African vermiculite is highly in demand worldwide because it is so pure.

The development of the phosphate project was just as successful. The South African Government established a mining company called Foskor to mine this deposit. Today its production covers more than 80% of the South African demand for superphosphate. As Merensky predicted, the area around the town of Phalaborwa has become a mining and industrial centre of the first rank.

And finally, what became of Merensky's farm, Westfalia, and of the many forestry and agricultural experiments that Merensky initiated?

It was a severe challenge for the trustees to fulfil both wishes of the testator at the same time, namely to continue the experimental work and to operate the farm(s) so efficiently that the Trust's capital resources would grow enough to form the basis for a foundation. They succeeded in doing both. The cultivation experiments were continued and there were even new ones, for example, a tea plantation in Natal, a series of experiments to turn blast-furnace slag into slag cement, or prospecting for asbestos, which led to the opening of the Eldorit Mine in the Bushveld in 1965.

At the same time, Westfalia was developed further, as Merensky wanted it to be. The two planned dams, the Von Bülow Dam (1957) and the Rosendal Dam, were built. Over time, the farm was enlarged, eventually reaching a size of 8000 hectares. The controlled planting of saligna and pine trees became very important in this period. The Trust's involvement in the timber industry was also strengthened: In Natal, the Trust purchased forest areas, acquired sawmills, and, finally, also got involved in building timber production. They also bought a furniture factory in Pretoria. Much of the legwork on these developments was done by Jürgen von Bülow, who, after his release from the internment camp, had intensified the forestry activities and played a prominent role in the Trust after Merensky's death. Sadly, he died much too young in 1972, only 61 years old, from complications after an operation to an intervertebral disc.

In the 1960s there were a number of changes regarding the spheres of activity of the Trust. The asbestos mine Eldorit, which had just started operations, had to close once the health risks posed by asbestos became public. The Transvaal Ore Company was sold to the Phalaborwa Mining Company. The mining of vermiculite was certainly profitable, but it had proved to be increasingly difficult to maintain a global marketing system. Westfalia also underwent a change. After more than 70 years, problems with the citrus trees led to their being phased out, to be replaced by more avocados.

On 26 November 1973, the Trust became the Hans Merensky Foundation. According to the 1949 founding document, the "objective of the Hans Merensky Foundation is to promote and assist in the development of the resources of South Africa and neighbouring territories – particularly such natural resources as soil, water, minerals, flora and fauna – and to promote the health and welfare of the inhabitants; more specifically by research, experimentation and demonstration and through the correlation and application of scientific knowledge". The Foundation awards scholarships for forestry and agricultural training at various levels and in respect of the related manufacturing or processing fields. For this purpose, the Foundation works with government organisations, all the South African universities and agricultural schools and colleges, as well as the German universities in Hohenheim and Göttingen. A special fund entrusted to the Hamburg Senate awards scholarships to German students who want to work in South Africa on one of the research interests supported by the Foundation. Moreover, the Foundation runs its own research programmes on forestry, the timber industry and subtropical fruit. So, for example, as its founder would have wanted, the Foundation is working on planting yellowwood plantations for the first time (yellowwood is highly prized by cabinetmakers, but thus far the tree has only grown wild, and has therefore become endangered). The first experiments look very promising. Meanwhile, similar attempts have also been made regarding East African mahogany and sawtooth evergreen oak. Where necessary, the Foundation also supports the research projects of third parties. From 1988, the Merensky Technological Services (MTS) have also offered global contract research on issues relating to the cultivation of avocados.

Today, the economic activities related to earning the finances needed to promote training and research focus on two main areas: forestry and subtropical fruit.

The companies belonging to the Foundation cultivate a total area of 101 600 hectares, of which 21 600 hectares belong to the Foundation itself. The remaining land is leased, or is land that belongs to the State Forests but for which the Foundation has timber rights. Of these lands, 11 200 hectares are under eucalyptus, and about another 60 000 hectares are under pine trees. Some of the land used for this purpose is situated on or around Westfalia, but a large part of it is in KwaZulu-Natal. The timber processing plants include five sawmills. The wood is processed into timber for the mines, building timber and laminates for the furniture manufacturing industry.

In the cultivation of subtropical fruit, the focus is on avocados and mangoes. With 1100 hectares under avocado cultivation, the Foundation is Africa's largest avocado producer. Westfalia also has a tree nursery which produces no fewer than 100 000 avocado trees every year, some for the use of the Foundation, some for the use of other companies. About 525 hectares are planted with mangoes. In the cultivation of both avocados and mangoes, ecological methods are increasingly used. The label "Westfalia" on avocados and mangoes has become much prized. Large parts of the production are exported to England, France and Germany. In order to manage the marketing and sales in Europe better, the Foundation has established its own sales networks. Since 1999, avocados are also sold in a processed form; and since 2002, the cosmetic industry has increasingly purchased and consumed avocado oil. All in all, the enterprise now employs 4700 people.

Of course, various things have changed on the farm itself. The development of the farm into a large industry is very clear from the packing halls and loading bays, which are hives of activity, and the adjacent cold storage facilities. In the old days, teams of mules drew the carts full of avocados. Today, huge lorries with trailers have taken their place. Every year, 2,5 million boxes of four kilograms each, ready packed for sale, leave the farm on pallets and are sold to consumers. Around this centre there are a nursery school, a crèche and a day care centre for babies where the mothers who work at the packing houses can leave their children. There is also a social centre, a doctor and the management building. The scientific laboratory is situated elsewhere on the farm.

The Top House that used to stand at the top of the slope is no longer there. It was replaced by the Hans Merensky Memorial Building in 1982. There were good reasons for making this change. There was a need for a functional, air-conditioned building to house the large herbarium of the plants on the farm and its environs as well as the valuable Merensky Archive under optimal conditions. This plan succeeded, and the damage to old documents that is so often observed in tropical countries could be prevented.

More than this: The Merensky Archive unites all the documents, correspondences and reports relevant to Hans Merensky. The American geologist Dr Katja Freitag, who is now working at Phalaborwa, has organised and catalogued the archive with remarkable clarity. Now a well-thought at system of cross-references makes reviewing and working with the Merensky papers easy.

Nevertheless, making the decision to replace the old house with this new building must have been very difficult indeed. But the view over the valley remains as beautiful as ever – a picture of peace and quiet.

Finally, as to the state of Merensky's current reputation: In Germany and in many other countries, Merensky's name is now only known in geological circles and among mining experts. The broader public has forgotten him, and current reference works no longer mention him. This is not true in South Africa and Namibia. Since platinum mining is flourishing, scientific research in this sector continues. On the one hand, the basic assumptions that Merensky proposed about the structure and extent of the platinum reefs have been confirmed, and on the other, detailed knowledge of the deposit has increased enormously. Of course, this means that the name of the discoverer is continually recalled. One example serves to illustrate this: the South African *Journal of Geology* entitled one of its volumes in 1999 a "Special Issue on commemorating the 75$^{th}$ anniversary of the discovery of the Merensky Reef". The glossy cover featured a colour facsimile of the first sketch Merensky made of the position of the platinum finds – a joy for every geologist! Merensky's fame as the discoverer of the platinum-bearing reef named after him endures. However, there are some serious experts on ore geology and industrial minerals who argue that it is not the discovery of platinum, but the conclusions that Merensky drew in the dunes above Lüderitz and that led to the discovery of the diamonds in the Oyster Line, that make him the most original prospecting geologist of all. Merensky's scientific assumptions with regard to the Oyster Line (the simultaneous deposit of oyster shells and diamonds, warm water fauna, a warmer climate, the important role played by the lifting of the subcontinent, etc.) are still valid. New discoveries have been added. Today, the geologists of the Consolidated Diamond Mines of Namibia (NAMDEB) know that there are probably seven beach terraces of different ages on which diamonds were deposited. At 2 million years, the Oyster Line is one of the younger placers, while the diamond deposit at Kolmanskop, at 70 million years, is probably the oldest deposit of its kind.

Be that as it may, Merensky's name is current among everybody connected even remotely to geology or mining in southern Africa. This is true also because Merensky was awarded high academic honours: he was awarded an honorary doctorate by the universities of Stellenbosch and Pretoria, as well as the Draper Medal of the Geological Society of South Africa, the highest honour that this Society can give to a scientist.

His name is also familiar to the broader public from the activities of the Hans Merensky Foundation, as well as by the places named after him: Merensky Street in Windhoek, the Merensky Dam in south-eastern Namibia, the building in which the Physics Institute at the University of Stellenbosch is housed, the generously built Merensky Library at the University of Pretoria, the Merensky Dam in the valley below Westfalia, the Merensky Lodge and the Merensky Game Reserve near Phalaborwa.

So, what conclusion can we reach about this great man's life? To put it in a nutshell, his life was exciting, perhaps even adventurous, but he was always focused on his goals and, in the end, very successful. He initially worked as a geologist to earn a living and because he enjoyed discovering things. Once he had made his fortune, he soon developed a sense that having so much money placed him under an obligation. For him, that meant that he wanted to use his wealth to promote "general progress" in the sciences and technology, particularly to benefit South Africa, which had become his second home.

Perhaps a few words about his relationship with Germany would be in order: He was born to German parents in South Africa, but was schooled in Germany and went to university there. He became a Lieutenant of the Reserve and, as a mining assessor, he was a Prussian official. There is no doubt about his original German citizenship. Around 1926 – he was then 55 years old – he decided to stay in South Africa for the rest of his life. Everything he said and did after that time left no room for doubt that he saw himself as a South African. That is the emotional perspective. The legal aspects are less clear. It is not quite clear whether he ever gave up his German passport and whether, since he was born in South Africa, he was automatically a South African citizen or whether he only attained citizenship around 1936. His South African biographers have paid scant attention to such matters of form. From their point of view, Hans Merensky was always a South African. An example of this approach can be cited from the article on Merensky in the *Dictionary of South African Biography*. In the last paragraph, the author of this article, W.P. de Kock, describes the aims of the Hans Merensky Foundation and he ends with the sentence:

"This is indeed a fine and enduring monument to a generous benefactor, a genial colleague, a charming host, and above all a great South African."

Hans Merensky's own attitude to South Africa is clear from his impressive comment in a speech made at the opening of the library of the University of Pretoria, named after him as the donor of the library:

"This country has given to me so much, that I am only too happy to be allowed to help it to develop in some way, and I am grateful to be able to give back to it a fraction of what it has given to me. I hope this Library will be a cornerstone in the building-up of a bigger South Africa for the future generations ..."

# Bibliography

Anhaeuser, C.R. and Wilson, M.G.C. (eds.). 1998. Mineral Resources of South Africa. *Handbook of the Geological Survey of South Africa* 16.
Arkin, M. 1972. Jeppe, Sir Julius Gottlieb Ferdinand. *Dictionary of South African Biography* II: 340–341. Cape Town.
Bardet, M.G. 1974. Gisements de diamant d'Afrique. *Mémoire Bureau de Recherches Géologiques et Minières* 83(II).
Biehler, W., Boos, R., Bosse, H.R., Krauss, U., Kruszona, M., Percy, A. and Schmidt, H. 1986. Industrieminerale. *Untersuchungen über Angebot und Nachfrage mineralischer Rohstoffe* XIX. Hannover/Basel: Bundesanstalt für Geowissenschaften und Rohstoffe/PROGNOS.
Blohm, E.G. 1986. My association with Dr. Hans Merensky. Unpublished manuscript. Westfalia: Merensky Archive.
Bolz, K., Harms, U., Pissulla, P. & Schmidt, H. 1985. *Gold, Platinmetalle und Diamanten in der sowjetischen Handelspolitik.* Bundesanstalt für Geowissenschaften und Rohstoffe, Institut für Wirtschaftsforschung Hamburg, Institut zur Erforschung technologischer Entwicklungslinien. Hamburg: Verlag Weltarchiv.
Braun, H. 2004. Der Schmuckdiamant als Veblen-Leibenstein-Gut. Vom Symbol der Reichen und Mächtigen zum Konsumartikel mit Wertillusion für das breite Bürgertum. In: Walter, R. (ed.). *Geschichte des Konsums. Vierteljahrsschrift Sozial- und Wirtschaftsgeschichte*. Beihefte vol. 175: 159–197.

Braun, H. 2004. Der Weltmarkt für Diamanten. Eine raffiniert inszenierte Wertillusion. *Frankfurter Allgemeine Zeitung* 9 September 2004: 25.

Bridges, R.T. 1942. The Geologist. His work in South Africa. Presidential Address to the Geological Society of South Africa. *South African Mining Journal*: 57–58.

Buchanan, D.L. 1979. Chromite production from the Bushveld Complex. *World Mining* 32(10).

Canton-Thompson, G. 1931. *The Zimbabwe culture. Ruins and Reactions.* Oxford: Clarendon Press.

Carstens, J. 1962. *A fortune through my fingers.* Cape Town: Howard Timmins.

Cawthorn, R.G. (ed.). 1999a. Special issue on commemorating the 75th aniversary of the discovery of the Merensky Reef. *South African Journal of Geology* 102(3): 175–302.

Cawthorn, R.G. 1999b. The discovery of the platiniferous Merensky Reef in 1924. *Ibidem*: 178–183.

Cawthron, R.G. 1999c. Platinum-group element mineralization in the Bushveld Complex – a critical reassessment of geochemical models. *Ibidem*: 268–281.

Cloos, H. 1937. Karl Mauch. *Geologische Rundschau* vol. 28: 357.

Cockburn, A. 2002. Diamanten. Die bittere Wahrheit. *National Geographic (Germany)* 3: 40–73.

Coetzee, C.B. (ed.). 1976. Mineral Resources of the Republic of South Africa. 5th Edition. *Handbook of the Geological Survey of South Africa* 7.

Cornell, F.C. 1920. *The glamour of prospecting.* London: T. Fisher Unwin. Reprint 1986, 1992. Cape Town: David Philip.

Damman, E. 1993. Merensky, Alexander. *Biographisch-Bibliographisches Kirchenlexikon* V: 1294–1295. Herzberg: Verlag Traugott Bautz.

*Der Spiegel.* 1989. Im Griff des Syndicats. 43(44): 151–166.

De Kock, W.P. 1977. Merensky, Hans. *Dictionary of South African Biography* III: 602–606. Cape Town.

Duparc, L. & Molly, E. 1928. Les gisements platinifères du Birbir (Abyssinie). *Schweizerische Mineralogisch-Petrographische Mitteilungen* 8: 240–257.

Du Plessis, J.S. 1968. Smuts, Jan Christiaan. *Dictionary of South African Biographie* I: 737–758. Cape Town.

Evans, A.M. 1993. *Ore Geology and Industrial Minerals.* Oxford: Blackwell Scientific Publications.

Freitag, K. 2002. Report on the Hans Merensky documents. Unpublished manuscript. Westfalia: Merensky Archive.

Gevers, T.W. 1968. Wagner, Percy Albert. *Dictionary of South African Biography* I: 860–861. Cape Town.

Giraud, P.N. 1983. *Géopolitique des Ressources Minières.* Paris: Edition Economica.

Glueck, N. 1938, 1939, 1940. The first campaign at Tell el-Kheleifeh (Eziongeber). *Bulletin of the American Schools of Oriental Research* 71: 3–18. The second campaign. *Ibidem* 75: 8–22. Third season of excavation. *Ibidem* 79: 2–18.

Grebe, W.H., Kästner, H., Kippenberger, C. *et al.* 1975. Chrom. *Untersuchungen über Angebot und Nachfrage mineralischer Rohstoffe* VII. Hannover/Berlin: Bundesanstalt für Geowissenschaften und Rohstoffe / Deutsches Institut für Wirtschaftsforschung.

Gregory, T. 1971. Sir Ernest Oppenheimer. In: Williams, E.T. and Palmer, H.M. (eds.). *Dictionary of National Biography 1951–1960*. Oxford: University Press pp. 781–783.

Gutschke, T. 1972. Phillips, Sir Lionel (Baronet). *Dictionary of South African Biography* II: 544–546. Cape Town.

Hall, R.N. 1907. *Great Zimbabwe, Mashonaland, Rhodesia*. London: Methuen.

Hall, R.N. & Neal, W.G. 1902. *The ancient ruins of Rhodesia (Monomotapae Imperium)*. London: Methuen.

Hallack, R.K. 1977. Beyers, Frederick William. *Dictionary of South African Biography* III: 67–68. Cape Town.

Hans Merensky Foundation (after 2002). The Hans Merensky Foundation: Prospectus. 70 p.

Harrington, A.L. 1972. Barnato, Barney. *Dictionary of South African Biography* II: 31–33. Cape Town.

Harrington, A.L. 1977. Jones, Guy Carleton. *Dictionary of South African Biography* III: 452–453. Cape Town.

Hartkopf, W. 1992. *Die Berliner Akademie der Wissenschaften. Ihre Mitglieder und Preisträger 1700–1990*. Berlin: Akademie-Verlag.

Herrman, L. 1968. Harris, Sir David. *Dictionary of South African Biography* I: 351–352. Cape Town.

Heyden, U. (ed.). 1996. *Alexander Merensky. Erinnerungen aus dem Missionsleben in Transvaal (Südafrika) 1859–1882*. Berlin: Edition Ost.

Hoffmann, U., Hoffmeyer, M., Kippenberger, C. *et al.* 1983. Phosphat. *Untersuchungen über Angebot und Nachfrage mineralischer Rohstoffe* XVIII. Hannover/Kiel: Bundesanstalt für Geowissenschaften und Rohstoffe / Institut für Weltwirtschaft.

Hotz, L. 1968. Albu, Sir George. *Dictionary of South African Biography* I: 9–10. Cape Town.

Jeppe, F. and Merensky, A. 1868. Original Map of the Transvaal or South African Republic. Combined with the results of their own explorations by F. Jeppe & A. Merensky. Reconstructed by A. Petermann, 1:1.850.000. *Petermanns Geographische Mitteilungen,* Ergänzungsband 5. Gotha: Justus Perthes.

Kayser, K. 1937. Alexander Merensky als Geograph und deutscher Kolonialpionier. *Koloniale Rundschau* 28: 385–394. Leipzig: Bibliographisches Institut.

Knetsch, G. 1937a. Beiträge zur Kenntnis der Diamantenlagerstätten an der Oranje-Mündung. *Geologische Rundschau* 28: 188–207.

Knetsch, G. 1937b. Übersicht über die Geologie des südlichen Lüderitzlandes. *Ibidem*: 208–228.

Kohl, H. and Schoeman, A. 2004. *Kolmanskop. Past and present.* Windhoek/Göttingen: Klaus Hess Publishers.

Krahmann, R. 1930. Magnetic investigations as an aid to economic geology. *Transactions of the Geological Society of South Africa* 33: 65–87.

Krahmann, R. 1936. The geophysical magnetometric investigations on West Witwatersrand areas between Randfontein and Potchefstroom, Transvaal. *Transactions of the Geological Society of South Africa* 39: 1–44.

Krüger, D.W. 1968. Hertzog, James Barry Munnik. *Dictionary of South African Biography* I: 366–379. Cape Town.

Lehmann, O. 1955. *Look beyond the wind. The life of Dr. Hans Merensky 1871–1952.* Cape Town: Howard Timmins.

Lehmann, O. 1965. *Hans Merensky. Ein deutscher Pionier in Südafrika.* Göttingen: K.W. Schütz Verlag.

Lissner, I. 1961. *Rätselhafte Kulturen.* Olten/Freiburg: Walter Verlag.

London, J. 1993. Wie von alters zog die Argo. In: *Meistererzählungen.* Zürich: Diogenes-Taschenbuch.

Lüert, H. 1971. Merensky, Hans. *Deutscher Bergbau im Ausland in der Vergangenheit, Gegenwart und Zukunft.* Köln/Berlin: Groote'sche Verlagsbuchhandlung pp. 41–49.

Lüert, H. 1971. Krahmann, Rudolf. *Ibidem*: 49–52.

Machens, E. W. 1968. Das Präkambrium von Afrika. *Handbuch der stratigraphischen Geologie* XIII(2): 414–551. Stuttgart: Enke Verlag.

Machens, E. W. 2007. The Merensky Archive on the Westfalia farm in South Africa. *World of Mining – Surface & Underground* 59(2): 110–113.

Mager, E. 1895. *Karl Mauch. Lebensbild eines Afrikareisenden.* Stuttgart: Kohlhammer.

MacIver, R.D. 1906. *Mediaeval Rhodesia.* London.

Mauch, C. 1870. Carl Mauch's Reisen im Inneren von Südafrika (nach Mitteilungen des Reisenden aus Potchefstroom vom 30.06.1869). *Petermanns Geographische Mitteilungen* 16: 1–8; 92–103; 139–142. Gotha: Justus Perthes.

Mauch, C. 1872a: Nachrichten von Carl Mauch im Inneren von Süd-Afrika bis zum 27. Juli 1871. Antritt seiner neuen Reise nach Manica. Die Gold- und Diamantenfelder in der Transvaal-Republik. *Petermanns Geographische Mitteilungen* 18: 81–82. Gotha: Justus Perthes.

Mauch, C. 1872b. Carl Mauch's Entdeckung der Ruinen von Zimbaoe, 5. September 1871. *Ibidem*: 121–126.
Mauch, C. 1874. Carl Mauch's Reisen im Inneren von Süd-Afrika, 1865–72. *Petermanns Geographische Mitteilungen.* Ergänzungsband 8(37): 1–52. Therein: Petermann, A. Originalkarte von Carl Mauch's Reise von Simbabye nach Senna 1871–1872, 1:2.000.000. Gotha: Justus Perthes.
Mendelssohn, E.M. 1972. Gelletich, Hans. *Dictionary of South African Biography* II: 258–259. Cape Town.
Merensky, A. 1875. Original Map of Transvaal or South African Republic including the Gold- and Diamondfields, 1:1.850.000. *Zeitschrift der Gesellschaft für Erdkunde.* Berlin/Bothabelo.
Merensky, A. 1884. Original Map of South Africa. Containing all South African Colonies and Native Territories, 1:2.500.00. Berlin: Simon Schropp.
Merensky, A. 1888. Akklimatisation des Pferdes in Südafrika. *Deutsche Kolonialzeitung.* Neue Folge 1(38): 304–305. Berlin.
Merensky, A. 1899. *Erinnerungen an das Missionsleben in Südost-Afrika (Transvaal) 1859–1882.* 2nd revised and amended edition. Berlin.
Merensky, H. 1905. The gold deposits of the Murchison Range in north-east Transvaal. *Transactions of the Geological Society of South Africa* 8: 43–46.
Merensky, H. 1909a. The diamaond deposits of Lüderitzland, German South-West Africa. *Transactions of the Geological Society of South Africa* 12: 13–23.
Merensky, H. 1909b. Vorläufige kurze Angaben über die Diamanten bei Lüderitzbucht. *Zeitschrift für praktische Geologie* 17: 79–80; 122–129.
Merensky, H. 1925a. The platinum areas of Lydenburg. *South African Mining and Engineering Journal* 76:474–476.
Merensky, H. 1925b. Report on the platinum occurrence on the properties of Potgietersrust Platinums Ltd. Unbublished report. Westfalia: Merensky Archive.
Merensky, H. 1926. Die neu entdeckten Platinfelder im mittleren Transvaal und ihre wirtschaftliche Bedeutung. *Zeitschrift der Deutschen Geologischen Gesellschaft* 78: 296–314.
Merensky, H. 1929. The discovery of the Namaqualand diamonds. (Dr. Merensky's replies to Dr. Reuning's statements). *The Mining and Industrial Magazine*: 436–439.
Merensky, H. 1936. Interviewed by B. Lombaard, Johannesburg, 11. January 1936. Unpublished report of the interview. Westfalia: Merensky Archive.
Niemann, M. 1999. *Mecklenburgische Großgrundbesitzer im Dritten Reich (1933–45).* PhD Thesis. University of Rostock.
Niemann, M. 2002. Dr. Hans Merensky. Geologe in Südafrika und Gutsherr in Mecklenburg. In: Niemann, M. (ed.). *Mecklenburgische Gutsherren im 20.*

*Jahrhundert. Erinnerungen und Biographien.* 2nd edition. Rostock: Ingo Koch Verlag.

Ovendale, R. 1972. Bailey, Sir Abe. *Dictionary of South African Biography* II: 19–20. Cape Town.

Potgieter, F.J. 1972. Jeppe, Friedrich Heinrich. *Dictionary of South African Biography* II: 338–339. Cape Town.

Priesner, C. 1994. Merensky, Hans. *Neue deutsche Biographie* 17: 131–132. Berlin: Duncker & Humblot.

Putzer, H. 1968. Aufsuchung. In: *Lehrbuch der Angewandten Geologie* II(1): 5–97. Stuttgart: Enke Verlag.

Reh, H. 1958. Dem Andenken des großen Prospektors Hans Merensky. *Zeitschrift für Angewandte Geologie* 4(4): 182–186.

Reuning, E. 1928. The discovery of the Namaqualand diamonds. *The Mining and Industrial Magazine*: 341–356.

Reuning, E. 1929. The discovery of the Namaqualand diamonds. An answer to Dr. Merensky's reply. *The Mining and Industrial Magazine.*

Reuning, E. 1931. Der Ursprung der Küstendiamanten Süd- und Südwestafrikas. *Neues Jahrbuch für Mineralogie, Geologie und Paläontologie.* Beilagenband A vol. 64: 775–828.

Roberts, B. 1972. *The Diamond Magnates.* London: Hamish Hamilton.

Schneiderhöhn, H. 1929. The mineragraphy and genesis of the platinum bearing nickel-phyrrhotite ores of the Bushveld Igneous Complex. In: Wagner, P.A. 1929: 206–246.

Schneiderhöhn, H. 1958. *Die Erzlagerstätten der Erde* I. Stuttgart: Gustav Fischer-Verlag.

Schumacher, 1954. Nachruf Hans Merensky. *Geologische Rundschau* 42: 316–317.

Skawran, P.R. 1971. Dr. Hans Merensky. Mens en voorbeeld. *Publication University Pretoria* 62: 53–58.

South Africa. Chamber of Mines. 2002–2006. *Annual Report, 2003/ 2004−2005/2006. Ibidem. Facts & Figures,* 2003−2005.

*Ibidem. The South African Mining Industry, Fact Sheet,* 2002−2003

Spies, S.B. 1968. Maritz, Salomon Gerhardus (Manie). *Dictionary of South African Biography* I: 513–515. Cape Town.

Trümpelmann, G.P.J. 1968a. Mauch, Karl (Carl). *Dictionary of South African Biography* I: 524–528. Cape Town.

Trümpelmann, G.P.J. 1968b. Merensky, Alexander. *Ibidem*: 532–535.

United States Geological Survey 2005, 2006. Mineral Commodity Summaries.

Vermark, C.F. 1976. The Merensky Reef. Thoughts on its environment and genesis. *Economic Geology* 71: 1270–1298.

Verwoerd, W.J. 1986. Mineral deposits associated with carbonitites and alkaline rocks. In: Anhaeuser, C.R. & Maske, S. (eds.). *Mineral Deposits of*

*Southern Africa.* Johannesburg: Geological Society of South Africa. pp. 2173–2191.
Viljoen, M.J. 1999. The nature and origin of the Merensky Reef of the western Bushveld Complex based on geological facies and geophysical data. *South African Journal of Geology* 102(3): 221–239.
Visser, D.J.L. 1972. Reinicke, Leopold. *Dictionary of South African Biography* II: 573–574. Cape Town.
Von Bülow, H. (ed.). 1994. *Bülowsches Familienbuch* III. Aumühle.
Wagner, H. 1989. USA-Stahlveredler 2. Mangan, Chrom, Nickel, Kobalt, Vanadium. *Rohstoffwirtschaftliche Länderberichte* XXXIII. Hannover: Bundesanstalt für Geowissenschaften und Rohstoffe.
Wagner, P.A. 1925. Notes on the platinum deposits of the Bushveld igneous complex. *Transactions of the Geological Society of South Africa* 28: 83–133.
Wagner, P.A. 1929. *The platinum deposits and mines of South Africa.* Edinburgh & London: Oliver & Boyd.
Wagner, P.A. & Merensky, H. 1928. The diamond deposits on the coast of Little Namaqualand. *Transactions of the Geological Society of South Africa* 31: 1–42.
Webb, T.H. 1824. New localities of tourmalines and talc (vermiculites). *American Journal of Science & Arts* VII: 55.
Williams, E.L. 1978. Diamond harvest of the Namib surf; the story of CDM. *Optima* 27(4): 84–105.

# INDEX OF People

Albu, Sir George 76, 87
Baerveldt, P.C. 103
Bailey, Sir Abe 158, 171, 177, 178
Becker, Gustav A. 103, 119–122, 129, 158, 171, 177, 178, 184
Beyers, Frederick William 164, 169, 171
Bismarck, Otto von 33
Braun, Dr Helmuth 181
Bridges, R.T. 240
Bülow, Bernhard Ernst von 196
Bülow, Bernhard Prince von 196
Bülow, Friedrich-Carl 195
Bülow, Henning von 192–194
Bülow, Jürgen von 192, 195–197, 219, 240, 243–246, 248, 250, 251, 255–257, 262, 271, 275
Bülow, Jutta von 195
Bülow, Karl von 196
Bülow, von, family 191, 193
Bülow-Dennewitz, Count von 196

Busschau, prospector 118, 137, 145, 160, 230, 231, 268
Cameron, Professor Eugen N. 255
Canton-Thompson, Gertrude 31
Caplan, C. & Caplan, M. (brothers) 149, 151–155, 157–159, 170, 174
Carstens, Jack, Captain 136, 147, 164, 168, 174
Cartier, Louis 93
Catherine the Great 139
Cawthorn, R.E. 7
Celliers, Dr I. 118, 137, 146
Churchill, Winston 212
Cleveland (old Cleveland) 233–236, 268
Coetzee, Jan & Coetzee, Theunis (brothers) 155, 156, 159, 175
Cooper, Schreiner 118, 119, 122
Cornell, Fred C. 147, 148, 174
Correns, Horst 191, 205, 206
Correns, Jr. 205, 206
David, King 26, 27

De Kock, W.P. 280
Dessau, Ignatius 134–138, 154, 155, 157
Dias, Bartholomeu 22
Douglas, Alexander 184, 271
Dunne, H.C. 98, 99, 101, 104
Eckener, Hugo 132
Elkan, M. 103
Ellis, J. 125
Erasmus, Adolphe 89, 125
Farquharson, Mr (British Commissioner) 121
Fick, Dr J.C. 256, 261, 262
Fonteneau, Captain Jean 53
Frederick August II, Elector 139
Freitag, Dr Katja 278
Gelletich, Dr Hans 236
Gernet, Hans von 118, 119, 122
Glueck, Nelson 27
Goethe, Wolfgang von 141
Gordon, I. & Gordon, J. (brothers) 149
Grober, Prof. Dr. med. 217
Hall, Richard Nicklin 31
Harris, Sir David 167, 170
Havenga, Nicolaas Christiaan 164, 249
Heeren, Arnold H. 23
Heine, Heinrich 194
Heraeus, Wilhelm Carl 93
Hertzog, J.B.M. (Prime Minister) 164, 173
Hiram, King 26, 27
Humboldt, Alexander von 28
Ibn Battuta 49
Imreh 50
Jeppe, Friedrich Heinrich (Frederick, Postmaster General) 21, 158
Jeppe, Sir Julius 157, 158, 177, 178
Jones, Guy Carlton 221
Jones, J.E. 54
Kaiser, Professor Dr Erich 216

Kennedy, R. 148–150, 170, 171, 174
Klugkist, Dr Carl-Theodor 198, 219, 241
Knacke, Friedrich 136, 137, 149
Krahmann, Dr Rudolf 221, 236
Kruger, Paul 133
Kurmakoff 91
Lacroix, Professor Alfred 53
Laubscher, prospector 149
Lecomte, Louis 54, 55, 58–60
Lehmann, Olga 7, 10, 212, 257
Lettow-Vorbeck, General Paul von 133, 243
Linhardt, Fräulein 82, 104, 128, 129
Livingstone, Dr David 21, 86
Lombaard, Andries 99, 101, 102, 104, 105, 107–111, 113, 268
London, Jack 161, 162
Louis XVI, King 93
Louw, Hon. E. 252
Louw (Prospector) 150
Lüderitz, Adolf 33
MacIver, David Randall 31
Maddison, Robbie 259, 260, 262
Malcomess, Major and Mrs 191, 192
Maritz, Manie (General) 146, 173
Mare, D. 125, 146
Mauch, Carl 24, 28–30, 65, 157, 158, 220
McKerrell, D. 125
Mecklenburg-Schwerin, Grand Duke of 193, 196
Meitner, Frau Professor Lise 132
Merensky, Albert 243
Merensky, Alexander 10, 17–25, 29, 33–35, 158
Merensky, Alexander Jr. 35
Merensky, Ernst-Adolf 199
Merensky, Hans 7–10, 13–15, 17–21, 24, 25, 35–39, 41, 42, 44–46, 54–71, 73–77, 79–83, 85–90, 95, 98–111, 113–125, 127–129, 131–

INDEX OF PEOPLE 291

138, 142–146, 150–167, 169–179, 183–199, 201–217, 219–227, 229–237, 239–263, 265–276, 278–280
Merensky, Margarethe 219
Merensky, Paula 19
Mermoz, Jean 48, 49
Metternich, family 194
Minister of Justice, 240
monks
  Bendectine 194
  Cistercian 194
Neal, W.G. 31
Ney, Marshall Michel 196
Obst, Professor Erich 216, 217, 240
Olthaver, H. 119–122, 158
Oppenheimer, Sir Ernest 142, 168, 170, 171, 177–180, 183, 184, 186, 250, 251
Oppert, Jules 28
Osten, Herr von der 199
Oudinot, Marshall Nicholas 196
Petermann, Dr August H. 29, 30
Peters, Carl 34
Phillips, Harold 188
Phillips, Sir Lionel 186–188
Phoenicians 27
Pirow, Dr Hans 164
Plange, C. 187
Pretorius, Andries (President) 43
Quatremère, Etienne Marc 23
Rabinowitz, Salomon 149–151, 155, 170, 171, 174
Reinicke, Dr Leopold 221
Renders, Adam 30
Reuning, Dr Ernst 145, 146, 150, 152–157, 159, 160, 172–175, 268
Rhodes, Cecil John 30, 141
Riemerschmid, Frau Dr. G. 217
Rifle Guards 36
Roeder, Carl von 87, 89, 90
Rolfes, Carl 271
Rothschild group 54
Rothschild, Lord Nathaniel 141

Ruh, Max 233, 256
Saint-Exupéry, Antoine de 48, 49
Solomon, King 23–29, 31
Saxony, Crown Prince of 199
Scaliger, Julius Caesar 91
Scheffer, Heinrich Theophilus 92
Schlimmer (Merchant) 100–103
Schneiderhöhn, Professor Dr Hans 123, 124
Schoeman, Schalk & Schoeman, Willem (brothers) 101, 102, 104, 105, 107, 109–111
Schweinfurth, George 132
Sekhukhune, King 19, 98
Sheba, Queen of 26, 27
Shepenupet, Queen 90
Smuts, Jan (General) 164, 169, 171, 204, 212, 240, 249
Solvay, Ernest 132
Stille, Professor Dr Hans 132
Thaer, General von (Sr.) 36, 37
Thaer, Albrecht von 36, 37, 193, 196, 272
Thaer, von (family) 36, 37, 199
Troye, Gustav, 116, 117
Ulloa y García de la Torre, Antonio de 92
Van der Bijl, Dr Hendrik Johannes 250
Van Wyk, digger 154
Veblen, Professor Thorstein 181
Wagner, Percy A. 123–125, 267
Warmback, William 184, 249, 271
Webb, T.H. 238
Weber, M. 125
Wipplinger (Merensky's assistant) 82, 83, 89, 90, 99, 101, 108, 116, 117, 128, 129, 136, 137
Wollaston, William H. 93
Wood, Charles 92
Wools-Sampson, Sir Aubry 58, 60
Zimmermann (Merensky's chauffeur and gardener) 206, 207, 209, 258
Zimmermann, Mrs 207, 258

INDEX OF

# Places, companies and institutions

Aandenk 222–225, 229
Addis Abeba 91
Adlon, Hotel 127, 131, 136, 137, 190–192
African and European Investment Corporation 119
African German Estate and Investment Company Ltd 184, 185, 188
African Metal Corporation 250
Agadez 49, 50
Aïr Mountains 49, 50
Akaba, Gulf of 27
Alaska 48, 63, 161, 162
Albania 227
Albertinenhof 191
Alexander Bay 14, 142, 148–152, 156–161, 163, 167, 168, 171–173, 177, 178, 187, 189, 206, 223, 226, 229, 240, 266, 268, 270, 273
Andes 48, 91

Anglo French Exploration Company 222
Anglo American Corporation of South Africa 120, 122, 168, 224, 225, 229, 250, 274
Angola 22, 180
Angra Pequeña 33
Anjeva 55, 58
Anosivola 55
Arabian Peninsula 26, 27
Argentina 128
Argyle 181
Arlit 50
Atlantic coast 63, 65, 67, 76, 135, 139, 144, 146, 174
Atlas Mountains 48
Australia 48, 134, 181, 189, 217
Austria 45, 82, 236
Baku 54
Barnato Group 122
Basal Reef 224

Bechuanaland 22, 28, 65
  *see also* Botswana
Beira 28
Bela-Bela *see* Warmbaths
Benguela current 144
Berlin 18, 33, 38, 41, 73, 127, 131, 132, 136, 190, 191, 193, 196
  Mission Society 18, 19, 25, 33, 34, 272
  University of 35
  Technische Hochschule 193
Berlin-Charlottenburg 236
Berlin-Lichterfelde 36
Berlin-Moabit 35
Birbir, river 91
Bochum 131
Bonn 196
Botshabelo 19, 23–25, 29, 202
Botswana 22, 28, 65, 181
Brandenburg 13
Brazil 48, 63, 64, 140, 238
Bremen 33, 205
Breslau 38, 199
  University of 57
Breteuil, Pavillon de (Sèvres) 93
British South Africa Company 30
Bruges 139
Buchuberg 149, 170, 174
Bulawayo 29
Bulgaria 135–137, 157
Bultfontein 141
Bureau de Recherches Géologiques et Minières 49
Bureau International des Poids et Mesures 93
Bushveld 8, 45, 62, 67, 95, 97, 101, 103, 107, 110, 115–118, 120, 122–125, 127, 130, 132, 135, 161, 223, 227, 230–233, 236, 240, 255, 267–270, 274, 275
California 63, 161, 162
Canada 94
Cape (Province) 147, 187, 254, 255

Cape (Colony) 166
Cape Town 18, 149, 164, 166, 167, 174, 177, 189, 206, 249
Carlton, Hotel 81, 202
Cartagena 92
Caspian Sea 54
Central Selling Organisation (CSO) 180, 181
China 49, 205, 238
Church of Our Lady (Dresden) 140
Cologne-Kalk 131
Columbia 91, 92, 94
Commisariat à l'Energie Atomique (CEA) 49, 50
Congo 50, 180
Congo Basin 217
Cornellsberg 148
Cornellskop 148
Dakar 48
Damaraland 87
Damascus 26
Dar-es-Salaam 128
De Beers 50, 141, 142, 167, 170, 178–181
De Beers Consolidated Mines 141
De Beers Mining Company 141
Dennewitz 196
Deutsche Bank 69
Deutsche Geologische Gesellschaft 132
Deutsche Kolonialgesellschaft 145
Drakensberg 18, 19, 28, 174, 187, 188, 217
Dresden 139, 140
Duiwelskloof 187, 259
Durban 28, 54, 59, 61, 74, 144, 174
Dutch East India Company 139
Dutch Reformed Church 176
Dutoitspan (mine) 141
East Africa 180, 205, 212, 243, 276
  German 34
  Portuguese 103
Egypt 31, 90, 91, 244

Eldorit (mine) 275, 276
Eloth 25, 27
Emmaus Mission Station (Zululand) 18
Emsland 272
England 44, 92, 94, 148, 187, 277
Erongo (volcano) 87
Erongo massif 87–89
Erzgebirge 38
Erz- und Kohle-Flotation (Bochum) 131
Ethiopia 91
Ethopian Plateau 91
Europe 25, 30, 69, 73, 74, 76, 113, 130, 133, 134, 139, 140, 146, 174, 183, 186, 188, 189, 214, 236, 239, 241, 242, 277
Ezion-geber 25, 27
Far West Rand 221
Fianarantsoa 55
Fish River 85
Fort Gouraud 48
Fort Napier 74
Foskor 275
France 23, 277
French Academy of Sciences 53
Friedlaender & Co. 54, 58–60
Friesland 214
Gartz an der Oder 35
Germany 9, 13, 20, 24, 28, 30, 33, 34, 41, 42, 45, 73, 82, 128, 130, 131, 133–135, 140, 145, 165, 181, 185, 186, 188, 189, 197, 203, 214, 221, 277, 278, 280
German Protectorate 24, 28, 34, 87
Gibeon district 85
Gießen, University of 145
Goldenbow 191, 192, 195, 198
Gold Fields Group 221
Goslar 39
Gotha 29, 158
Göttingen, University of 23, 276
Green Vault (Dresden) 139

Grootemist 150
Großbeeren 196
Große Randstufe 217
Guinea 48
Gütersloh 35
Gutzmin 199
Haakdoorndrift 230
Hamburg 131, 205, 276
Hannover, Technical University of 216
H.M. Association 157, 166, 167, 170, 171, 173, 177, 178
Hans Merensky Foundation 8, 9, 271, 272, 276, 277, 279, 280
Hans Merensky Dam 210
Hans Merensky Physics Block 217
Hans Merensky Trust, 199, 214, 256, 271, 272, 275, 276
Harz Mountains 38
Heidelberg, University of 35
Hohenheim, University of 276
Humboldt AG 131
Hungary 134
Hyderabad 27
India, 27, 28, 139, 147
Indian Ocean 27, 31, 65, 187
coastline 144
Industrial Development Corporation 250, 251
Inyanga, Ruins of 31
Iran 227
Israel 26
Ivory Coast 48
Jagdlust 230, 232, 255, 268, 274
Jamaica 92
Japan 180
Jena, Institute for Clinical Medicine 217
Jeppestown 178
Johannesburg 29, 42–45, 53, 59–61, 66, 67, 74, 76, 77, 79, 80, 82, 83, 89, 90, 98, 99, 102, 108, 111, 113, 117–121, 127, 134, 137, 138, 144,

146, 155, 156, 174, 177, 178, 184, 186, 191, 202, 204, 206, 220–223, 235, 236, 255, 256, 262, 268
Johannesburg Consolidated Investments 120
Johannesburg Stock Exchange 61, 121
Johnson Matthey (platinum dealer) 273
Judea 26
Jwaneng 181
Kalahari 50, 148, 212
Kalkfontein 213, 257, 272
Katanga 50, 217
Katanga line (railway) 217
Kazakhstan 227, 232
Kimberley 43, 45, 93, 140, 141
Klerksdorp 221, 222
Kloster Eberbach 194
Kolmanskop 64, 66, 135, 136, 143, 144, 172, 223, 279
Krupp-Gruson works 131
Kuwetshwane 108, 109
Lecomte Madagascar Gold Concession 54, 58–60
Leopoldina (German Academy of Science) 35
Letaba river 248
Libby (Montana) 237, 238
Lichtenburg 165, 173
Limpopo river 22–24, 29–31
Limpopo Province 28, 187, 227
Lisbon 139
Lombaard farm 99, 107, 111
London 121, 134, 136, 137, 143, 148, 169, 197, 205
London Stock Exchange 121, 134
Loolekop 233–238, 242, 244–249, 251–254, 256, 266, 268, 269, 274
L.P. Syndicate 103, 104
Lourenço Marques 174, 231
Louvre 91

Lowveld 204, 233, 237, 244, 248, 259
Lüderitz 33, 64, 66, 76, 87, 135, 143–146, 150, 172, 279
Lüderitz Bay 33
Lulu Mountains 99, 101
Lydenburg 19, 98, 99, 101, 114, 116–118, 120, 123, 125, 230, 267, 268
Lydenburg Platinum Ltd. 109, 120, 135
Lydenburg Platinum Areas 135
Maandagshoek (farm) 99, 101, 104, 107, 109, 113, 114, 130
Madagascar 53, 54, 56, 58–61, 220
Madras 27
Magdeburg 131
Magoebaskloof Pass 188
Mananjary 54
Maputo *see* Lourenço Marques
Marseilles 48
Matabeleland 23, 30
Matadi, port 218
Mauchberg 28
Mauritania 48
Mauritius 54
Mecklenburg 191, 193, 194, 196–198, 243
Merensky Archive 9, 75, 216, 278
Merensky Reef 62, 95, 114, 116, 118, 120, 124, 125, 158, 230, 278
Merensky Technological Services (MTS) 277
Messina 260
Middelburg 19, 21, 29
Mining and Finance Corporation 119
Ministry
  of Agriculture 214, 256
  of Economic Affairs 252
  of Finance 164, 249–252
  of Trade 250, 251
Mokopane *see* Potgietersrus

Monomotapa, kingdom of 29
Montana 233, 237, 238
Mooihoek 107–110
Morocco 241, 242
Mozambique 18, 22, 27, 65, 67, 86, 174
Mpumalanga 18, 28, 29, 227
Munich, University of 216
Murchison Range 220
Museum of Indian Art, New York 91
Mysore 27
Namaqualand 76, 124, 135–139, 144–151, 157, 163–166, 168, 169, 171, 173, 174, 176, 220, 256
Namaqualand Diamond Company 136, 149, 171
Namib (desert) 148
Namibia 13, 14, 48, 65–67, 85, 87, 135, 172, 220, 273, 278, 279
  see also South-West Africa
Natal (KwaZulu-Natal) 67, 74, 166, 214, 275, 277
Native Affairs Department 119
Netherlands, the 44, 139
Niger, Republic of 49
Northam 213
Odendaalsrus 222, 225, 274
Oder (river) see Gartz an der Oder
Office for Land Acquisition 198
Olifants River 248
Onverwacht 110
Ophir 23–31
Opperculum 170
Orange Free State 45, 166, 221–225, 232, 236, 268, 273
Orange River 66, 135, 154, 160, 163, 165, 172, 273
  mouth of the 14, 144, 146–148, 150
Otavi Mining Company 250
Ouallaga (province) 91
Oyster Line 63, 144, 150, 151, 155, 156, 158–160, 170–172, 174, 175, 177, 179, 184, 216, 270, 273, 279

Paris 93
Pawonkau 37
Phalaborwa 8, 238, 251, 252, 274–276, 278, 279
Phalaborwa Mining Company (PMC) 274–276
Phalaborwa Phosphate & Vermiculite Company 251, 252
Philippines 227, 255
Phosphate Development Corporation 252
Piccadilly 134
Pietermaritzburg 74
Pietersburg 230
Pilgrim's Rest 107
Poland 199
Polokwane see Pietersburg
Polynesia 217
Pommerania 199, 205
Pomona Formation 150
Portuguese settlement 22, 30
Port Nolloth 147–149, 152, 163–165, 169, 174, 176
Potchefstroom, University of 272
Potgietersrus 116–118, 120–123, 125, 137, 145, 267
Potgietersrus Platinum Mines Ltd. 122
Pretoria 21, 43, 45, 177, 206, 216, 256, 275
Pretoria, University of 9, 13, 217, 240, 272, 279, 280
Prussia 13, 38, 39, 42, 73, 74, 280
Prussian Academy of Sciences 132
Rammelsberg (mine) 39
Rand Club 67, 68, 74, 82, 100, 186, 202, 220
Randfontein 221
Red Sea 25, 27
Rems Valley 28
Rheingau 194
Rhodesia 212
Richtersveld 148

Riesengebirge 38
Rio Pinto (Columbia) 91
Rio Tinto 274
Rodenwalde 191–193, 195, 197–199
Rosendal Dam 275
Ruhrgebiet 39
Russia 93–95, 101, 102, 106, 138, 181, 189, 227, 238, 273
Russian Foreign Trade Bureau 94, 131
Rustenburg 118, 122, 125, 230, 267
Saarland 38
Sahara 24, 49
SASOL 86
Saxony 199
Schloss Johannisberg (vineyard) 194
Schwerin 192, 195
Sena 30
Serra Pelada, Brazil 63
Sèvres 93
Shinkolobwe 50
Sierra de Minas, Argentina 128
Silesia 36–38, 186, 206
Sofala 28
South Africa 7–10, 13, 14, 18, 22, 25, 28, 30, 34, 39, 41–43, 45, 48, 53, 59, 62, 64, 65, 69, 73–75, 80, 90, 95, 97, 103, 106, 113, 121, 123–125, 131, 134–138, 140, 141, 144, 147, 148, 155, 169, 170, 174, 177, 181, 185–187, 189, 190, 192, 193, 205, 212–214, 216–222, 224, 227, 230, 232, 234–236, 238–244, 248–251, 257, 261, 265, 266, 269, 270, 272–274, 276, 278–280
South African Custodian of Enemy Property 199, 250
South African Geological Survey 123
South African Phosphate Company 242, 247
South African Townships 119, 122
South African Townships, Mining and Finance Corporation 158
South African Soil Conservation Board 261
South America 91, 134, 242
South Carolina 238
South-West Africa 66, 87, 98, 135, 143, 145, 150, 172, 174, 220, 250
Southern Rhodesia 28, 30, 31, 65, 86, 220, 255
Soviet Union 131, 137, 138, 242
Soviet-occupied zone 199
Spitzkoppe 87
Springbok 176
St Cloud 93
St Helena 224
Steelpoort River 110, 111
Steinberg (vineyard) 194
Steinkopf 149
Stellenbosch, University of 13, 217, 272, 279
Stetten 28
Straschimir (Bulgaria) 135
Stuttgart 30
Sumatra 128
Süßwinkel 199
Swakopmund 87, 89
Swaziland 18, 65
Tati 29
Thebes 90
Timbuktu 49
Top House 204, 205, 212, 259, 262, 263, 278
Transvaal 13, 18, 19, 21, 28, 29, 34, 42–44, 79, 86, 89, 103, 115, 118, 120, 122, 125, 131, 158, 165, 166, 187, 188, 196, 201, 112, 214, 220, 221, 224, 229, 263, 274
Transvaal Land and Exploration Company 110, 119
Transvaal Ore Company 252, 256, 276

Tsumeb 87
Turkey 227, 255
Tzaneen 13, 210, 216
Union Carbide Corporation 232, 255, 274
United Nations 212
Upper Silesia 38, 206
Urals 93–95, 97, 131, 137, 138
USA 94, 180, 238
Usakos 89, 90
U.S. Geological Survey 95, 274
USSR 131
Vaal River 25
Varkvlei 230
Venice 139
Ventersdorp 165, 173, 223
Ventersdorp System 223
Vlakpoort 213, 230
Von Bülow Dam 275
Voorspoed 66, 68
Warmbaths 213
Waterberg 89, 125
Waterloo 196
West Wits Line 221
Western-Australia 181
Western Holdings 224

Westfalia 14, 187, 188, 197, 201, 202, 204–210, 212–214, 219, 225, 232–235, 239–241, 243–246, 252, 255–257, 261–263, 266, 270, 273, 275–277, 279
Windhoek 87, 89, 90, 149, 272, 279
Winterveld 231, 232, 255
Wisconsin, University of 255
Wit Extensions 222, 223, 225
Witwatersrand 43, 54, 61, 64, 67, 158, 220–223
Witwatersrand
  formation 64
  sequence 64
  System 221–223
Witwatersrand, University of 272
Woodbush Hill 187
Württemberg 30
Yeoville 104
Zambezi River 23, 30, 31
Zimbabwe 24, 27–31, 65, 227, 238
  *see also* Rhodesia
Zimbabwe Ruins 23, 24, 28, 30, 31
Zobten (mountain) 38
Zululand 18

# INDEX OF

# Concepts and events

acclimatisation (European horses) 34, 257
aerial photographs 50
agriculture 14, 37, 79, 194, 195, 198, 199, 205, 207, 209, 219, 230, 232, 238, 241–243, 267, 270–272, 276
  activities 20, 37
  experiments 275
  techniques 210, 216
agrochemical
  industry 248
  plant 249
alluvial
  deposit 62, 63, 91, 93, 151
  placer deposits 54
  soil formation 140
Anglo-Boer War, First 21, 75
Anglo-Boer War, Second 74, 75, 133, 146, 173
animal husbandry 272
apatite 88, 242, 244, 247, 274
  ore 245, 246, 248
  rock 246
aqua regia 92
aridity 49, 87, 143, 146, 148, 169, 207, 245
asbestos 237, 238, 275, 276
Ascania-Magnetometer 221
asphalt 85
avocados 214, 234, 276, 277
bankruptcy 14, 71, 203, 265
basic rocks 93, 97, 101, 108, 115, 116
beach placers 63, 64
bear market 70, 85, 173
bedding planes 47, 49
bee-keeping 215, 216
beryl 88
beryllometer 50
biographer 212, 257, 280
bitumen 85
blue ground 140

breccia 89, 140, 141
breeding 211, 213, 214, 256, 257, 272
  stock 214
British 24, 28, 30, 31, 33, 34, 74, 75, 95, 121, 212
building timber 214, 218, 256, 275, 277
carat 63, 139–141, 149, 151, 156, 159, 166, 167, 174, 179–181
carrier
  of fertilizer 238
  of insecticides 238
cartel 179, 180, 182
cassiterite 62, 88, 89
catchment area 209
cattle 213, 214, 230, 272
  African domesticated 256
chalcopyrite 109
Charter of Human Rights 212
chemical 94, 99, 108, 115
  compounds 97
  elements 15, 92
  engineering 134
  formula 237
  industry 226
  leaching 62
  reactivity 226
Christianity 34
chromates 226
chrome 80, 226, 227, 255
  ore 226, 227, 229–232, 236, 255, 268, 274
  oxides 226, 227
  salts 226
  world market for 274
chromite 62, 107, 117, 227, 230, 231, 268, 269
Chrysoprase, Silesian 38
citrus 213, 243, 256, 272, 276
clarity (diamonds) 180
coal 38, 39, 42, 47, 103
  deposit 43, 67, 86, 217

liquefaction 86
  outcropping seams 86
columbite-tantalite 88
compost 213
compound interests 127
concentration camp 75
concession 43, 44, 54, 55, 57–59, 66, 87, 100, 186, 235, 236, 249, 253, 266, 268, 274
consolidation 120, 121, 141
consulting commission 128
conventional wet ore dressing 131
copper 26, 27, 47, 49, 50, 87, 147, 217, 233, 235, 247, 252, 259, 274, 275
  mines 87, 147
credit 70, 71, 81, 100
creditor 76, 98, 125, 127, 128, 132
debt 70, 71, 76, 81, 98, 103, 127, 128, 132, 266
deforestation 209
desertification 210, 244
diamond 13, 14, 25, 42, 43, 45, 48, 50, 62–68, 76, 93, 135–137, 143, 144, 146–151, 153–161, 163–175, 177–184, 186, 187, 189, 190, 192, 202–204, 212, 219, 220, 223, 224, 229, 240, 244, 251, 266, 268, 270, 273, 278, 279
  -bearing pipe 50, 62, 137, 141
  Brazilian 64, 140, 224
  cartel 179–182
  deposit 14, 87, 93, 124, 136, 139, 160, 172, 175, 179, 220, 270, 279
  history of 139–142
  industry 167, 168, 170, 179, 180, 251
  market 70, 167, 168, 178, 189
  placer 63, 160
  rush 45, 166
  seekers 138, 145, 163–165
  South African 64, 140, 224
digging licence 145, 168, 179

digging rights 100, 168, 230, 235, 252
diggings 29, 30, 45, 141, 150, 159, 173, 234, 268
dikes 47
diplomatic service 195
doctorate honoris causa
  Alexander Merensky 35
  Hans Merensky 132, 193, 240, 279
Draper Medal 279
dressing plant 185
drilling 48, 54, 116, 128, 222–225, 229, 232, 235, 268, 274
dry sieving 89
dumping strategy (Russian), 190
dune ridge 66
dunes 64, 66, 136, 143–145, 151, 223, 279
economic
  activity 56, 85, 146, 277
  crisis 142, 266
  development 94, 119, 239, 266
  growth 80
  viability 15, 16, 48, 131, 242, 269
economy, war 80
erosion 14, 47, 64, 99, 188, 207, 208, 210, 211, 261, 271
eruption channel 140
eucalyptus 209, 217, 218, 240, 256, 277
European banks 44, 58, 69
expansion (of vermiculite) 234, 237, 238
expansion factor (of vermiculite) 237
expert appraisal 43, 66–69, 80, 87, 128, 135, 137, 241
exploration 22, 46–48, 80, 125, 172, 221–223
extraction process 130, 131
farming techniques *see* agricultural techniques
fault zone 89
feeding-pipe 140

fertiliser 241, 242, 244, 248, 251
field geologist 123, 248
financial adviser 184, 249, 271
financial plan 157, 250
financier 44, 54, 85, 87, 90, 100, 101, 115, 134, 135, 157, 169, 202, 220
flotation 131
forest 38, 190, 191, 197, 199, 205, 211, 256, 263, 275, 277
forester 38, 192, 193, 195, 198, 209, 219
forestry 37, 193, 199, 209, 217, 241, 256, 267, 270, 272, 275–277
fortune-hunters 79, 140, 144, 147, 148, 164, 165, 168, 173
funding 30, 81, 90, 100, 102, 121, 138, 272, 276
furniture factory 275
garnet 88
geochemical prospecting 47, 50
geological environment 55, 147
geologist 16, 25, 38, 42–47, 49, 50, 53–59, 61, 66, 68, 71, 74, 77, 80, 81, 85, 89–91, 95, 97–99, 106, 117, 118, 122–125, 132, 134, 135, 137, 145, 146, 160, 164, 172, 186, 193, 201–203, 216, 220, 221, 225, 233, 240, 243, 244, 248, 255, 265–267, 269, 278, 279
geophysical depth exploration 221, 222
global market 8, 90, 276 *see also* world markets
global marketing sytem 276
gold 23, 25–31, 42, 43, 45, 48, 53–65, 67, 69, 70, 80, 87, 90–92, 95, 120, 128, 129, 147, 158, 161, 162, 168, 184, 187, 220–226, 229, 232, 236, 244, 251, 268, 273, 274
-bearing layers 221–224, 268
-bearing vein 82, 104, 129
deposit 27, 29, 53, 62–65, 90
diggers 29, 30, 43, 67, 161, 186

prospecting 86, 220
prospecting techniques 162
prospector 22, 25, 29, 43
  rush 63, 161
Gospel 34
granite 45, 87
grass farm 212, 213, 256
grazing 187, 188, 231, 233, 234, 244, 257
grenadillas 214
Gross Domestic Product (Namibia) 273
hand sorting 88, 89
health risks (posed by asbestos) 237, 276
honey production 215, 216
house arrest 240, 241
humus layer 187, 218
hunting 22, 25, 30, 36–38, 136, 183, 186, 191–193, 195, 197–199, 203, 205, 243
hydrological balance 238
hydrothermal process 238
immigrant 41, 74, 134, 186, 221, 236, 265
improvement (of soils) 198, 238, 271
industrial complex 269
industrial firms 82
internment 74, 87, 133, 206, 239, 240, 241, 265, 266, 275
investment 46, 56, 68, 70, 74, 79, 102, 119, 129, 140, 168, 177, 184, 185, 188, 190, 208, 210, 215, 224, 225, 249, 250, 271
iridium 92, 93, 99
iron ore
  crusts 47
  deposits 47, 48, 50
joint committee 250
journalists 127, 189, 190
Karoo formation 89
Karoo system 86
kimberlite 141
kimberlite pipes 50, 62, 63, 141

laboratory 56, 99, 108, 237, 238, 278
land reform 199
landowners 42, 68, 76, 110, 123, 145, 150, 188, 191, 199, 208
last will 14, 256, 270
lawyer 70, 71, 76, 98, 99, 149, 179, 184, 271
layered deposits 227
lead 38, 56, 87, 135, 157
lead and zinc mine 38, 87, 135
leaf cover 209
legacy 133, 265, 270
legislation 42, 168, 169, 224
Leibniz silver medal 132
leprosy 34
liberty 38, 74
lode deposit 125
magnetic anomaly 48
malaria 34, 61, 257, 258
manufacturing industry 82, 93, 134, 145, 185, 226, 229, 276, 277
manure 213
mass-produced goods 181, 248
melioration 235, 238
melting point 92, 226
memorandum of understanding 250
metal extraction procedure 130, 131
metallurgical procedure 274
metallurgy 238
metallurgist 92, 95, 231, 269
mica 233–235, 237
  rotten 233, 234, 237
military service 13, 36, 37
mineral deposit 13–16, 29, 39, 41, 43, 44, 46, 47, 64, 138, 212
mining 13, 15, 38, 39, 55, 59, 62, 63, 65, 66, 69, 70, 73, 77, 79, 82, 86–90, 98, 100, 101, 119, 122–124, 127, 131, 136, 137, 145, 147, 166, 168–170, 174, 177, 179, 183, 185–187, 220–222, 225, 229, 231, 235, 242, 247–249, 251, 256, 269, 273–275, 278, 279
  assessor 13, 33, 39, 280

commissioner 107
company 42, 46, 47, 54, 58, 59, 61, 63, 67, 69, 79–82, 85, 115, 120, 122, 130, 132, 134, 149, 165, 167, 168, 202, 224, 225, 235, 250, 251, 275, 276
engineer 41, 42, 44, 54, 60, 89, 91, 221
enterprise 44, 68, 131, 157
legislation 173
   in the Orange Free State 166, 22 4
   in the Transvaal 42, 166
machinery 185
magnates 14, 67, 158, 178, 204
project 68, 100, 134, 251
rights 166, 171
scene 83, 220
school 44, 45
student trainee 38, 206
techniques 45, 80, 272
Miocene period 143
mission station 17–20, 22, 25, 29, 34, 68, 202, 208
missionary 13, 17–24, 29, 34, 98, 133, 158, 176, 196, 208
molybdenum 47, 67, 226
monopoly 94, 95, 131, 141, 167
mortgage 70, 198
motorisation 86
mudflow 62, 210
mussel beds 144
Namaqualand ponies 256
national cultural monument 202
native platinum 121
newspaper 127, 131, 189, 259
noble metal 92
norites 121
norite bands 121
nuggets, gold 62, 162
nutritive elements 213
occurences
   apatite 247
   platinum 108

October Revolution 94
oil
   fields 47, 54
   reserves 86
   shale 85
Old Testament 23, 25, 26, 27, 29
open cast mine 141
option
   agreement 119, 223
   area 58, 120, 136, 145
   hunters 118
ore
   dressing plant 131, 145, 185
   dressing procedure 130, 131, 134, 185
   reserves 46, 54, 80, 252
   seekers 67, 186
Orlov diamond 139
orogenetic zones 227
osmium 92
*Ostrea prismatica* 144, 151
oversupply 142, 180
oxidation zone 47, 49
oyster shells 144, 151, 152, 155, 156, 160, 175, 279
paleoplacers 64
palladium 92, 93, 95, 273
panning 43, 48, 56, 63, 91, 99, 105, 106, 163, 204
parent rock
   for platinum mineralisation 97, 98, 106
   of diamonds 140
partnership agreement 152
peas 213
pecan nuts 214
pegmatites 87, 88
pegmatite rubble 88
pentlandite 109
phosphate 86, 213, 241, 242, 248–254, 266, 268, 269, 274, 275
   mining industry 242
   occurrences 241, 247
   raw 241, 251

super- 241, 248, 275
phyrrotite 109
plantation 208, 209, 213, 214, 217, 219, 243, 244, 252
  citrus 213, 243, 256
  eucalyptus 209, 217, 240
  pine 209
  sugar cane 214
  tea 275
  yellowwood 276
placers
  aeolian 64
  fossil 64
  residual 64
Platina del Pinto 91
platinum 14, 48, 62, 89–93, 95, 97–99, 101–108, 111, 113–116, 120–122, 124, 128–132, 138, 145, 161, 164, 177, 190, 220, 223, 225, 229, 240, 244, 255, 267, 268, 273, 278
  boom 120, 121, 123, 158
  business 115, 121, 129, 131
  companies 120, 190
  content 97
  deposit 90, 95, 99, 102, 109, 110, 121–123, 137, 160, 189, 220, 266
  diggers 114
  group 95, 99
  market 94, 95, 131, 138, 189, 190
  metal 92, 125, 273
  mineralisation 97, 115, 118
  parent rock 97, 106
  price 94, 95, 131, 190
  production, world's annual, 95, 273
  prospecting 42, 97, 103, 109, 111, 139, 157, 204, 230, 270
  project 102, 105, 110, 115, 157, 184
  seekers 114, 203
  share 115, 119–121, 128
  speculation 121, 128, 158
  -bearing layer 109–111, 113, 114, 116, 117, 118, 122, 267
  -bearing reef 117, 118, 120–123, 267, 270, 278
  -iridium alloy 93
precious metal 62, 92, 93, 95, 104, 130, 229
prehistoric stone tools 236
price
  dumping 131
  of diamonds 139, 141, 142, 168, 173, 174, 179–182
  of gold 95
  of metals 80, 89, 94, 95, 131, 190
  of shares 45, 46, 59, 60, 69, 70, 120, 121, 128, 178
  war 190
primary deposit 62, 63, 98, 125, 137, 143
primary mineralisation 57, 93, 105
prisoner 74, 75
processing plant 88, 89, 249, 277
progress, promotion of general 202, 211, 215, 217, 272, 280
project plan 250
prospecting 14, 42, 45–48, 50, 51, 57, 58, 60, 61, 65, 66, 81, 85, 86, 97, 99–101, 103–105, 107, 109–111, 113–115, 118, 120–123, 128, 137–139, 144, 148, 151, 153, 154, 156, 165, 166, 168, 172, 174, 177, 184, 186, 204, 213, 219–221, 225, 229–232, 235, 236, 243, 246, 249, 253, 255, 266–270, 274, 275
  commission 80
  handbook *see* textbook
  holes 48, 146
  lines 104–106
  methods 47, 63, 105
  pits 172
  plan 145, 254
  project 45, 157, 184, 213, 226, 235, 254

shafts 48, 119, 248
techniques 162
textbook 147, 162
trenches 175, 234
work 81, 99, 137, 172, 248, 274
protection (of game) 193
pyrite 109
pyroxenite 109, 121
radioactive minerals 50, 247, 274
railway
  sleepers 218
  system in the Lowveld 248
rainy season 248
rationalising 80, 88
raw materials 15, 54, 80, 86, 92, 95, 127, 147, 177, 194, 220, 243, 244
  market 14, 16, 44, 85, 94
  industry 69, 220
reserves
  chrome 274
  oil 86
  ore 46, 54, 80, 227, 252
  phosphate 252
  platinum 95, 131
  water 210
rest magma 88
Rhine wine 81
rhodium 92, 93, 99
rights
  concession 274
  digging 100, 168, 230, 235, 252
  discoverer's 99, 107, 170, 171
  finders' *see* discoverers'
  mining 166, 171, 251
  phosphate 251, 252
  timber 277
river
  sands 56, 91, 98, 139
  terrace 154, 162
River Theory 143, 146
Roman emperors 139
rubellite 53
ruby 202

ruthenium 93
sapphire 202
satellite images 50
sawmills 275, 277
scholarships 276
scientist 122, 123, 279
scurvy 161
sea route (to India) 139
secondary
  deposit 61, 62, 64, 93, 140, 168
  diamond concentration 137
  gold concentration 57
  market 180
  mineral concentration 64
semi-precious stones 38, 53, 88
shaft 48, 119, 124, 224, 235, 248
share 44–46, 59, 60, 68–70, 95, 115, 119–121, 128, 129, 133, 150, 152, 158, 170, 171, 177–179, 183, 184, 215
shareholders 70, 141, 179
shock-heat 237
shortage
  of fertilisers 242, 244
  of food 242
  of platinum 94, 95
  of superphosphates 241
silver 90–92, 132, 135
sintering point 238
slag cement 275
smallpox 23
smelter 27, 88, 89
soil erosion 14, 207, 211, 261, 271
speculation 46, 59, 60, 70, 121, 128, 129, 158, 161, 184, 223
speculators 45, 46, 59, 100, 186, 224
stainless steel 226
standard kilogram 93
standard metre 93
start-up
  enterprises 157
  funds 102, 122, 138, 205
  operations 134

state monopoly 95, 131
steel industry 169, 229, 269
stock exchange 43–46, 61, 68, 69, 113, 115, 119, 121, 134, 135, 184, 265
  collapse 265
stock market 68, 69, 120, 121, 129
  crash 121
stockbrokers 121
stockpile 142, 168, 180, 181
  of raw materials 80, 142, 241
stock-taking 208
stream placer 62
sugar cane
  plantation 214
  processing 214
sugar industry 214
sulphide minerals 109
sunlight (in South Africa) 217
syndicate 103, 104, 108, 109, 111, 113, 115, 120–122, 128, 135, 149–154, 158, 159, 165, 167–171, 180–182, 190, 235
synthetic diamonds 190
take-over
  negotiations 183
  bid 153
tantalite 67
teamwork 47
telegram 59, 60, 67, 82, 136, 137, 255
tenant farmer 120
tennis 75, 197, 202, 204
terraces 145, 154–156, 162, 170, 175, 213, 234, 268, 273, 279
test shaft 248
test trenches 48, 149
testament 199, 256, 266, 271, 272
timber
  building 218, 256
  industry 275–277
  production 217, 275
  resources 198, 209, 214

supply 209, 214
tin 45, 46, 48, 62, 63, 70, 80, 87, 89
  deposit 67, 87
  mine 88, 89
  ores 62, 88
  rush 45
tourmaline 53, 202
traders 22, 90, 94, 95, 100, 139, 141, 180, 182
train 89, 90, 101, 117, 217
tremas trees 214, 234
trenches 48, 119, 149, 151, 155, 156, 159, 160, 165, 175, 234–236, 245–247, 254, 260
tropical diseases 34
trustee 271, 272, 275
tungsten 67, 226
ultrabasic rocks 97, 98, 141, 227
uplift 216, 241
uranium 49, 50
valuation categories 174, 180
vegetable garden 187, 206, 216, 258
veins 47, 82, 89, 104, 109, 129, 190
vermiculite 233–238, 244, 246, 247, 251, 252, 256, 268, 272, 274–276
village elders 119, 208, 211, 215
vineyard 194
viticulture 194
volcano 87
water (for mining activities) 88, 89, 148
weathering 62, 238
white gold 92
World Exhibition, Paris (1900) 53
world markets 8, 93–95, 121, 131, 147, 167, 181, 189, 227, 231, 274
World War, First 14, 87, 94, 142, 147, 174, 178, 196, 203, 233, 243
World War, Second 48, 180, 181, 199, 216, 224, 232, 241, 259, 273
yellow ground 140
Zeppelin 50, 132
zinc 38, 87, 135, 157